Surviving Game School… and the Game Industry After That

Surviving Game School... and the Game Industry After That

Michael Lynch
Adrian Earle

Illustrations by
Diana Nguyen

CRC Press
Taylor & Francis Group
Boca Raton London New York

CRC Press is an imprint of the
Taylor & Francis Group, an **informa** business

CRC Press
Taylor & Francis Group
6000 Broken Sound Parkway NW, Suite 300
Boca Raton, FL 33487-2742

© 2018 by Taylor & Francis Group, LLC
CRC Press is an imprint of Taylor & Francis Group, an Informa business

No claim to original U.S. Government works

Printed on acid-free paper

International Standard Book Number-13: 978-1-138-56809-9 (Paperback)
978-1-138-56813-6 (Hardback)

Library of Congress Cataloging-in-Publication Data

Names: Lynch, Michael (Computer game designer), author. | Earle, Adrian, author.
Title: Surviving game school ... and the game industry after that / Michael
Lynch and Adrian Earle.
Description: Boca Raton, FL : CRC Press, Taylor & Francis Group, 2018. |
"A CRC title, part of the Taylor & Francis imprint, a member of the Taylor &
Francis Group, the academic division of T&F Informa plc." |
Includes bibliographical references.
Identifiers: LCCN 2017045268| ISBN 9781138568099 (pbk. : alk. paper) |
ISBN 9781138568136 (hardback : alk. paper)
Subjects: LCSH: Computer games--Programming--Vocational guidance.
Classification: LCC QA76.76.C672 L95 2018 | DDC 794.8/1525—dc23
LC record available at https://lccn.loc.gov/2017045268

Visit the Taylor & Francis Web site at
http://www.taylorandfrancis.com

and the CRC Press Web site at
http://www.crcpress.com

To Francine Jackson, noted astronomy educator, planetarian, writer, science historian, and longtime friend and companion.

Michael Lynch

I would like to dedicate this book to Carole for her support during the long periods I was buried in my study wrangling with it.

Adrian Earle

*"There are at least two kinds of games;
one could be called finite, the other infinite."*

— James Carse
*Finite and Infinite Games
The Free Press, A Division of Macmillan, Inc. 1986*

Notice of Rights

Notice of Liability

Trademarks

Contents

Foreword

THIS BOOK, AS YOU are about to find out as soon as I shut up, or you just skip past this zestful preface, is jam-packed with practical advice. It's contemporary, highly relevant, and frequently wryly humorous.

So, where did it come from? Mike and Adrian are entertaining, opinionated, avuncular, and, most assuredly, experienced. These guys know game schools. I work with Mike at RPI in upstate New York, where we teach courses on game development and collaborate on various and sundry projects. They also know the game industry. Adrian designed one of my favorite games from my teenage years—the Napoleonic wargame *Fields of Glory*— and has a long list of other video game credits, as well as credits on board games, rules for miniatures, and now designs for escape/mystery rooms in Albany, New York, a number of which I've been in (and managed to get out of).

Together they are a trove of sagacity, both deep and trivial (do not play *Trivial Pursuit* with these guys—you have been forewarned), with opinions sometimes contentious and always real and drawn from life. You may not always agree with them, but you cannot deny their years of working in and observing the very world they are telling us about. And, oh my, do they have much to say!

If you're interested in the game industry, this book will tell you things you want to know, and many things perhaps you wanted not to know. It illuminates and demystifies, opines, explains, and entertains. Short of time travel or an ethically dubious cloning experiment, this may be your best bet to understanding what you're letting yourself in for if you really do intend to open the portal and find out what your first years in game school or the game industry may be like. Not only that, but what you have here is also a survival guide, with tricks, tips, and advice that will help you level up your career faster than doing irrelevant side quests. Reading this book might even help you determine what is and isn't an irrelevant side quest in your own life.

So, what I'm saying is, you've struck gold in hitting upon this book. Now all you have to do is listen to them. Become informed. Then chew it over. Take it on board. Apply it. And survive game school, and the game industry after that (and become a more productive, more charming, and more compassionate human being).

Maurice Suckling
Professor of Practice, RPI, NY, and games industry veteran
www.mauricesuckling.com

Acknowledgments

ADRIAN WOULD LIKE TO acknowledge the thousands of gamers who bought Adrian's games over the years and whose indirect support enabled him to survive for twenty-five years in the games industry.

Mike would like to acknowledge the hundreds of students who have passed through the Games and Simulation Arts and Sciences (GSAS) program at Rensselaer Polytechnic Institute. They were a pleasure to work with, and may they all become superstars in the industry.

Mike would also like to acknowledge his colleagues in GSAS, most notably Marc Destefano, Kathleen Ruiz, Shaun Lawson, and Ben Chang, program director. It's been a wild fourteen years. Mike especially wants to thank colleague and game writer Maurice Sucking, who helped to set us up with our publisher.

We certainly want to acknowledge the work of our illustrator, Diana Nguyen, who created all the artwork for Taylor under some tight time constraints.

We would also like to thank those folk who read early drafts of this work, especially Dom Cristaldi, Andrew Dunetz, Spencer Johnson, and Chris Lynch.

A shout-out to the many fine people who work at game studios in and around the hip little city of Troy, New York. Thanks go out especially to Karthik and Guha Bala, founders of Vicarious Visions and now Velan Studios, and to Tobi Saulnier, founder and head of 1st Playable Productions. Their enthusiastic support for the GSAS program over the years has helped make it what it is. Thanks also go out to the greater business community of Troy, who work tirelessly to help a tired old northeastern mill town get back on its feet.

Finally, we would like to acknowledge the work of Laquana Cooke, PhD, Assistant Professor of Digital Rhetoric at West Chester University, for her thoughtful quotes, which we were, regrettably, in the end not able to use in this book.

Authors

Michael Lynch, Ph.D., has for the past fourteen years been teaching various video game design courses in the Games and Simulation Arts and Sciences (GSAS) program at Rensselaer Polytechnic Institute and enjoying Troy, New York.

Mike's checkered career began in the nuclear power industry and ended in that industry following the Three Mile Island accident in 1979.

Switching gears entirely, he went on to renovate a small planetarium in his hometown of Providence, Rhode Island, and then created programs for it. In the years following, Mike designed and built two recording studios and a concert lighting system.

He was an early adopter of personal computers, starting with a hobby machine in 1976. Later on, he got to write a lot of code, first for a major computer company and later for a successful Internet startup.

Mike has been a gamer ever since Pong, or, more precisely, ever since Clue. During his boyhood, Mike almost never lost a Clue game – because he had better algorithms. He regrets that he never had the opportunity in life to work in the game industry, but he is making up for that now.

Heading off to graduate school late in life, he finally settled down as an academic, which he has been ever since. His research interests center around the construction of a system for interactive storytelling, something that, he freely admits, is not ready to ship.

Academic Qualifications
BSEE (Honors), Electrical Engineering, Worcester Polytechnic Institute, Worcester, Massachusetts
Ph.D., Communication Science, University of Connecticut, Storrs, Connecticut

Adrian Earle, a lifelong avid gamer, Adrian has worked professionally in the video game industry for over twenty-five years. He has over thirty published products to his credit, including four original intellectual properties (IPs).

Adrian has worked as a designer, producer, senior manager of a major design studio, and freelancer and ran his own company for over three years.

He has been involved in the production of video games covering many genres, across several platforms, from the early rubber-keyed Spectrum through to modern PCs, SNES, PS2, Xbox, DS, 3DS, and, most recently, on phones and tablets for both iOS and Android devices.

In addition to his work in the computer games industry he has been involved with board games, compiled and published two sets of miniature war games rules, and was a consultant designer on a published card game.

He served on external committees for the master's program on game design at SMU Guildhall, and the associate degree course on game development and animation at Mildred Elley College.

Adrian has given innumerable talks and lectures on the game industry to schools, colleges, and the general public and was an adjunct faculty member for a semester teaching a course on the history and culture of games at Rensselaer Polytechnic Institute.

He is currently the game developer for All In Adventures, designing live action puzzles for a series of different themes.

Academic Qualifications

B.Sc. (Econ.) Honors—International Politics and Strategic Studies, from Aberystwyth University in Aberystwyth, Wales.

A Note to Parents

I F YOU ARE READING this, then maybe you have a son or daughter soon to be of college age who is just crazy about games.

To you, who may be about to pay out an extraordinary amount of money, in many cases to a top school so that your son or daughter can learn how to make games, this may seem like pure folly. Perhaps it is, but if you yourself went to college, try to remember what it was like simply to pursue some kind of learning just for its own sake.

If your son or daughter won't have it any other way, may we suggest that they double major? That is, they pursue an undergraduate degree in game design or game development and at the same time pursue a degree in a more traditional area. Computer science and game design often go together, and a solid training in computer science makes it a lot easier to find a job after graduation. The same would be true of other traditional areas like visual arts, although perhaps not to the same extent.

Keep in mind, as we'll keep mentioning, that the game industry is merely a branch of the entertainment industry, and it is just as wildly competitive as the film industry, the television industry, or the music business.

Ultimately, making games is a high-risk, high-return proposition, yet every year thousands of students find employment doing just that.

A NOTE TO STUDENTS

Dear student, please read the preceding section, *A Note to Parents*.

Introduction

WHAT COULD BE COOLER than working in the video game industry? Certainly not much else to a gamer, and if you're a gamer, you've probably already at least thought about it. Maybe you are already working in the industry or working on your own game project, what many call a "hobby project" or a "passion project."

If you are a high school student and you ask your parents, they might tell you to get real. They might advise you to do something serious where you can actually land a job. Maybe your parents are more supportive than that. If so, count yourself lucky, and go for it.

I.1 THIS… IS… SHOW BIZ

The video game industry is part of what people call show business, that is, the entertainment industry.

It doesn't quite seem like it, though, does it? When we think of show biz, we think of movies and television, Broadway plays, and rock stars. Once upon a time video games were looked upon as a weird, geeky fringe thing, where teenage boys (and they were mostly boys) would hang out in arcades and scare parents, while towns all across America were trying to shut the arcades down.

THE FIRST AMENDMENT

Pinball machines and the arcades that often housed them were long regarded as social problems ever since the pinball machine was introduced in 1932. Things weren't too bad during the early years, though, until slot-machine-style "payouts" were added to some machines.

Payouts meant gambling, and gambling meant organized crime. City after city (even New York City)—with good reason—banned the machines. The industry quickly pivoted—removing the payout mechanisms and inventing the *flipper*, thus inserting player skill into the games. Over time, cities and towns eventually lifted the bans, imposing stiff taxes along the way. NYC did not lift its ban until decades later, in 1974 (Paul 2016).

There matters stood until Atari's *Pong* was introduced in late 1972. It was wildly successful, and a number of new manufacturers were drawn to this "arcade video game" business. Through the 1970s, the number of available machines exploded, as did the arcades. For a while, it seemed like every strip mall with rentable space had an arcade in it.

And the historical pattern repeated. A number of cities and towns attempted to ban arcades. This time, the outrage was over the loud, raucous nature of the arcade itself, not to mention the theme of some of the games. This seems to be something that happens whenever teenage and twenty-something males (and they were over-whelmingly male) congregate.

But these new digital entertainment devices never had slot-machine payouts on them. On some occasions, arcade operators with deep pockets fought back on First Amendment grounds. The courts, in most cases, agreed, and arcades were able to continue operating. But none of these cases ever made their way to the Supreme Court. Other towns, like Marshfield, Massachusetts, kept the ban in place since it was never challenged, finally eliminating it in 2014.

(Eventually, most of the arcades disappeared, but that was due to market pressures. The arrival of home game consoles and the personal computer did them in.)

Fast-forward to 2011. In the landmark case *Brown v. Entertainment Merchants Association*, 564 U.S. 786, the Supreme Court ruled 7-2 that video games were works of art, entitled to full protection under the First Amendment (Totilo 2016).

Note: Some material adapted from For *Amusement Only: The Life and Death of the American Arcade* (June 2013).

Personally, we, the authors of this book, are glad those efforts didn't succeed. In the years since those dark days, video gaming has grown up, and video games (at least some of them) are now usually recognized as an art form in their own right, rivaling that other great technological art form, the motion picture.

As time went on, video gaming became more mainstream. Many other kinds of people started playing, not just teenage boys. Other kinds of games were getting made, too. Eventually, major entertainment corporations like Warner Brothers, Sony, and Vivendi got into the act. Video gaming became very profitable, just another way to reach into the entertainment consumer's wallet.

Little gaming companies became giant gaming companies. Still, even now, little studios manage to survive—barely—making it by taking chances, while the big outfits, working with big budgets, often prefer to play it safe.

But make no mistake, the video game business is show business, and there's the rub. As with any business, development studios and game publishers stay alive by making games that a lot of people want to buy. And even though there's no business like show business, the video game industry has a lot more in common with movies and television than we might care to admit.

I.2 WHO WE ARE

One of us, Michael "Mike" Lynch, teaches various game design and game storytelling courses at Rensselaer Polytechnic Institute (RPI) in the Games and Simulation Arts and Sciences (GSAS) program, one of the oldest, highest-ranked undergraduate game design programs, according to the *Princeton Review* (date unknown).

The other one of us, Adrian Earle, is a 25-year veteran of the game industry. He has credits on over thirty published video games, in addition to working on board games and publishing rules for miniatures. His job titles have ranged from assistant designer to senior designer, producer to senior producer, and head of the design group at a major games studio.

We got together to bring you this book based on our collective experiences. Hence the title: *Surviving Game School... and the Game Industry After That*. We hope that, above all, it gives you a realistic understanding of this industry, how to prepare for it, and how to break into it.

I.3 ONLY A FEW MAKE IT BIG, BUT THERE IS STILL PLENTY TO DO

Watching talent shows like *American Idol* or *America's Got Talent* can get depressing. They've largely run their course by now, but the idea here still holds.

It was fun to watch people make fools of themselves (maybe that was even the best part), but what was depressing was seeing how few people actually have what it takes to be a star, to be that person in front of the camera, adored by millions.

The game industry has its own stars, too, and if you are any sort of regular gamer, you probably know some of their names: Toby Fox, Jenova Chen, Gabe Newell, Irv Levine, Jonathan Blow, and Tim Shaffer, to name just a few. Maybe *you* have what it takes to be the next star.

Next time you're watching the latest big CGI-laden blockbuster at your local cineplex, on your Blu-ray player, or streaming off Netflix™ or Amazon™, stick around and sit through the end credits. Get a sense of just how many people it took to make that movie. While you're at it, look at all the job categories, too. So many different arts and crafts are involved.

Another reason for sitting through the end credits is you might get rewarded with a nice Easter egg* at the end.

Do you do this with your favorite games? Have you actually looked at the "credit crawl" that you can find somewhere in your favorite game? If you do, you'll see dozens, maybe even hundreds, of names listed. Check out the job categories, too. Later in this book we'll get into what those jobs are, and maybe you can see yourself fitting into one of them.

So the good news is that you don't have to be a superstar, although it helps. There is plenty of work to do for people with all sorts of talents and skills. You might not be the lead designer or the vision keeper or the big-picture person (at least not right away), but those dreamers and visionaries need lots of help bringing their visions to life. And whether you are a coder, an artist, or a writer, there is probably enough work out there to keep you busy.

I.4 ARE YOU A STAR?

But maybe you think that deep down you really, really have star power. There's only one way to find out, and that's to give it your best shot. Eminem's *Lose Yourself* from the film *8 Mile* is all about that. Listen to it a few times to get yourself fired up.

---

* In movies, an Easter egg is a bit of bonus footage placed after all the end credits to reward those patient enough to sit through them. In video games, an Easter egg is a bonus "cut scene" (a mini-movie) or bit of game play that rewards the player clever enough to find it. Among gamers, Easter eggs don't stay secret for very long.

But it doesn't come easy, even, or especially, for superstars. Whatever your particular strategy, you should probably plan on solidly mastering one skill, to the point where people take notice. Then you blossom from there.

Now, entire books have been written about motivation, and so we supply a list of some of the better ones in the appendix, but just talking about motivation is not the primary purpose of this book.

I.5 MAYBE YOU DON'T KNOW

More likely, though, you're at a stage in your life where you really don't know what you're good at, or what you want to do, or even what you'll be doing a few minutes from now. Entire books have been written about how to find your way in life, too, and we list a few of the good ones of those in the appendix as well.

But let's get into this a little before we move on.

Many young people we've met, both in school and those just starting out in the game industry, aren't always entirely sure what it is they ought to be doing in life. We think this is completely normal. You might be someone who, all your life, has thought that you were destined to be one thing, only to discover later on that you were really better suited for something else.

In the world of work, it is not uncommon for people to shift their entire careers several times over the course of their life. One of us (Mike) has done exactly that, only going back to graduate school later in life to get his Ph.D. Before that, he worked in the power industry, built special-effects projectors for planetariums, designed concert lighting equipment, had an Internet startup business, and wrote a lot of code. It's been a fun ride.

Your life may go like that, too; you just don't know how it will end up. The main thing is to go with your honest and sober assessment about *what you ought to be doing* and make sure to pay attention to what your gut instincts are telling you. Use your brain, too, but don't ignore your gut. Don't worry about getting this right the first time. Very few people get this right the first time.

Then, the main thing will be to *dive in and get going*. Change will come to you as it needs to.

I.6 LUCK AND SERENDIPITY

The world operates more by random chance than we realize. We moderns do not like randomness, although perhaps not at a casino or when rolling d20's (twenty-sided dice) in Dungeons and Dragons®, but most of us *hate* randomness in real life. We want to think that if we can only plan everything just right, control all the variables, get into the right schools, and make all the right decisions, things will turn out just peachy. Perhaps the ancients knew better. They were much more subject to natural disasters, plagues, and famines and so understood they really didn't have that much control over their lives. They didn't have valid scientific theories to explain lightning, thunder, or contagious diseases. The events of their lives, good and bad, were credited to or blamed on various gods.

There's a lot to say in favor of good planning and making good decisions, but in life *you never know*. One of us (Adrian) got started in the game industry through a chance encounter. He was studying for his Master of Arts in International Politics and Strategic Studies when he happened to mention to someone in a bar that he was a gamer and designed games on the side. That person was a games programmer and knew his company needed a designer. He arranged for a meeting between Adrian and his boss, and his plans for a career in academia as a college professor turned into a career spanning twenty-five years designing and producing video games. This can also happen to you, because *you never know*.

So one of us bounced around a lot during life while the other got lucky and discovered his life's destiny early on. Well, okay, maybe not that early on: Adrian had already spent ten years in the fire service as a dispatcher.

There is an old saying in motivational speaking circles: "Luck is what happens when preparation meets opportunity." This quote isn't modern, but goes all the way back to the Roman philosopher Seneca, and what he is simply telling us is that we make our own luck. Seneca had his head screwed on right.

ON THE SHORTNESS OF LIFE

Lucius Annaeus Seneca, also known as Seneca the Younger (4 BCE to 65 CE), was a noted dramatist and humorist, statesman, and Stoic philosopher. A prolific writer, he left a large body of work during his life, both fiction and nonfiction. One of his "dialogues" (a short philosophical work) was *De Brevitate Vitæ,* or, *On the Shortness of Life*.

Tl;dr: The key takeaways are (1) time is the only commodity that you cannot get more of in your life, and (2) a life lived wisely and well is a good life, no matter how long or short it is.

You can read it in Seneca (1932).

So go ahead, be thinking about what school to attend and what skills you most want to acquire. Think about it a lot until you feel convinced this is the best thing you can possibly be doing at this stage of life. Work hard and get yourself ready.

I.7 HOBBY OR PROFESSION?

It might be that you love games and want to make games but just don't see yourself doing it for a living. Maybe you ought to go to med school instead.

You can still make games, though, and it's never been easier. There are plenty of resources out there to get you started, much of it cheap and much of it free. We have a list of those in the appendix.

If you're in high school and reading this, one thing we want to ask is: *what's keeping you?*

This is especially true if you want to be a programmer (by the way, programmers in the game industry are usually called "engineers"). Have you learned Python yet? Have you visited www.python.org and downloaded everything you need to start programming in that wonderful Python language? Why not?

Have you downloaded the Unity® Engine yet? You can get it at https://unity3d.com/, and the engine is entirely free, at least until you get to the point where your game actually earns some money.

If you want something simpler to get started, there are Construct 2®, GameMaker Studio 2®, and RPG Maker®. If you want to build story-based games, there are Twine® and inklewriter®. All these are great for students of all ages to get started with. They are also good enough for professionals to use for fast prototyping.

And there are plenty more besides those.

We bring this up to get you to think about the question: *where is your passion?* If you really want to learn how to code and make games, there is nothing—repeat: nothing—stopping you except maybe your own fear, or laziness, or lack of curiosity. Or maybe you don't have a computer (even though any reasonably recent clunker can get you started). But this is the twenty-first century, and those excuses will no longer fly. These days we think everybody should know some code, or at least the fundamentals of how code works, even if that is not your life's mission.

So even if you don't see yourself doing this for a living, you can still make games.

What's Keeping You?

I.8 REMEMBER, IN THE END IT IS A BUSINESS

Never forget, if you work in the game industry, you're working in a business, one that needs to make a profit to stay alive to make more games. Much as we, as gamers, might scoff at those yet-another-sequel games that keep getting pumped out by the major studios, people keep buying them, and so the major studios are only too happy to keep supplying them.

ABOUT THAT WORD, "GAMER"

On the surface, a gamer is simply someone whose lifestyle involves playing a lot of games: games of any sort, whether board games or video games. But "gamer" has also picked up a lot of negative baggage over the years, accumulating such negative stereotypes as the overweight, antisocial dude who spends his life living in his parents' basement, wasting away his life playing shooter games. The term has also picked up connotations of "racist," "sexist," and other negatives as a result of various scandals and controversies that have sprung up over the years.

We are not about to go down that rabbit hole here. In point of fact, nearly half the U.S. population plays games of one sort or another, and it is unfair to attach such overly simplistic negatives to this huge population of people.

For our purposes, we prefer to think of "gamers" as people who simply love playing games and who make sure to leave time open in their busy lives to do exactly that.

The really lively sector of the industry, though, has for a few years now been indie gaming. This is where insane chances are taken by tenacious developers who believe in what they are doing and are willing to make some substantial sacrifices to get there. Even then, very few indie games actually make money, but some stand out and hit big with gamers.

These days, the space containing someone making a game purely out of passion shades imperceptibly into the two-guys-in-a-garage indie studio (where "guy" can refer to anyone of any gender). It's pretty amazing to think that one of the most talked-about games of 2015 was *Undertale*, developed by Toby Fox. This is one person, with the help of some friends, using GameMaker Studio 2, who made a game that impressed top industry people. Although it didn't win any of the big awards at the Game Developers Choice Awards ceremony at the 2016 GDC, it got a few nominations—and a lot of respect.

More recently, *Owlboy*, made by just a handful of people at D-Pad Studio, scored big with indie game fans. It was under development for nearly a decade (it launched in 2006), but many fans felt it was worth the wait. This is passion gaming at its finest.

We find it interesting—and more than a little gratifying—to see how the game industry has in some ways returned to its roots: a handful of people making something amazing in their parents' basement or garage.

You might have a game concept that appeals to a pretty narrow niche, maybe just yourself. What's great about being alive today is that there really isn't anything stopping you from making that game. Of course, it's another question whether or not other people will find it fun, or give you money for it or not—another issue we return to later.

So sometimes an individual project, built out of passion, turns into a major hit. *Minecraft*, anyone?

I.9 GETTING YOU READY

The rest of this book will be all about helping you to get ready to dive into this wonderful, dynamic, infuriating, crazy, difficult, rewarding, and FUN industry for that amazing day when all your hard work pays off and opportunity crosses your path. Let's hope you don't miss it.

HENRY ROLLINS...

… is one of the more controversial figures on the pop culture terrain. He came to fame as the incendiary front man of the seminal hardcore SoCal punk band Black Flag, continuing later as the leader of his own Henry Rollins Band.

He's also hosted his own talk show (which isn't quite the term for it) on the IFC cable channel and regularly tours the world standing in front of a mic, regaling the audience with his unique perspectives on culture, politics, and life in general.

He made a short video for the Big Think YouTube channel, explaining how all this came together for him early in life. It's worth a look:

https://www.youtube.com/watch?v=BkvEpoqFx6c

Welcome aboard!

CHAPTER 1

High School

OK, SO IF YOU are reading this chapter, you're probably in high school, right? If you are considering a career in the game industry, this chapter is for you. If you're done with high school, you could read this chapter for amusement.

Meanwhile, meet Taylor, who will be our companion during our journey.

Hello everyone, my name is Taylor and I am a gamer. That's me, fishing my backpack out of my locker.

I play a lot of games and think it would be awesome to become a game developer.

I know these two old guys who have had a lot to do with games, and they are going to help me achieve my ambition.

Why don't you follow me in my adventures as I move from high school to a career in games?

1.1 YOU CAN DO ANYTHING

Were you ever told when you were younger that you could be anything you wanted to be, like an astronaut or president of the United States? You've probably figured out by now that that's just about as true as (spoiler alert) Santa Claus.

Still, we all need dreams and aspirations to keep ourselves going, and getting into the game industry can be one of our dreams. After all, a lot of people *do* work in this industry, which directly employs about 42,000 in the United States alone, with another 100,000 people employed indirectly (Videogames 2014).

If you've made it this far, you are probably convinced that making games for a living is what you must do, and we don't want to rain on your parade; we just want to drizzle lightly on it, a reality check on whether your plan has a fighting chance.

You may also have grown up being told to "do what you love, and the money will follow" (Sinetar, 1987).* This one actually has a grain of truth to it, but it is not the whole truth. Look at its opposite: Doing what you hate might make you a lot of money, but you will be miserable, so what's the point? This seems to happen, for example, to a surprising number of people who go to law school, although solid data are hard to come by. Real lawyering isn't like *Law and Order*; much of it is exhausting, tedious paperwork, but it can be a great way to make a lot of money.

What is more likely to happen is that doing something you hate will sooner or later drive you out of that career. At least that's the way it would work in an ideal world. But once you get out of school, start paying off student loans, buy a house, and start a family, you might find yourself trapped instead. You might want to keep your options open.

So is the game industry right for you? Let's see.

We're assuming that you are an avid, maybe a rabid, gamer. So far, so good. But have you actually tried to *make* a game? That is, instead of merely playing someone else's creation, have you tried creating your own?

It doesn't have to be *Fallout 4*. It doesn't have to be *Pac-Man*. It doesn't even have to be *Pong*. Creating a game counts even if it's "only" a board game (and we deeply respect modern board game designers). It counts if it's a mod† or a level for a game that supports modding or player-created levels. It counts if you've picked up one of the many free game engines and design tools (e.g., Construct 2, Unity, Unreal Engine 4) and made a game using that. We have listed a number of these resources in the appendix.

If you've done this and, better, are still doing this, then you are showing the world that you have passion. Trust us when we say that this is going to count for a lot.

---

* *Do What You Love, The Money Will Follow* was the title of an immensely popular book by Marsha Sinetar, first published by Paulist in 1987. It sounds good, but in our experience the real world doesn't usually cooperate.

† "Modding" or making a "mod" refers to modifying an existing game using design tools (generally called "level editors") supplied by the game's publisher. Sometimes mods are unauthorized, with fans of the game constructing such tools and sharing their creations without the approval of the publisher. With so many cheap or even free game engines out there to play with, modding is less popular than it once was, but it is hardly dead.

1.2 CROSSING THE GREAT DIVIDE

Something funny, and a bit sad, happens when you Cross the Great Divide. We use that term to refer to what happens when you go from being a mere player to one who has picked up deep knowledge and experience about what makes games actually tick.

When you were "only" a gamer, you could have your mind repeatedly blown by each next, new great game. Of course, over time you begin to develop a critical sense and can start to tell the difference between good and bad game play, brilliant or cheesy stories, great or terrible character models, intelligent or stupid non-player characters (NPCs). It helps if you read a lot of game reviews, visit the fan sites, and exchange recommendations with friends.

All of us develop this critical faculty to some extent, and some of us are better at it than others. We do it with everything: cars, restaurants, music, movies…and games. Some people get so good at it that they get paid to be movie reviewers or restaurant critics. Nice work if you can get it.

But something happens once you pull back the curtain and start to learn the actual secrets (that aren't so secret anymore) of what parts go into a game and how they are all put together.

This happens to people who learn how to make movies, whether they went to film school or not. Once you begin to understand how stories are structured, how camera shots are carefully composed, how lenses and lighting and panning and dollying work, and all the rest of the filmmaking craft, some of the magic goes out of going to the movies.

Go through this process and you can no longer look at a movie the same way again. Part of your brain will be picking it apart, analyzing it, finding how some lame story exposition got snuck into the dialogue, or noticing how convenient some plot coincidence was, or why that background was so badly lit.

Do this with making games, and the same thing will happen. Why do the combos in this fight game tie my fingers in knots? Why do those textures look so stretched out of shape? What's with that annoying lag? Why is the frame rate so low? Why was I able to find a perfectly undamaged health pack in the rubble of an oil tank I just blew up? (This last one is from famed game designer Ernest Adams, who uses it as an example of especially stupid level design from an old James Bond game.)

But it's not all bad news. One kind of magic goes out of your life, but a new, deeper, richer kind of magic enters. And this works very much like learning stage magic and learning how tricks (or "illusions") are done. The gee-whiz goes out of it, to be replaced by a new-found respect for the brilliance and skill of the magician. Welcome to the club!

That's the deal you make once you choose to go pro, and there's no getting away from it.

1.3 WHAT'S A "PLETHORA"?

So here you are, a high school student trying to figure out what to do with your life. You are "paralyzed by a plethora of possibilities." According to thefreedictionary.com, a "plethora" is "an abundance or excess of something."

In the old days you probably did what your parents did, maybe farming or blacksmithing or baking. Life today, at least in the developed world, is different: You usually actually get to choose what you're going to do when you get older. That's the theory, anyway. But just as not everyone is actually going to grow up to be an astronaut or president of the United States, not everyone is cut out to work in show business, or the game industry in particular. If you want to do that, decide right now, and plan on working your butt off on your way to that first industry job.

Oh, and have some talent, too!

1.4 THIS SOUNDS PRETTY SCARY

All the things we just talked about, along with everything else that makes adolescence so rough, make for a pretty scary scenario.

You may be one of those teenagers who swaggers around, acting brave and in control, but, shhhh, we're all friends here, and deep down you are scared, and you know it. It's all a matter of being honest with yourself. In your innermost thoughts, you know you're going to have to confront a world that is a lot more confusing, complicated, and frightening than you ever imagined.

You are not alone. Everyone has to go through this. You are faced with making some really critical life choices, and you want to get it right. Of course, if your choices are between going to Harvard or Oxford, or buying the Lamborghini or the Maserati, or working at Goldman Sachs or Morgan Stanley after you graduate, well, this book wasn't for you anyway.

The rest of this chapter, and much of this book, is all about helping you figure out what you need to be doing to get ready, at least as far as getting into the game industry is concerned.

1.5 THINKING STRATEGICALLY

So you've gotten this far and are convinced that you are absolutely, positively going to go to Game School. The next chapter helps you select one, but before we get into that, you will want to "game" the rest of your four-year sentence in high school for maximum pay-off. What follows are some of the things to pay special attention to. All of them are about *showing initiative*, raising yourself above the pack so that you stand out. Adrian calls this being the "shiny cog," a phrase he heard in a talk* at GDC and that he feels exemplifies the attitude needed for a new entrant in the game industry.

Good Grades. Yes, we sound like your parents. Unfortunately, getting into good schools has gotten so competitive that you don't have much of a choice. This includes not only the grades you actually get in your courses, but also your SAT scores, the quality of your college application (including the essay), the letters of recommendation you line up, and all the rest. We have more to say about this in the next chapter.

YOUR COLLEGE ESSAY

It is perfectly natural to want to lard your college admissions essay with a lot of high-sounding phrases about changing the world and why you are just the person to do it. Admissions officers and their staffs read thousands of these, and they've heard it

---

* Adrian would really like to credit the speaker, but he did not make note of his name.

all before. If your essay reads like most of the others, it probably won't do much to boost your odds of getting in.

What works a lot better is to actually stay away from the grandiose boilerplate and speak about who you are as a person and what motivates you. To offer up a made-up tragic example: If one of your siblings or parents died from cancer, and that is what is motivating you to go into pre-med, then say so. You don't need tragedy in your life for this: Anything that lets the reader know what makes the genuine you tick will work better than fancy but generic boilerplate.

Advanced Placement (AP) Credits. If at all possible—and assuming you are a decent enough student—load up on AP credits. The best reason for doing this is to open up slots during your college career where you can take courses that are going to be a lot more interesting and useful to you than anything your high school likely offers. We can't stress this one enough.

It goes without saying that the AP credits you go for should be the ones that are going to be required of you once you actually get to college anyway. Good ones to load up on are calculus, physics, biology, and "Computer Science 101" or other starter courses in computer programming.

THE IMPORTANCE NUMBERS PLAY IN EVERYDAY LIFE

"If you learn nothing else, learn to speak the language of Math; you will need it everywhere…Spreadsheets, burn down charts, animation frames, colors, hit points, physics, file sizes…Learn to communicate well using numbers. No matter what career in the games industry you want, you need Math."

SPYROS GIANNOPOULOS
Software Engineer & Game Industry Veteran

Also, make sure these credits will actually be accepted by the schools that you are applying to. While taking any AP course is worthwhile and satisfying in its own right, you want it to do double duty for you by having it count toward graduating college.

Extracurricular Activities. What you do with your free time, besides playing and making games, says something about your character and your level of commitment to your community. College admission folk look at these as one of the factors that play into whether you get admitted or not.

It isn't quite so important what these extracurricular activities are. Of course, if you are a programmer and are a member of the Chess Club, well, that's hardly surprising. But it might be more interesting to at least some people looking at your application if you are a programmer and a member of the Ballroom Dancing Club.

Performing charitable work or community service also counts for a lot with admissions officers. If you devote part of your free time working with Meals on Wheels, that also says a lot about who you are.

See how this works? You're sending a signal that you are a well-rounded, community-minded person. And you are.

Summer Courses. Depending on where you live, you may be able to take courses for college credit at a local community college or take various "enrichment" courses offered through some colleges, museums, and art centers.

Taking courses for college credit is risky if you are still in high school. Besides the problem of actually getting to take one, you don't really have any guarantee that you can transfer these for college credit later on. If you go this route, and you've already been accepted somewhere, check with your college beforehand. Get it in writing. If you get into a really top school, they are going to be picky as to what other schools they will accept credits from.

Summer enrichment courses are another matter. They are usually shorter and much more affordable than a course that awards college credit. Courses that carry college credit are nearly always more expensive; what you will earn here instead is a certificate of completion of some sort, suitable for framing but not for putting on your college transcript.

These courses can be about practically anything: How to use Adobe™ Photoshop®, how to code in Python, how to write a short story. If your budget and work schedule allow for it, you may want to give them a try.

A third thing you can do with your free time is to take courses that attract your interest on sites like www.Coursera.com or www.Udacity.com. These online schools offer courses in practically everything, and they are a great way to ramp up a skill quickly and relatively painlessly.

Finally, there's the Internet. You can find endless tutorials on YouTube and other places, and they are a great way to skill up in something, like Photoshop or Adobe After Effects®, you need to start acquiring right now. Even professionals do this, and it isn't cheating.

Regardless of how you load up on all this knowledge, make sure you let people know about it on those college applications.

Your Portfolio. This item is so important that we devote a whole section to it later in this chapter. While not all schools require that you submit a portfolio of your work, many do, and you want yours to stand out.

Making Games. This goes without saying. One of us (Mike) is constantly amazed when a student comes along who wants to major in computer science but has never written a program. Thirty or even twenty years ago, that might have made sense, but today there is no excuse. More and more high schools even offer programming courses, although—if what students tell us is true—a lot of them aren't particularly good. Go back to the section on summer courses for a way out, or just look for programming tutorials and books on the Web.

Same goes for making games. It's never been easier or more affordable (as in, free) to get started. It is also possible that someone in your area offers summertime "boot camps" in coding or game design. Ask around.

Showing Initiative. All of the above are about making you look good to a college admissions officer, and all have value in their own right; we would be the last ones to disparage them.

But what you are ultimately trying to do here is "game" the college admissions process. You want to look so compelling to a college that they want you, need you, to be one of their students. (They also want your money, but that's another story.)

And this business of showing initiative doesn't stop here. If there is one theme you are going to run into again and again in this book, it is how important it is to devise brilliant and inventive ways of separating yourself from the herd.

1.6 THE ALL-IMPORTANT PORTFOLIO

Basically, a portfolio is a carefully assembled collection of your own, original, best work. You want to be working on your portfolio, early, hard, and often, with the intention of including it with every college application you fill out.

Nowadays this is usually a link to a website you construct that shows your work. Some schools prefer that you upload your best work to a specific site that lets them look at all the applicants in one place. One such site is www.slideroom.com.

Your portfolio has many more uses than just getting into a good school, however. You will want to maintain a solid portfolio of your work through college and during your time in the industry.

What goes into a portfolio? Traditionally, the portfolio is something artists assemble from the best works they have created. If the artist is a filmmaker of any sort, the portfolio often gets called the "demo reel." If the artist is a musician, the portfolio is usually called the "demo tape."

But the portfolio is not limited to the visual arts. Writers can create portfolios for their best writing examples: short stories, poetry, essays, and the like. Programmers can show off their best coding projects. Designers can show off their best design projects, including completed games.

What you want to put into your portfolio needs to be your best, repeat *best*, work. A tight portfolio, filled with excellent work, is a much better tool for convincing admissions folks than a bloated, sloppy one made up of everything you have ever created, good, bad, or ugly.

You need to be ruthless about this. Remove work that you know in your heart is substandard. If you cringe when you look at it, others may, too, and you might want to consider dropping it altogether.

One thing you *do* want to do is show works in their finished states, or as close to finished as possible. If you want to show off a game that you built, try to get it into the most polished, well-balanced, and fun shape that you can. One complete game that really does look complete is far more effective than a half-dozen partially finished games. This is true regardless of what you want to show: a painting, a musical composition, or a piece of software.

Unfortunately, anything you include in your portfolio that is an .exe file, that is, a piece of executable code like a game, will likely never get tried by someone reviewing your work. In this age of aggressive computer viruses, most admissions officers (and later, any game studios you are applying to) will be reluctant to launch your game. It's too dangerous.

So for games in particular, you may want to include a video clip of the game play itself so that the reviewers can watch that instead.

At this early stage of your career, when trying to get into a good college, you want to begin the career-long process of building an amazing portfolio. This is a topic we will return to several more times before we're done.

1.7 NOW LET'S GET ORGANIZED TO GET OUT OF HERE

If you are in your senior year, you need to be applying to colleges. Between your parents, your teachers, your guidance counselors, there really isn't much for us to add that you don't already know. We will just touch on the topic here.

The process ought to start sooner than you think, ideally, at least during the summer between your junior and senior years. For a more thorough checklist, check out:

bigfuture.collegeboard.org/get-started/for-parents/parent-action-plan-12th-grade

Summer—check out schools, see how expensive they are, maybe visit the most promising ones. Take the SATs.

Fall—get started on writing those college applications. Have people who know what they are doing review your work and heed their suggestions. Don't forget those all-important letters of recommendation. Begin lining up scholarships and financial aid.

Winter—keep after the financial aid. Take the SAT subject tests and the AP placement tests. Send out applications.

Spring—wait for those letters of acceptance. What you want to get in the mail is the thick envelope, not the thin one. Spend time with your parents deciding which school is going to be your best bet. Start locking down the money.

1.8 TAKING A YEAR OFF

You may have heard that maybe you ought to take a year off between high school and college, just so you can experience the world a bit and spend some time reflecting on your future. Traditionally, this has been done by backpacking in Europe, but you could backpack anywhere, but be sure to get your shots. The world can be a dangerous place, but a wonderful one as well.

Taking the year off can be good for the heart and soul, not to mention the mind. There is value in learning another language, for example.

So if you are able to afford it, we heartily recommend it, although we understand that not everyone will be in a position to do this.

You could instead take some time off later in your academic career, perhaps during the summer after you graduate college. You're older and more worldly and have better friends and more sophisticated tastes, not to mention more common sense. Besides, you will have earned it.

Of course, if a major game studio is dangling a job in front of you as soon as you graduate college...well, we don't have to answer that one, do we?

1.9 GRADUATION DAY

Graduation is an emotional time for most people, even if you're one of those swaggering, brave students we talked about earlier. And why not? You've just finished up four of the most harrowing, annoying, frustrating years of your life (so far) and you haven't even really started living yet.

Now you get to look forward to the next phase of your life, and for most of you that's college. But between graduation and your freshman year at college, there is this matter of the summer vacation, the subject of Chapter 3.

Just a note for our overseas readers. In the U.S., the term *college* includes what in Europe is usually referred to as *university*. We're going to use the word "college" for that higher education experience toward an undergraduate degree that follows high school.

CHAPTER 2

Paralyzed by a Plethora of Possibilities

Tʜɪꜱ ᴄʜᴀᴘᴛᴇʀ ɪꜱ ᴀʟʟ about helping you decide on a game design program. We saw what a "plethora" was in the last chapter, and with more than 700 colleges now offering programs in game design or game development, there is no shortage of possibilities to get paralyzed over. This chapter should certainly not be your only guide to selecting a good school, but we hope it will help you separate the wheat from the chaff.

2.1 GAME SCHOOLS, GOOD AND BAD

This is going to be a large section, so hold on.

When we last checked in on this, there were at least 700 colleges and universities offering undergraduate programs in a game-related degree. Just a decade ago there were only a few dozen. Undergraduate programs are the ones that award associate's and bachelor's degrees.

Frankly, quite a lot of these are "me-too" programs designed to cash in on the video game craze and, to be blunt, some of them are not very good at all. What you want is a solid program that, in the end, will actually help you land a job in the game industry.

Sometimes the situation is so bad that it veers into fraud. In 2016, the *Wall Street Journal* ran several articles about for-profit schools that did such a bad job of "educating" students that students were completely unable to land industry jobs. This, despite the glowing promises in the schools' promotional literature. The worst offender (already bankrupt) was Corinthian Schools (Douglas-Gabriel 2016a). Another one, ITT Tech, also recently went down the tubes (Douglas-Gabriel 2016b). The federal government has its eye on several others.

FOR-PROFIT VERSUS FLY-BY-NIGHT SCHOOLS

Let's be clear. We sharply distinguish here between schools that offer genuine value for the money you pay them (even if they are not chartered as "nonprofit" or "not-for-profit" schools) versus those schools that offer a shoddy, low- or no-value education for the money.

The former includes fine schools like DigiPen, while the latter includes the likes of Corinthian, which the federal government has, justifiably, shut down.

But don't dismiss for-profit schools altogether, as some are excellent. One school, DigiPen, stands out as offering one of the best programs available, nearly always ranking in the top five game schools overall.

How good is DigiPen? Two students from DigiPen created a "mod" of Valve Software's® terrific game *Half-Life* using the game engine that Valve Software kindly makes available for modding by the fans of the game. They made a game called *Narbacular Drop*. These two talented students were quickly hired by Gabe Newell, the CEO of Valve Software, where they went on to build *Portal*, one of the greatest video games ever made. Gabe has an excellent track record for spotting talent.

The for-profit model, *when it is legitimate*, works you hard…very hard. Going to school there is essentially like working a full-time job, one with lots of unpaid overtime. If you want to hit the ground running and get schooling over with in about two years, rather than four, then you may want to consider programs at schools like DigiPen or Full Sail.

At Full Sail you can complete a Bachelor of Science degree in Game Art in just 20 months, or online in 29 months.

At DigiPen you can choose from several interrelated majors. You can go for a Bachelor of Arts in Game Design or a Bachelor of Science in Computer Science and Game Design. There are also degree programs in Computer Science and Digital Audio, Digital Art and Animation, and Music and Sound Design, among others.

Keep in mind, though, that for-profit schools and traditional four-year programs offer very different experiences and promise somewhat different outcomes. The for-profit schools are all about getting you ready to get into the job market as fast as possible. The four-year programs claim to do a better job of making you a "more well-rounded person." If you learn programming at a for-profit school, you'll learn programming, but much less about a subject like art history or philosophy or what impact video gaming has on society. For that kind of knowledge, you are on your own. A four-year program, by contrast, provides many more opportunities to takes courses in these subjects.

2.2 WHAT TO LOOK OUT FOR IN A GAMES PROGRAM

First off, you want a program where you actually make games, lots of games. Ideally, this begins practically the moment you walk into your first class. And why not? More and more students these days are making games on their own, and so they are already, to an extent, "plug and play."

Any program that calls itself "Game Studies" should probably be double-checked for game industry relevance. Game studies is like film studies, in that it isn't generally about teaching *you* how to make games, but having you study what others who make games do.

Now, this is an entirely legitimate activity, because we do need people in academe who make it their life's work to consider important issues like sexism, violence, addiction, income inequality, and other social matters that video games might have an impact on.

But we assume you want to make games, not study how other people make them, and that's why we caution against anything that sounds like "studies," unless that's your thing. If you go this route, you are probably signing up for eventually completing a Ph.D. and becoming a faculty member at a college or university.

The same is true of programs that call themselves "digital media." There is nothing wrong with digital media, and some courses with that in the name talk about video games as well. But games are "interactive," and that is a whole other matter. Digital media embraces all the terrific—but still noninteractive—media made and distributed using digital hardware and software, which is basically everything these days.

What you *do* want to see are solid offerings that combine theory and practice in meaningful ways. While there are a lot of theoretical materials to get through in many of the courses, those materials need to be matched to practical exercises and projects to bring them to life. Making games is a lot like writing computer programs or making a movie: There is no substitute for actually making them. There is no such thing as games appreciation. That would be a lot like game studies.

So let's have a look at the basic kinds of courses you can expect.

2.3 CORE COURSES IN GAME DESIGN

Here we look at many of the courses you are likely to encounter during your stay. The names may change, but essentially you ought to be getting at least these.

"One of the biggest things graduates get from game development schools is a solid foundation, the ability to teach themselves, and the skill to rapidly adapt to whatever's needed. I always told my students that there are 100 things to keep in mind when designing and by the time they graduate they'll only be able to do 30–40 of them without thinking. That leaves 60–70 things for them to constantly think about, which is a daunting task. Every year after graduation they'll add another 10–20 things to the "done automatically" list, freeing up more of their brain for innovation and creativity. This means graduating school is only the beginning of becoming the developer they'll eventually be."

MICHAEL McCOY, Jr.
Designer and Lecturer, Boss Fight Entertainment

Game Design. Where it all begins. Designing games is what game designers do, but what does that mean? Well, you'll never get total agreement on this, but in essence a designer is someone who scrutinizes a "problem" from as many angles (you might hear them called "lenses") as possible, seeking to find a "solution," ideally the optimal solution. Design is all about making things useful, workable, productive, profitable, or, in the case of games, fun and entertaining.

As you will no doubt have this hammered into you in game school, designers cycle iteratively through a process of: (1) prototyping, (2) testing, (3) getting feedback, (4) refining the design. Rinse and repeat as often as necessary until everyone agrees (or insists) the design is "done." Or, you run out of time or budget on the schedule. Then you actually build the game.

"If I could give a new designer to the industry only one piece of advice, it would be to learn the difference between *good* design and the *right* design. Within our personal gaming history of board games, video games, party games, formal lessons in classrooms and lecture halls, we are inundated with what solid, elegant design is. In this day and age, we have a healthy amount of literature on the subject. When a designer comes out of school today, they should have a fairly robust knowledge of what quality design is, and the ability to create it.

The reality of the industry is that perfect design is not enough alone to make a viable product. Always consider what the goals of your design are. Is it simple enough? Does it make enough money? Does it support the play style you are trying to appease? Is it compatible with your art style?

In the end, commercial game design is customer driven, even if you are trying to make a political statement, or when your players don't even know what they want. Sadly, this a lesson that is typically learned the hard way, when we see our best designs pried away from us because they were not right for that product. Don't worry though, if you were brave enough to enter the game design field, then I'm sure you will come up with an even better design before you know it."

ROBERT GALLERANI
Design Principal @ Vicarious Visions

Design, which we like to call the D-word, is a fascinating, sprawling, inspirational mess, and we can hardly do it justice here. We've listed a few recommendations in the appendix.

Game Programming. You might not necessarily see this as a course separate from what the computer science department offers, but a course like this specifically exposes you to the kinds of programming challenges unique to games. It might use Python along with modern Python-based game engines, like Cocos2D or Pyglet. Or it might center on the powerful C# ("C-sharp") programming language as used in the Unity engine.

This course may or may not involve another important programming language, C++. You will encounter C++ if you set about learning Epic's Unreal Engine 4® (UE4). C++ is the native programming language used in that engine.

If you don't learn C++ here, and you are also majoring in computer science, we certainly hope you learn it in some other course. You're going to need it.

If you are planning on majoring or double-majoring in computer science, it is *essential* that you master some C++ and its predecessor language, C. We say "some" because many experienced programmers feel it takes years to get really good at it. C++ is easily among the fastest, most powerful, highest-performing, and trickiest languages out there. But with great power comes great responsibility. It is immensely difficult to learn. It is a serious programmer's programming language. It is truly hardcore.

You won't be taken seriously in a game industry job interview if you cannot demonstrate some skill in this language. The inner workings of nearly every modern game engine are implemented in C++. Many games (for the coding needed beyond that in the core game engine) are also written in C++. Every game built using the Unreal Engine (UE4) is coded in C++. As part of the interview process for programmers, most studios will give you a tough programming problem or two to solve as "homework," and your solution will need to be written in C++.

JAVA

What about Java, you ask? Skill in this language is valuable for so-called enterprise programming, such as banking and air travel reservation systems. It's also useful for developing Android apps, where it is more or less the "native language." But it is far less valued in the game industry, and it is used far less often to make games.

We would even go so far as to say that when you go shopping around for a solid computer science program, go for the ones that feature C++ as the major teaching language over Java.

By the way, we are not speaking here of JavaScript, which is a rather different language used for different purposes, notably for programming on the World Wide Web and, increasingly, for "single-page" apps, as might be found on a mobile device. Unlike Java, knowing some JavaScript may well come in handy.

Incidentally, as we saw, you're likely to get a good dose of Python as well wherever you go. We approve: Python is another of those must-know languages to clip onto your tool belt.

Even if you don't plan on programming for a living, we think everyone should get a little exposure to the art and craft of programming. This has been called by some "procedural literacy." You don't want people to think you are illiterate, do you?

Game Mechanics. You might not see a course like this offered, but this subject covers a lot of technical matters that you'll need to pick up at some point. These include establishing the core mechanics of a game, understanding the fine points of probability and random number generators, how to clean noisy data from accelerometers and motion detection devices (like the Wii Remote from Nintendo™, the Kinect from Microsoft™, and mobile devices), and a lot more.

Game Storytelling. Some games don't need a story; others are all about the story. A shooter game might have no more story than "kill all the zombies." A heavy story-based game will ideally have a well-crafted plot with nicely developed characters speaking intelligent dialogue. Writing stories for games is quite a different matter than writing for film or television because of the interactivity and that thing called "player agency." The player is in the story, and so the player affects how the story evolves. This leads to a lot of interesting challenges for the game writer that writers of noninteractive works never confront.

History and Culture. Games didn't just show up in the 1970s. Humans have been playing games of one sort or another for as far back as we have recorded history. A course like this surveys how it all began and how we got to where we are today. Also, since games are part of our culture, are affected by culture, and can have a big impact on culture, this is something to dive into as well.

Game Production. How do games get made? A course like this has you and your team build a substantial game while following the typical development cycle in use in industry (preproduction, production, postproduction, and so forth). One of us (Mike) teaches this course with actual game industry professionals (we call them *clients*); the other (Adrian) has played the role of client on numerous occasions. During the course, each student team has to keep its client and the instructor happy. Students learn a *lot* from a course like this.

Game Development. This is the core of your game school experience. Here you make games, a lot of them, and nearly always in small teams. There could be two or even four semesters of *game development*, with each installment setting the bar higher. Toward the end, you will likely be making a semester-long game, with the goal of producing something substantial, a game you will be proud to put in your portfolio.

It is often during the game development courses where the "human" side of teamwork bursts out. Yes, you will have to work with others, learn how to persuade others that your ideas are worth taking seriously, deal with creative but difficult people, and learn how to compromise without pouting or excessive drama. You will also have to get better, much better, at personal time management and those game development skills you've decided are the most important to master.

Level Design. Many games are built around the notion of the player advancing through a succession of levels, starting with the easily mastered and ending in the insanely difficult. In older games, these levels were "in your face": The player would explicitly reach the end of a level and get rewarded with a "cut scene" or other important piece of information. During that time the next level would load, and the player might see the word "Loading…" and maybe a progress bar. This was all forced on the designers because of the hardware memory limits of the time.

More recent games don't necessarily have levels in this old-fashioned sense, but in the background the levels are still there. It's just that they are stitched together seamlessly into a much larger continuous world, and the loading and unloading happen in such a way that the player is less likely to notice the interruption.

Someone has to construct all those pieces of a giant open-world environment and stitch them all together, and this is the job of the level designer.

In a course like this, you get to construct these pieces using appropriate software tools (level editors). Level editors come in many sizes and shapes, but the end goal of such a course is to have you learn what makes a level "good" or even "great." You might think this is pretty straightforward, but it's not.

Artificial Intelligence for Games. AI for games is not like the traditional AI found in the computer science department. GOFAI ("good old-fashioned artificial intelligence") only partly overlaps with what is needed for games. If you are at all interested in programming non-player characters (NPCs) or other parts of a game's intelligence, this course is for you.

AI, whether for games or not, is a vast and important field of study. Why, artificial intelligences may even be taking over the world! A course like this one only gets you started on this endlessly fascinating journey.

Experimental Games. In a course like this, you get to go wild trying out new game concepts, game mechanics, new art styles…whatever you want your experiment to be "about." This is an art-school kind of class, one where you get to be all-out creative while still working within deliberately imposed "constraints." Constraints, as you will learn, are a good thing, as they impose some discipline on your wild ideas, plus help you keep your project grounded in reality.

Many of the most remarkable indie games in recent years have the flavor of an experiment. We're thinking of games like *Super Meat Boy, The Stanley Parable, Antichamber, Don't Starve, Her Story,* and *Brothers: A Tale of Two Sons.* These are the sorts of games that could only come about as a result of somebody tinkering with the usual assumptions of what a game can be.

Research Project. This kind of course is relatively uncommon, but well worth it. Here you get to work with a faculty member on some research project somehow tied in with games. You might be writing a lot of code, conducting experiments on experimental participants (usually students from "Psych 101"), creating art or animation, or anything else that needs doing.

In other cases, you get to decide what to research, with the faculty member guiding you on how best to go about it (searching through the academic literature, constructing surveys and questionnaires, running experiments, and so forth). Either way, you'll get to experience a different side of academic life.

Senior or "Capstone" Project. As the names suggest, here you get to integrate all your talents and skills into something truly substantial. Usually this is a massive game development project involving a team for at least a semester-long commitment. The team could be small, four or five students, or quite large, a dozen or more. The project might take place in one semester or bridge several semesters. It can even be a game that shows commercial potential.

It is probably going to be the strongest item in your portfolio.

These are most of the courses you are likely to run into in a game design or development program. Every program is different, and you will undoubtedly see many other offerings than the ones we have touched on, courses such as Character Modeling, Advanced Artificial Intelligence for NPCs, Music Composition for Games, Sound Design, Writing for Games, and User Experience Design for Games. With 700 colleges involved, a complete list would be enormous, and at the end of the day you are just going to have to really look at what a particular course will teach you and decide if it will help get you to where you want to be.

Also keep in mind that you will be taking courses outside the games program. If you are a computer science type, you will have required courses to take in order to meet your course requirements. Most CS programs follow a fairly standard curriculum first established by the Association for Computing Machinery (ACM). Nowadays, it is jointly developed and revised from time to time by both the ACM and the Institute of Electrical and Electronics Engineers (IEEE) (ACM 2013). This is a massive 518-page report, so clearly those folks have given it a lot of thought.

If you are more on the art or music side of things, the course offerings are much less standardized, because, hey, it's art. It is safe to say that each art school has its own distinctive personality and puts its own unique stamp on what it considers a proper art education. Check out the art and music departments of your chosen schools to see what awaits.

2.4 CONCENTRATIONS AND MINORS

Most four-year universities offer packages of courses variously called *minors* and *concentrations*. There are many variations on these. Obviously, a minor will require fewer courses in some subject than its corresponding major, perhaps half as many, and will cover less material. Still, the idea of taking a coherent sequence of courses in some topic area makes sense, and other minors are designed to give you an overview of the central ideas in some field of study.

As such, this sequence is usually spelled out for you, and you'll need to take whatever core courses are required for the minor. There is then usually a handful of choices you take in the minor to complete the total number of required courses. In general, you will need to fill out paperwork to "declare" a minor, and you may additionally need approval from the department offering the minor. This is all so that your completion of the minor will appear on your diploma.

Since you are in college anyway, you can certainly add a minor (or even two) to your regular workload. If you are in visual arts, for example, you could minor in filmmaking, or even computer science if that works for you. The idea here is that opting for a minor in general makes you better educated than simply taking a random assortment of courses all over the map. It's a matter of getting a deeper understanding of some particular subject rather than a superficial understanding of a lot of unrelated subjects. There is nothing wrong with being interested in all sorts of things, mind you, but the idea is for you to get a more solid foundation in something specific.

A concentration, if your school offers them, is an even more lightweight kind of minor. It's based on the same idea, that of going into more depth in one subject, but fewer courses are required, perhaps as few as three.

One thing to keep in mind is that completing a minor will usually appear on your actual diploma, whereas a concentration appears on your transcript but isn't shown on the diploma. If this sort of official recognition matters to you, then take the extra course or two and be in a declared minor.

One final point about minors and concentrations. Whichever one you pick, you should be comfortable doing that work in its own industry, one not related to games. Don't choose a writing concentration if you wouldn't be happy writing for other entertainment media or as a journalist, advertiser, or blogger. It's a tough reality to face, but the hard fact is that you might need to start in a related field before you can move into the game industry. This is quite all right! Many people in the industry (including some of our dearest friends) came from somewhere else, like film or television or sculpture, then made the switch. They bring to the industry the unique perspectives they gained elsewhere, and the industry is better for it.

So make your work in the minor or concentration part of your Plan B in case you are unable to land an industry job right after graduation.

CHAPTER 3

Before You Start College...

S O YOU GRADUATED HIGH school and are looking forward to college in the fall, but first to having a nice summer vacation. Maybe you have an internship or a job.

We suggest you enjoy at least some summer vacation before heading off to college in the fall. You will get very busy once that starts. But even if you have the whole summer off, you can't rest too easy.

3.1 WHAT ABOUT THE PORTFOLIO?

We brought up portfolios before, and so of course you've followed our advice from the previous chapters and put a killer one together.

Consider doing some maintenance on your portfolio. No one is going to see your latest efforts just yet since you've already been accepted to college, but it helps to keep your portfolio fresh and up to date. Basically, you'll be doing that for as long as your career advancement depends on keeping it up to date, which, if you are lucky, could be over twenty years. ☺

An old trick a lot of professional writers use is to write something and then "throw it in the drawer." The writer lets some time interval go by, perhaps several days or even weeks, before looking at it again.

This is especially shocking to young writers when they first employ this trick, but even experienced writers become chagrinned at how lousy that first draft was. *All writing is rewriting*, as they say.

Your portfolio works the same way. You probably haven't looked at it since last winter when you were applying to colleges. Since then you have hopefully done some new work that is better and more polished than your earlier work. This is one reason to work on your portfolio continuously.

So as you review your portfolio, expect the occasional cringe or facepalm.

But we know you guys. You've graduated, it's party time, and you're not going to do this now, are you?

3.2 AREN'T YOU CODING YET?

Let's get into that idea of procedural literacy some more.

Procedural literacy is a term popularized by noted game designer Jesse Schell, although he didn't coin it.

Procedural literacy is a skill, a kind of literacy, like ordinary reading, in which you are able to think in terms of *processes* and *procedures* as a series of definable steps. Breaking down and understanding those steps is how you come to understand complex processes— ones that at first glance seem too mysterious to figure out. This is how programmers—and engineers in general—build complicated things. They break down complicated projects into simpler, more manageable, more understandable steps.

JESSE SCHELL

Jesse Schell is Distinguished Professor of the Practice of Entertainment Technology at Carnegie Mellon University's (CMU) Entertainment Technology Center (ETC) and the author of the indispensable game design book (Peters 2014). His studio, Schell Games, is a widely recognized builder of so-called serious games.

He is also the person who popularized the word *gamification*, something we'll talk about later.

Jesse Schell believes that *everyone* who works at developing games needs to develop some level of procedural literacy, and we wholeheartedly agree. People who already love to program don't have a problem with this, but other creative people often struggle with attaining some mastery over it.

It's all a matter of unwinding big problems into a lot of little problems. There's an old joke: how do you eat an elephant? One bite (or byte) at a time.

Two fundamental ways of looking at the world through the lens of procedural literacy involve *loops* and *conditionals*.

In programming, the ubiquitous **for** loop handles looping, and we all do this constantly in our everyday lives. Curiously, though, it seems quite difficult for some people to grok how a **for** loop works when considered abstractly. It's the kind of thinking that programmers routinely engage in but that nonprogrammers sometimes struggle with.

"GROK"

"Grok," a word once popular in the computer programming community, is a Martian word that appears in Robert Heinlein's classic novel *Stranger in a Strange Land* one of the landmark science fiction novels from Sci-Fi's Golden Age (Heinlein 1961). "To grok" literally means "to drink," but it means much more than that: to "drink" so deeply about something that one comes to a state of total understanding. We think this useful word deserves to come back into popular use.

Let's start with an easy, real-world example to show you what we mean:

```
for each the_item in grocery_bag:
    put the_item away
```

This doesn't quite read like regular English, but the key ideas are there. And it isn't a particularly elegant piece of coding, either. We call code that looks like this *pseudocode*, a rather brittle and formal version of English or other language that expresses the idea of what a program is supposed to do in a more-or-less human-readable way. Unlike real English, it's very formal, so that we can get from it to actual computer code in a reasonably straightforward way. There is no poetry about it at all.

That, in a nutshell, is what a **for** loop does. And this is just the beginning of what procedural literacy entails.

Another basic idea is the *conditional*, basically an **if-then** sort of statement. Actually, it is better thought of as **if-then-else**, because you nearly always want to handle both situations. To continue with our example:

```
if the_item is perishable:
  put the_item into the refrigerator
else:
  put the_item into the pantry
```

We can now combine the **for** and the **if** to produce the pseudocode for what we do when we return home from grocery shopping:

```
for each the_item in grocery_bag:
  if the_item is perishable:
```

```
    put the_item into the refrigerator
else:
    put the_item into the pantry
```

This is what procedural literacy is all about.

3.3 ARE YOU A WRITER OR AN ARTIST? KEEP A JOURNAL/SKETCHPAD!

This is another way to spend your summer. Buy a beret, hang out at Starbucks™, nurse a latte, and scribble or sketch in your journal as you people-watch and eavesdrop on their conversations. This is the clichéd stereotype of the writer, but there is some truth to it.

The practice by writers of maintaining journals and of artists keeping sketchpads is ancient, and people still use it because it works. Whenever you get an idea, overhear someone say something clever, or are told about a book or movie, you write it down in your journal. If you see a cool character or event, make a sketch of it. Over time you amass a vast amount of raw material for your next great story, screenplay, poem, song lyrics, or exhibition.

If you are trying to be a writer and are getting frustrated by the process, it may be because you haven't started a journal. While you may think that you don't need one, that you can keep all the cool stuff you encounter in your head, you probably can't unless you have one of those trick photographic memories.

So keep a journal or sketchpad! This practice isn't only for writers and artists, either. Anyone can benefit from this.

3.4 MAKE GAMES!

You can be doing that, too. You already have a lot to work with, and you can continue developing your best ideas with all that free time.

But if you'd rather skateboard, we understand.

CHAPTER 4

Day One

4.1 THIS… IS… COLLEGE…

First thing you're going to get smacked with is, college is not very much like high school. At all. And you are going to like that very much.

One thing we recommend is putting some space between you and your parents when you go to college. You won't be able to do this if your college is near your home. Once you are in college you may notice that some of your friends with parents close by don't really seem to be living their own lives. College is a chance to learn to be an independent person in a safe environment. We think a lot of students take advantage of that.

"Game development schools are very intense experiences and routinely push students to their limits… but why? It's because every project in the game industry is an experiment, with developers struggling to overcome challenges they've never encountered. If graduates struggle with the daily work load, how can they possibly overcome these unexpected challenges and complete their projects? While existing skill sets are useful, developers constantly adapt to the needs of the project, making teaching yourself a most valuable skill."

MICHAEL McCOY JR.
Designer and Lecturer, Boss Fight Entertainment™

4.2 WHAT YOU CAN EXPECT

After you get over the initial shock and confusion, you'll quickly settle into a routine. You have classes to go to, meals at the cafeterias, and all sorts of extracurricular activities to choose from. You have "freedom" to run (or ruin) your life, but with that comes responsibility.

One of these activities, no doubt, is playing video games. Did you bring your Xbox® or PlayStation® with you to your dorm? Maybe your roommates did. The temptation will be to play a lot more video games now that your parents are not around to stop you, and this is why you need to be careful.

It is all too easy to fall into this trap, playing games so much it starts to interfere with your schoolwork. You need to face this fact right away before it becomes a problem. One of us (Mike) once had a student who boasted he played a well-known MMORPG 14 hours a day. Our lawyers didn't want us to tell you which game that was, but maybe you can guess. As the instructor, I was not impressed, and sure enough, he basically washed out after only one semester.* You simply cannot sit in your room all day playing *League of Legends* or *Overwatch* or any other popular MMOG and expect to graduate college on time.

It is one uncomfortable reality that games and, more importantly, game developers have to confront. Games really can be addictive (just like a lot of other human activities like running, junk food, or sex). This shouldn't be surprising because there is such a thing as gambling addiction. Machines such as slot machines, especially modern video slot machines, are expressly designed to get people to keep feeding money into the machines. This all works through a process called *operant conditioning*, which psychologists have studied for decades and which is now well understood.

TURNING A RAT INTO A JUNKIE

Operant conditioning, first identified by behavioral psychologist B.F. Skinner, is the basis for the classic laboratory rat behavior. Put a lab rat into a box, and reward it with a pellet of food whenever it pulls a lever. At first it won't know how to do that, so early on, you reward the rat if it just gets close to the lever, then later touches the lever, then later actually pulls the lever. Before long the rat will happily pull the lever over and over again until stuffed.

Then you start the rat on a *reinforcement schedule*. Reinforcement is just another way of saying "reward." You don't always reward the rat for every lever pull. You skip

---

* If you are a true gamer, this is a challenge you will have all your life. When he had his own company, Adrian and his business partner had to ban the playing of *DOOM* at work because not enough work was getting done. (Yes, they were both guilty of playing it too.... ☺)

a couple at first, then more and more, stretching out the number of times the rat has to pull before getting a pellet. Putting the rat on a *variable reinforcement schedule*, having each reward arrive only after an unpredictable number of pulls, is the most powerful technique of all. Congratulations, you've just created an addicted rat.

This is how slot machines work.

This is one ethical consideration you may have to confront during your working career: Just how to balance making a game intensely fun against the risks that playing something too much fun might entail for some people.

If you already have this problem, if you are doing too much of anything that is affecting your school work, or you think you are sliding into this problem, you need to catch yourself as soon as you can. Try to trick a part of your brain into noticing the problem so you can take the appropriate steps *before* it gets serious. It's a lot more difficult to get out of an addiction than to slide into one. If people keep telling you that you have a problem, then maybe you do have a problem. Will you act on that? Unfortunately, we humans seem to be wired to reject such advice and erect a wall of denial, right up to the point where denial is no longer possible.

Good colleges and universities these days offer student health programs, including mental health programs, which are there to help. There is no shame in making use of these, and medical privacy laws let you be discreet about it. Depending on where you live and the policies at your school, it may even be possible to get with a handle on the problem without involving your parents, because if you are over 18, then you are technically an adult. But if you have a healthy and honest relationship with your parents, it is certainly best to involve them.

And it goes without saying that the same is true if you are having a problem with drugs or alcohol.

Obviously, this is not something we can advise you about in a book like this, but we do want to warn you about the hidden dangers of all that new-found freedom you get in college. At the very least, become aware of the support services your college offers.

Finally, one paradoxical reality that will hit you is that, once you start making games, you will end up playing games much less often. We make this point several times in this book. You may be saying to yourself, "That won't be me," but sooner or later it will.

Despite everything we said about game addiction, though, *not* playing games when what you do is make games is actually a bad thing. At the very least, you need to keep up with the competition and what's going on the industry, so leave some time in your schedule to play games.

4.3 MAKING NEW FRIENDS

You will make a lot of new friends (and maybe an enemy or two) at college as well. The hormonal storms you've been experiencing as a teenager are quieter now, but still raging, so some of your new relationships may occasionally get dramatic and stormy, too.

College is a good opportunity to develop your "emotional intelligence" (Goleman 2006). There won't be a college course called that, but you are at a point in your life where you can form some excellent friendships, ones that will last well past graduation. Don't expect this to be entirely painless, as some people will try to screw you over or fill your head with nonsense. Choose your friends wisely!

4.4 FORMING NEW TEAMS

Just as you can get better at forming long-lasting friendships, you can get better at finding like-minded people to work with on team projects.

Most game design programs, just like real-world projects at game design studios, are heavily team-based. Most of the games you make will involve your being a member of a team and making your contributions to the final project. But many different kinds of people, people with different talents, skills, and passions, make up these teams. When we say "like-minded" we really mean people *you can work with*.

Even so, there are usually a handful of "lone wolves" prowling amongst the student body, and you may be one of them. A lone wolf is someone who wants to do it all himself, without aid or assistance of any kind. Certainly this is possible. Jonathan Blow, who made the game *Braid*—and essentially launched the indie game movement—comes to mind.

For this to work, you need to be (1) extremely talented and (2) not too abrasive.

4.5 MEETING THE PROFESSORS

This is one of the big differences between high school and college. If you go to a decent school, you can expect to have some quality interactions with the faculty. We hope these will be the pleasant kinds of interactions, not the unpleasant kinds.

Some courses (like our iconic Psychology 101) may be a "factory" class where you listen to lectures in a room with 300 other students. Your exams may be multiple-choice questions on "bubble sheets" (like the old-style SATs) or online, or essays graded by teaching assistants (TAs), who are overworked and underpaid graduate students. Not much chance to get to know the professor here, except for the occasional question you get to ask during class time.

But the game courses should be better than that, with a much more favorable student-teacher ratio. It is much more likely that you both can get to know each other better. This is especially true if you stand out as an exceptional student. You may get to work on cool projects and be given opportunities that might not be offered to others.

Your professors are human, too, so don't be so afraid of them. Most of them are not like your high school gym teacher or vice principal.

"I've been in the industry since 1995 and done every game team job save hard core programming, animation, and detailed art. I've seen and experienced just about everything, but by far the hardest job I've ever done is teaching. Students routinely challenge you to grow and stray away from business as usual. I always approached teaching as a presentation of my knowledge with the caveat of 'I'm not infallible.' When students disagreed with something I said, I allowed an open discussion to see if I could poke holes in their theory and prove my way of thinking, which was usually the result; however, when they successfully defended their point, it forced me to look at things from a different perspective, which was an amazing thing!"

MICHAEL McCOY Jr.
Designer and Lecturer, Boss Fight Entertainment

4.6 GETTING CHALLENGED BY NEW IDEAS

If your school is doing its job, you will be exposed to all sorts of new ideas and new ways of thinking. Some of these may challenge deeply held beliefs and make you uncomfortable. In our opinion, college shouldn't be about so-called safe spaces. It is about giving you new ways to grow.

Now, if you're tempted to throw this book against the wall in disgust, please hear us out. We want to save you from a world of hurt. The real world is a much harsher place than you think it is, and it will quickly punish you every time you mess up. If you develop a reputation for complaining about every little thing, taking offense at the mildest remarks of others, requiring "trigger warnings" before any content that might challenge your current world views, then be prepared to be unemployable when you get out. Acting this way is a luxury you can maybe afford while in college, but it won't get you very far once you get out.

CHAPTER 5

Year One

5.1 JOIN THE CLUB

If your school has a game development club among its student clubs, then we suggest joining it. These are a great way to hook up with other students who make games, especially students who are further along in the program than you are. Most of the time these people are happy to help.

Many, though not all, of the colleges that have game design or game development programs are in close proximity to at least a handful of game studios, some of which are going to be small and independent operations. If your club's leadership is suitably dynamic and resourceful, they will occasionally bring in outside speakers from these studios to give talks.

No matter what the subject of the talk is, you want to go to these. Hearing from an industry professional, even someone who has only been out of school for a year or two, will give you insights that you won't get from the classes you take. Plus, you get to ask questions and maybe converse with them privately afterwards. Just don't be too pushy. This sort of contact might later lead to a nice internship or a job if you play your cards right.

5.2 THE INTERNATIONAL GAME DEVELOPERS ASSOCIATION

The International Game Developers Association (IDGA) has local chapters all over the world. Student membership rates are quite affordable, and if you ever get to the Game Development Conference (GDC) in San Francisco, you'll be able to attend IGDA events—and get free stuff, too!

Visit www.idga.org to learn more. Even if you can't afford to join, this site offers a wealth of information about the industry that you can tap into. Plus, you can usually sneak into monthly meetings because in most places they don't check for ID at the door, and even when they do, you can usually get an invitation as a guest of a member for at least a couple of visits. The IGDA booth at the GDC is rather stricter about memberships (there are only so many free T-shirts, after all), but it is still worth going and chatting to the booth staff. Remember, this is about building up your network of professional contacts, as well as listening and learning from the talks.

5.3 GAME JAMS…DO THEM!

One very valuable event your on-campus game development club will probably offer is the *game jam*.

You probably already know what these are. In a game jam, you get to work together with others to form a small team (or you can work solo if you insist). The jam starts and ends at fixed times. Typical durations for game jams are 8 hours, 24 hours, 30 hours, and even 48 hours.

Your club might host one, two, or possibly more game jams in a semester, each usually of different durations.

At the start of the jam, the theme (think of it as the "secret ingredient," as you might see on a cooking show on the Food Channel®) is announced. You and your team then have the stated number of hours to make a game that somehow incorporates that theme. At the end, time is called and the teams show their stuff to the judges. The judges disappear for a while to discuss what they have seen and then return to announce the winners.

The judges can consider any number of factors, but creatively incorporating the secret ingredient is definitely going to be one of them. They might also judge on originality, aesthetics, game play, sound design, or whatever else they've agreed on.

Then prizes are awarded. These are usually something quite nominal, like a MatchBox® truck or something, although occasionally the prizes are more substantial.

We strongly recommend doing game jams as often as you can manage. A game jam brings together a number of desirable things that make them especially valuable for game students.

> "Go to lots of game jams and hackathons. You'll meet great people and learn much more than you plan to."
>
> JON MESCHINO
> *Game Developer*

First, you are put under some intense time pressure, and you will be surprised how much you can do when the pressure is on. Somehow your creative juices really kick into high gear when a deadline is looming.

Second, only finding out about the secret ingredient at the last minute also helps fire up your creative juices. The secret ingredient works as a constraint, one that forces you to focus on finding a creative solution.

Third, related to that, you are forced to devise solutions to problems you likely haven't encountered before. The secret ingredient might force you to build a game in a genre that you don't normally play or have you confront a design challenge you never confronted before. This is all good.

Fourth, you will be thrown in together with interesting people you may not have worked with before, and you will learn all sorts of useful things just by working with them.

Fifth, game jams are a great way for you to get some valuable exposure and visibility. You may be able to make new contacts and open up new possibilities just by showing up and participating.

Sixth, and most important, it makes you a much more attractive prospect for potential internships, co-ops, and employment.

In our experience the students who did multiple game jams tended to land the best jobs at the best companies. *We cannot recommend these enough!*

THE GLOBAL GAME JAM®

The Global Game Jam (GGJ), founded in 2008, is an annual event that takes place in late January.

Every year, thousands of game makers—students, amateurs, and professionals—gather in various physical locations around the world to make a game in 48 hours. If you live or attend school near any large urban center, chances are there will be a GGJ going on.

To quote from the organization's website, "Think of it as a hackathon focused on game development. It is the growth of an idea that in today's heavily connected world, we could come together, be creative, share experiences and express ourselves in a multitude of ways using video games—it is very universal" (Global Game Jam 2017).

The GGJ is a very high-profile affair, with winners becoming well known internationally. It is great to win one of these and is a terrific career boost, but just going through the experience is well worth your time.

Interested? Visit globalgamejam.org.

By the way, the GGJ is not the only game jam event held regularly, merely the best known. Another is Ludum Dare at www.ludumdare.com. To see a list of game jams going on all over the world, check out www.indiegamejams.com.

5.4 MAKE GAMES ON THE SIDE

Even with the games you make as class assignments and the games you make in game jams, you could be doing even more. These are the games that are going to be games you're most passionate about. Not surprisingly, these are sometimes called "passion games."

Sure, you will be making the games you want to make in your courses (unless the instructor tells you otherwise), but these don't usually quite fit the bill. Games you make on the side will be the ones you care most about. They are the ones you will be most willing to see through to completion. Remember what we said about having that finished, polished game in your portfolio. Incidentally, that final phase, balancing and polishing, is actually quite tedious and time consuming. It is fussy work: you hammer away at it, tweaking settings, crafting better textures, adjusting color palettes, balancing the game, and a whole lot more, until you reach the point, finally, where you declare it *done*, and you can move on.

Sometimes, this game can be a continuation of a game you made initially for a course or a game jam. This means you probably teamed up with other students, and this is going to introduce some interesting problems. At the same time, it will let you develop some very useful skills.

First of all, because this is your passion game, you will get to exercise your powers of persuasion. You are its vision keeper. If you liked working with your teammates, and you can convince them to keep going on this game, you just might be able to pull it off.

In situations like these, though, your teammates will very likely have their own ideas for their own passion games. If so, you might find it better to part company (amicably) so they can pursue their own visions. You might want to add other people to the team who are more attuned to your vision.

But since this chapter is titled "Year One," you are probably not quite at the point where you can pursue your own passion game effectively. You are skilling up, and you are just getting started with that, so continue to make games on the side, but help others make their games of passion, too. These will be people in a later year than you, and you can learn a lot just by being a member of their team.

How do you find such people? Through your game club. This works, because most of the time in your classes you will be in the same year as everyone else, but the game club will have members in different class years and at different stages in the program. Later on, when you become an upperclassperson yourself, you will find younger students at the game club to help you with *your* passion game.

So whether you are in a position to make your own game or can help someone else, just make games, outside of class and outside of game jams. Bear in mind that while you are learning about video games, and they are your ultimate career goal, there is nothing wrong with making other types of games, too. Board games and card games still require all the game mechanics and fun factors that a video game does, but in some ways they are harder to design because any "math" that can't be handled by the computer has to be handled by human players.

5.5 READ THE "TRADES"

Very few industries are as dynamic (some would say crazy) as the game industry. Things are constantly changing, and keeping up makes busy people even busier.

All the latest industry news can be accessed on the web. Some of the material is quite high-powered and usually only available to industry insiders, who pay hefty subscription rates to access it. Quite a lot of these involve the business side of the industry, items like marketing research data, which are expensive to produce but quite valuable to senior game management. You really won't have much need to read these at this stage of your career.

But besides all those fan sites (and there are thousands), a few stand out as important resources anyone can access. In no particular order (and there are more besides these), they are as follows:

- *Gamasutra* (www.gamasutra.com). This is probably the granddaddy of trade resources on the web. Not only can you get the latest news as to what industry leaders are up to, you can access a massive archive of well-informed articles about all aspects of game development, design, and marketing.

- *Game Industry Biz* (www.gamesindustry.biz). This site not only offers straight game industry news but also articles that get more into background discussions and analyses about more long-term industry trends.

- *Game Insider* (game-insider.com). This site is more fan-oriented, supplying plenty of content about the latest games, the latest trailers for games, and so forth. It is a bit more enthusiastic and less outright critical (in the good sense of "critical").

- *Grand Text Auto* (grandtextauto.soe.ucsc.edu). This is an academic site, specializing in the matters of "computer narrative, games, poetry, and art," to quote from the site's banner. If you are interested in the more out-there issues of how stories can be generated procedurally, for example, this site might be of interest.

- *IGDA* (www.igda.org). We discuss the International Game Developers Association in several places elsewhere in this book. The IGDA is a nonprofit organization dedicated to serving the people who make games. This includes matters of "quality of life," for example, working to eliminate 100-hour workweeks and permanent crunch time. The various activities are organized around special interest groups, aka SIGs. A student membership is affordable and definitely worth your while.

- *Kotaku* (www.kotaku.com). This is another constantly updated news site with plenty of content that relates more to the popular-culture side of video gaming, but it has breaking industry news as well. Tune in here to see what's going on in the minds of gamers at the moment.

5.6 GETTING OVERWHELMED

We bring this up early because it is so important. College is stressful, and college isn't high school. Don't expect to be babied or cut much slack compared to high school. And why would you want that anyway?

If you didn't enter college with good "time management" skills, expect to have a rough time of it. In our experience, good time management skills among college students are pretty rare. The ones who have them tend to be the ones with the great GPAs or who took a year out between high school and college. Whether they worked, volunteered, or just traveled, it all involved learning some personal time management, even if only so they didn't miss their flights.

Sure, talent and raw ability count for a lot, but being able to manage your time effectively goes a long way toward closing the gap.

This is something you need to have out with yourself. If you procrastinate, find yourself slapping together assignments at the last minute, or never doing the kind of quality work you know you are capable of, then you may have a problem.

What's great about good time management skills (and good "discipline" in general) is the enormous amount of time and energy they release. When you are able to keep on top of things and not spin your wheels over useless activities, suddenly the whole day just opens up.

Just don't think of time management "discipline" as some sort of unpleasant punishment to endure but as liberation of the one thing you are given only a finite supply of: the minutes and hours of your life.

If what we just talked about sounds like you, then get onto your favorite bookseller's website and order *Getting Things Done* by David Allen (Allen 2002). Don't procrastinate! It will change your life.

Getting Things Done

Yes, this indispensable little book has the power to change your life. This is not a book about making better to-do lists. In fact, the author doesn't particularly like to-do lists, at least not the usual kind.

What the author does do is take you through the process of turning those giant projects into a series of smaller steps, ones that you can actually work on. He'll teach you how to best carve up that elephant into easy-to-digest pieces.

Even if you don't have a problem with time management, this book is worth a look.

5.7 BURNING OUT

If, after all this, life seems like an endless treadmill you can't get off, you may be tottering on burnout. Burnout is serious.

It can take a while to recover from burnout (in school or in life), so you want to be able to read the warning signs and take action before things become critical. This is a common theme in this book—learning how to act on things before they blow up in your face. Burnout is no different.

How do you know if you are tottering on burnout? One checklist you can check yourself against can be found here:

www.psychologytoday.com/blog/high-octane-women/201311/the-tell-tale-signs-burnout-do-you-have-them

As we noted earlier, most schools these days have some sort of student health facility, and they are equipped to help you deal with this. *Please*, don't be afraid to ask for help.

You are usually much less at risk of burnout if you've made the effort to master time management. But even with that, you might still feel overwhelmed. One reason for this that we've seen at times is the loss of a beloved family member. Curiously, this seems to be just as true for grandparents as for parents. If you were close to a family member who has recently passed away, you have to deal with not only missed classes and homework but the emotional turmoil you find yourself in. No matter how strong you are, it will take time to work through your loss. And please seek help; there is no substitute for getting help from others.

Consider the possibility that your looming burnout may be due to an essential mismatch between where you want to be and what your school is throwing at you. You may discover, for example, that you were happier being a gamer more than working on making games. Perhaps you miss the magic and wonder of being "just" a gamer. Or you may discover that making a game, and learning all the other stuff related to that, is much harder than you were prepared for.

Whatever the reason, perhaps you need to step back (once the semester is over and the torture has ended) and carefully rethink where you are going in life. There is absolutely no shame in doing this. It is far better that you discover this mismatch before you spend more time and money on something that won't ultimately pay off.

But you might not be ready to call it quits just yet, so perhaps just check yourself on how you feel once the next semester begins. Before you walk into that first classroom, are you experiencing elation or dread? Anticipation or anxiety? Read and heed these signs.

Please note that we are **not** talking about quitting. It really is true what they say, that perseverance is the way to make it in the long run. But if you come to the conclusion that making games is just not your thing, cut your losses and get out now before it becomes expensive, and persevere at something else. Maybe you were meant to go to med school or into engineering after all. You'll be glad you did.

To borrow a bit of biz speak, what you are doing instead is *pivoting*. Pivoting is what successful start-ups do to better match what they think they ought to be doing as a business with what potential customers actually want them to do. Pivoting is not quitting. It is not giving up. It is simply making a necessary, hard change of direction to get you off a road that would ultimately prove unproductive and unprofitable. You can apply that business principle here.

So if you see warning signs of burnout showing up in your life, don't be afraid to ask for help, and take positive steps to deal with it.

And even if you do decide in the end that a career in the game industry is not for you, you can still make your passion game in your spare time.

CHAPTER 6

Teamwork, Part One

6.1 GO TEAM!

The game industry is relentlessly interdisciplinary.

Interdisciplinary means that the members of the team have to utilize many different skills simultaneously. In the creation of a great game, this usually means having to get many different people working together. And hence... *The Team*. The team is more than merely a group of people assembled together.

Most good game programs have you work on team-based projects as part of the course work. Not 100% of your college work will involve this, certainly. You will also need to demonstrate your own personal competence in other ways, via things like exams, papers, programming homework, and so forth.

But maybe you're saying to yourself, "I'm socially awkward and don't really like working with other people." Maybe you run with scissors and don't play nice with other kids. If so, you are what is commonly called the "lone wolf."

There is (mostly) nothing wrong with being a lone wolf, and we will have a lot more to say about the lone wolf later. On the other hand, if you are someone who likes people and works well with others, you're already ahead of the game.

Expect, therefore, to be part of a lot of student teams during your time in school. In the previous chapter we talked about collaborating on game jams and the like, and you will find teams there as well.

What's the point of having you do all this team-based work? For one thing, this is how games (and movies and television shows and stage plays) get made in the real world. From the game educator's point of view, learning how to work with other people is yet another valuable outcome that goes beyond just learning how to code or how to use Maya®.

The lessons you learn by working with other people will serve you well in many areas of life. You will learn the art of communication: how to package and present your ideas clearly to others. You will learn the art of persuasion: how to get others behind your ideas, without bullying or arm-twisting. You will learn the art of compromise: being willing to meet others partway and settle for less than 100% of what you want, without throwing a tantrum. You will learn the art of negotiation: how to engage in the give-and-take process of arriving at a consensus (in biz speak, "getting to yes") about the issue at hand.

In short, you will learn how to get along with other people.

This is *far* more important than you may realize. Game studios absolutely look for this in job applicants. Your ability to be a team player is essential to career success. It may come as a shock to you, but even if you are the greatest computer scientist since Alan Turing, if you can't work with others, you *will* be passed over. Or, if they didn't know this about you when you got hired, you just might be among the first to be let go during a downsizing, if not fired outright. Trust us, we've seen this happen far more often than we care to recount.

"As a career coach at a college, I meet with a lot of game recruiters to talk about how students can best present themselves in the career search process. No matter what the company's size, genre, country, or reputation is, they all want the same traits: your specific talent, positive attitude, team-oriented focus, and fit for the company culture."

"In other words, job candidates need to present both their discipline-specific skills and their social skills in order to be considered. Getting into game careers does happen, but it takes persistence plus these personal attributes I've mentioned. With your commitment, these attributes can be learned through life experiences such as jobs or classes involving teamwork, clubs, working on projects with others, and other interactions where you spend time with people face-to-face. It's a very social industry where people like to have fun and enjoy their colleagues while working on a shared goal: making great games."

DAPHNE WALKER
Assistant Director & Career Coach, Champlain College

RHETORIC

Techniques for getting people to do what you want them to do go all the way back to the ancient Greek philosopher Aristotle. He called this "rhetoric." The objective of rhetoric is to get another person to adopt a position about some topic or issue different from what they currently hold. This can range from the simple (like what laundry detergent to buy) to the more complex (like what political beliefs to hold), all the way to the deepest questions in religion and philosophy.

These days the word "rhetoric" has picked up a lot of negative connotations, but back in Aristotle's time it was the preferred alternative to using violence or coercion, which Aristotle called "politics." Aristotle may have been on to something.

As President Dwight D. Eisenhower once said, "Motivation is the art of getting people to do what you want them to do because they want to do it." (Eisenhower date unknown)

What you do on a team often consists of engaging in a lively back-and-forth airing of ideas and visions, bringing up problems and proposing solutions, and heaping praise or scorn (more about the scorn later). This works best when everyone on the team is pulling in the same direction, but, as we shall see, sometimes people have hidden agendas, psychological issues, or personal problems that interfere with their performance at work.

Being on a team requires a certain level of maturity because you will not always get what you want, and things will not always proceed according to plan. Problems will inevitably surface. Acting maturely and treating others with respect (*especially* when things are going badly) goes a long way toward keeping teams running smoothly. It also sends a clear signal that you are a professional.

"Arguably the best skill you can have in this industry (and most others) is the ability to work well with your team. This entails communicating your thoughts clearly, asking questions, negotiating ideas, and remaining respectful of each other. This may seem like a no-brainer, but it can be hard to manage when you're under the pressure of a deadline or having a difficult day. In my career I have seen many newcomers take an idea or concept to heart and become offended when it doesn't pan out or has to be altered. You're entering a world of ever changing ideas, stake holders, and goals. Teach yourself early to accept it so you can move forward."

JON MESCHINO
Game Developer

A lot of these skills are ones you should have learned at a much younger age, especially on the playground during recess (assuming your school hadn't abolished recess altogether). Playgrounds nowadays often have adults constantly hovering around so that when little

Kevin or little Susie gets upset over some trifling matter like losing a game, a nearby adult can be summoned to make everything right.

We personally think it is better for kids to learn to work out their differences among themselves, on their own, with adults stepping in only when the situation really calls for it (like when it escalates to the point of physical violence). To run to an adult every time you get into a scrape does not help you become a more autonomous, reasonable, resilient, and independent adult. There was even a song about it. See the sidebar.

Certainly, behaviors like bullying can be a serious matter, but adults need to allow space, with some measure of supervision, for children to learn how to solve social interaction problems on their own.

By the time you get to college, you will have little choice but to get over your well-meaning—yet unintentionally sabotaging—upbringing. If you think there's too much drama on a student game development team, just consider what it will be like when millions of dollars are on the table and careers, livelihoods, and reputations are at stake.

Robyn Hitchcock— "Uncorrected Personality Traits" https://www.youtube.com/watch?v=s5sUfV1Mi7w (Try not to take this too seriously.)

Robert Fulghum's *All I Really Need to Know I Learned in Kindergarten* can be thought of as a proto-life-hack book (Fulghum 1988).

We hope you agree with us at least a little here and realize that success on a team, as in life, depends on your acting like a grownup. Of course, you'll make mistakes, which is one reason why student game teams are so great. They let you fail in a way that doesn't actually lead to wiping out your bank account, closing down your studio, or losing your home. All the same, while you are in the midst of it, you can sometimes get the feeling that what you're doing is the *most important thing in the world* and that any failure will result in your *utter and eternal ruin*.

Well, it won't. We've experienced our share of dramas on teams (we may have even been the cause of it once in a while), and it is simply a part of life. The thing to do when something goes wrong is to pick yourself up, figure out what broke, and fix it. After that, swear to yourself that you won't ever make *that* mistake again.

Also, if you were the problem, apologize, and admit you were wrong. Curiously, people will be surprisingly forgiving—and cut you more slack—when you have the courage to admit you were wrong.

6.2 BRAINSTORMING

One creativity exercise teams of all sorts engage in, especially during the early stages of a project, is "brainstorming." Let us state up front that not everyone thinks that brainstorming, as we are about to describe it, is the best way to go (Greenfield, 2014). A quick search of the term "brainstorming" will turn up hundreds of improvements and alternative ideas.

Brainstorming is a process of getting a bunch of creative people in a room together to dream up all sorts of wild and innovative ideas and designs for just about anything: new software, ad campaigns, the spring fashion lineup, the production design for a movie, and, of course, games.

The idea is to get ideas flowing by creating a space where peoples' imaginations can cut loose in a supportive environment. A good place to have a brainstorming session is in a room well equipped with things like a projector, lots of white board, maybe some cork-board, flipcharts, and a supply of pens, Sharpies®, Post-Its®, and other such materials.

The room should ideally be quiet and located far away from the usual office hubbub.

And because we need to be creative here, there are no rules. Well, there are a couple of rules. First, everyone needs to understand that there *is* an end goal in mind—to come up with something new—and so everyone's creative juices need to flow in that direction. Things to think about include: What is our objective? Why do we need to solve this? Are there limits to what is suggestable? What would happen if…?

These are important questions to keep the session on track.

It is unusual to have *no* limits; there are almost always going to be time or budget constraints. But on occasion, for example, you will have what are known as "blue sky" brainstorming sessions. These don't have limits and can lead to a wealth of completely new and innovative ideas. After that, you just need to find a way to implement them!

The other major rule—and it is sacred—is this: *Don't be critical!* Ideas should simply flow without constant interruption by critics and nitpickers. This is one place where heaping scorn on someone's idea is inappropriate.

Someone has to record what's going on, and so it might be a good idea to record sessions with strategically placed microphones or even cameras, although it's often not worth going that far.

Once the session is under way, as ideas come up, they are written on a white board or perhaps a flipchart or maybe typed into a doc file on a computer and projected onto a screen. Although we are both entirely computer savvy, we actually prefer the old-school pencil-and-paper method during these early stages. Having someone typing away during the sessions can slow things down and be distracting.

A new wrinkle on brainstorming has surfaced in recent years that could make brainstorming even more effective. Here's how it works: Essentially, it consists of conducting more than one session. At the end of the first session, the team will not have figured out every aspect of the matter at hand. When the meeting wraps up, everyone is charged with the task of "thinking about it" until the next session, and they then go their separate ways. During the time away from the session, each person comes up with a list of ideas to bring to the next brainstorming session.

At the next session, all participants present their lists, and the meeting moderator writes them down on the flipchart or white board or projects them onto a screen. Similar ideas are boiled down to a single idea, and the number of "hits" that idea gets is scored. The ideas with the greatest number of hits win, and these form the nucleus of the solution, at least for the time being. After this, the team might decide to have another go-round, which is continued until a solid, stable solution—one that everyone buys into—is attained.

This process works quite well, and we now routinely use it in our own work and recommend it to others. We aren't entirely sure why this works, but we've heard of theories that, despite the no-judgment discipline of a brainstorming session, there is still a kind of pressure on people to "produce" while on the job, and some people can't quite fully open up in the brainstorming climate. When off by themselves and given quiet time to devote to producing ideas without pressure, many people find that their creativity does finally open up. It may be that everyone is like this to different extents: able to pump out ideas in the excitement of a brainstorming session, and able to pump out ideas when left alone for a while.

6.3 SCRUM

Scrum is one of the so-called "agile methodologies" widely used in modern software development projects. Agile methodologies evolved within the software engineering field in the 1980s because too many large-scale software projects were failing, sometimes in spectacular and embarrassing (not to mention expensive) ways. One key reason this kept happening is that the development team would start work on a massive project by first being handed a "requirements document," a complete statement of what the completed system was required to do.

That was the idea, anyway. What kept happening was that the requirements would inevitably shift under the feet of the developers, and the way they went about developing couldn't cope with that. Development was done under the so-called waterfall model, and there is a nice Wikipedia article about it (Wikipedia 2018).

The waterfall model sounds good on paper, but in real life it had problems. Now, there is nothing wrong with locking down requirements as early as possible, even when building a video game, but where the waterfall model came up short was when some of the requirements kept changing, even as the developers were already building the system. Agile methodologies came about in part to correct one of the major shortcomings of waterfall. Even with agile, every effort is made to pin down requirements whenever possible, and to be able to gracefully redirect development on those occasions when they can't… in ways that don't threaten the whole project.

There are many ways to "do" agile development. In one sense, agile is a state of mind, a way of thriving on chaos. Changes come along all the time, some of them quite disruptive to any work already completed. This certainly characterizes development in the game industry, and so agile solutions have been widely adopted as a result. If you are doing it right, changes can be "absorbed" into a project without derailing it altogether.

Scrum is just one way of doing this, and we've put some links about it, and agile development in general, in the appendix.

So how does Scrum work? In essence, it is a process by which a development team can make steady progress on a project even as the requirements shift all around them. The workload (as determined by the producer with buy-in from the team) is organized as large blocks of work to be done, called "sprints." A sprint is typically on the order of one to four weeks in duration, with two weeks probably the most widely used, and the one we'll use in our discussion here. The sprint is said to be "time-boxed," meaning that it has specific start and stop dates, with a specific set of goals to be accomplished during that period.

The work to be done is determined at a fairly lengthy meeting held at the start of every sprint. Using best historical data for how much code a programmer can write in a day or how much art an artist can create in a day, the most important things that can be worked on *right now* are determined and the work parceled out to the team members—just enough work per person so that everyone can be kept reliably busy for the duration of the sprint.

What constitutes "the most important things"? This is a matter of judgment and experience, plus any information the team can obtain about what requirements are stable and what requirements are likely to change. One thing that goes on the list are any "backlogged" items, tasks that, for one reason or another, did not in fact get finished during the previous sprint.

The idea here is for the team, at the start of the sprint, to go into the two-week time period with a clear roadmap of what can be done and what has to be done. The objective is for everyone to finish everything on their task list, no more and—certainly—no less, during the sprint. (Actually if more can get done, great, but that is handled differently.)

To make sure everyone is making steady progress, the team then holds a daily meeting called the "scrum meeting." This is where the analogy with the sport of rugby comes in. In rugby, a scrum is a way of restarting play after an infraction. In the Scrum methodology, the daily scrum meeting is a way for the team to start fresh every day.

A scrum meeting is intentionally short, ideally no longer than ten minutes (that's the usual rule). In many outfits, to help enforce the need for shortness, the meeting is held standing up so no one gets too comfortable.

What happens during the daily scrum meeting? Essentially, everyone on the team reports on their progress from the day before and indicates whether they ran into any problems. If there are no problems, then no problem! Everyone indicates what they are planning to work on that day. The meeting moderator takes note of all this, and the meeting disbands.

If something goes awry and is taking longer than expected, you also report this at the daily scrum meeting, but it is not fixed then and there.

A key point of the scrum meeting is that no attempt is made to resolve problems right then and there. Instead, the affected parties, certainly you and the producer or the "lead" you report to, and only the affected parties, meet separately to address the issue. Nothing is allowed to fog what the daily scrum is trying to accomplish.

And so, over time, the team makes steady progress toward the goal. Complications and changes to the project requirements are dealt with in a graceful and reliable way. If things go reasonably well, then team members mostly don't have to engage in crunch time (Chapter 20), although someone having a technical setback might have to stay late a few evenings.

The great thing about Scrum, especially with regard to the game industry, is that *it works*. It has been proven in such large organizations as Activision™, and we hope that you get to build at least one project during your time at game school under the Scrum discipline.

One thing that distinguishes Scrum from other agile methodologies is that it also works with both engineers (programmers) and contributors from all other disciplines, like the various kinds of artists, that are part of game development. There is a wrinkle to Scrum that uniquely suits the needs of the game industry: The engineers can be given a daily roadmap of what to work on *today*, whereas it seems better to just give the artists the list of what is to be done over the two-week sprint and let them decide the order they will do them in.

Learning how to build complicated things like games using the Scrum methodology is a valuable skill to acquire, and you can even get additional training in it to become a Certified Scrum Master. We know of one student who went for this training, at his own expense (about $900). When it came time for him to interview for a job after graduation, he mentioned that he had become a Certified Scrum Master, and that was enough to land him the job. Your school might offer such training, so check into it. We've also put a link to this training in the appendix.

There is, of course, much more to say about the Scrum methodology than we can get into here, so please investigate the resources in the appendix.

6.4 THE LONE WOLF

This is the person who simply likes to do it all by himself. We say "himself" advisedly because this is something we've observed rather more often in men than in women [!!!!!].

Sometimes the lone wolf comes off as arrogant. Let's correct that. Oftentimes the lone wolf comes off as arrogant. Sometimes it can be hard to read this accurately. A truly gifted individual, someone who seems to be operating on some elevated plane the rest of us can't quite grasp, can be seen as arrogant, or at least aloof, when the lone wolf really doesn't intend to act that way at all.

Other times the lone wolf will indeed be just plain arrogant, and he'll demonstrate that (there's that "he" again) at every opportunity. Someone who constantly criticizes the work of others, who publicly belittles others, who thinks that everyone else is an idiot is arrogant. This might just be tolerable if the lone wolf happens also to be brilliant—but only just. The business world has a term for such people: the "difficult person" (Brinkman and Kirschner 2003). The business literature contains entire books about how to deal with them.

Don't get us wrong here. We are in awe of those brilliant lone wolf designers, people like Jonathan Blow (*Braid*) or Toby Fox (*Undertale*). If you are truly as brilliant as these designers, more power to you, and we look forward to playing your games.

A worse problem arises when the person is (a) arrogant but (b) not as brilliant as he or she believes. Even worse is the person who is (a) arrogant but (b) not brilliant at all. This person suffers from the Dunning–Kruger effect. Woe be to any team with a member who careens from crisis to crisis and is too dimwitted to notice what (or who) is the cause of the problem.

THE DUNNING–KRUGER EFFECT

The Dunning–Kruger effect gets its name from a landmark paper in 1999 by Justin Kruger and David Dunning, "Unskilled and Unaware of It: How Difficulties in Recognizing One's Own Incompetence Lead to Inflated Self-Assessments" (Kruger and Dunning 1999). The title says it all.

The Dunning–Kruger effect is regarded as one of the many "cognitive biases" that plague us humans. Although Dunning–Kruger is the modern name for this bias, perceptive people have taken note of the phenomenon for centuries, as William Shakespeare did, for example, in his play *As You Like It*. It is so prevalent, in fact, that it is one of the character archetypes found in comedies of all sorts (Sedita 2014). It shouldn't be hard to come up with examples.

We mentioned earlier that not playing well on a team is a great way to not get hired, but what if you genuinely, truly, find it difficult to work with others, or simply prefer to work alone? Here you might benefit from a little honest introspection.

If the matter is one of your being intensely shy or uncomfortable around people, take heart, as you can actually learn to overcome this. We're not talking here of psychological problems that might require counseling but the kind of shyness that many naturally introverted people experience. Are you an introvert? You probably already know whether you are, but if you're not sure, you can take a test.

THE MBTI

The Myers–Briggs Type Indicator (MBTI) is a psychological inventory that measures four key aspects of personality (reason/emotion, sensing/intuition) and four less important aspects (extraversion/introversion, perceptual/judgmental), resulting in four "scales" that claim to reveal one's personality. It is based on the teachings of Carl Jung, one of the founders of the field of modern psychology.

The results of the four scales can be boiled down to four letters drawn from eight letter pairs. Thus, **INTJ** is someone who is *Introverted*, is more *iNtuitive* than someone who simply lives in the moment, prefers *Thinking* to feeling, and is more *Judgmental* than one who takes things as they come without passing judgment.

The MBTI is quite popular with managers and business consultants as they believe it helps them to understand people on teams. This is controversial, perhaps, but the test can tell us something about ourselves if we are open-minded about its results.

If you are an introvert, you are not alone, and while it may be painful at first, learning to interact with others is something you can gradually improve. There are TED Talks and "life hack" resources abounding on the Internet. As you gain more confidence in your ability to communicate, you will begin to feel more comfortable about interacting with your teammates. Once you find yourself successfully communicating one of your own original ideas to your teammates—and they accept the idea—you are on your way. It can be tough, but keep at it, and you will eventually figure it out.

On the other hand, if you are one of those people who think most of the people around you (and, again, most often a "him") are idiots, then you have an entirely different kind of problem. Basically, you're arrogant (we'll refrain from using stronger language here). You probably know this about yourself already, but, then again, maybe others have been too put off to tell you to your face.

Now, arrogant people can do very well in life, very well indeed, like certain founders of certain successful high-tech companies. It's almost unfair, isn't it?

The trick with being arrogant, though, is that you also have to be brilliant, and very focused. Steve Jobs' laserlike focus was legendary, and his demand for excellence in everyone around him made him supremely difficult to work with, but all that allowed him to surround himself with the best of the best. If you are truly brilliant, maybe being seen as "arrogant" is merely self-awareness about one's brilliance.

If you are that arrogant, make sure you are also ridiculously gifted and single-minded in purpose. You will scare off a lot of people, but if your brilliance outshines your arrogance, you just might be able to pull it off. You might even change the world.

But if you are arrogant without that matching level of genius, you may well be setting yourself up for a long succession of painful failures.

6.5 GOING OFF THE RAILS

Sometimes, despite everyone's best efforts, things go badly awry on your team. This is sometimes called going off the rails. It happens, sooner or later, to the best of 'em. The issue then becomes: What are you going to do about it?

The first step is to diagnose what is going wrong. The next few paragraphs discuss some of the problems we've seen over and over again in student teams and what steps you can take to fix them.

6.5.1 Lack of Clarity

Starting with fuzzy plans leads to fuzzy (read "failed") results, which is why game dev teams go through the massive effort of creating a clear and detailed game design document (GDD) and technical design document (TDD) early on. On real-life teams these efforts are also made so that the publisher commissioning the game (and paying all the salaries) doesn't have any misunderstandings, either.

This never works perfectly, but the idea is to get as close to that ideal as possible. As an illustration, let us just write a simple GDD intro description paragraph for the game of checkers.

```
The game is played on a board with sixty-four squares colored
black and white.

There are twelve pieces for each player, and they are placed on
the white squares in the three rows closest to the players.

Each player takes turns moving the pieces.

Pieces can only move one square at a time, unless they are
capturing an opposing piece, when they can "jump" over them to
the next square.

The object of the game is to capture all of your opponent's
pieces by "jumping" over them during a move.

If a player moves a piece into the row nearest the opponent,
then the piece becomes "crowned" and can now move backwards.
```

OK, as we said, it's a simple description, but on the surface it does cover all the basics of the game of checkers.

Or does it?

In reality, the preceding text is a terrible description of checkers.

One of the main problems is that it makes the unjustifiable assumption that the reader already knows the game, and so it leaves out crucial details.

The assumption that the reader knows what you are talking about is one of the most common errors that new designers make. You should always start with the assumption that the reader knows NOTHING about your game, simply because that is usually the case.

So that was the first error, and it leads to dozens of others.

We are not going to outline them all; that is an exercise you may want to try yourself—see how many you can find. Challenge your friends to find more.

Here are a few to get you started.

The description of the board:

- It leaves out the fact that the game is to be played on an 8 × 8 grid, so it could validly be made to be a rectangle or a cross or any shape that has 64 squares.

- It does not say how many of each color there are, so you could end up with different numbers of black and white squares. Was there supposed to be a pattern of alternating colored squares? The GDD presented above doesn't say so.

The description of the position of the pieces:

- This description does work if the board was made correctly, but not otherwise.

- It does not say that a player can have only one piece on a square, so the reader might assume it would be valid to place them all on a single square.

Moving Pieces:

- It does not say that a player can only move one piece at a time, then the other player moves one piece.

- It does not say whether the players can move each other's pieces.

- It does not say that pieces can only move diagonally, always remaining on squares of the same color on the board.

- It does not say they can only move forward, although this is alluded to in the description of a crowned piece.

A not so obvious but BIG mistake: This GDD never actually says it is only a two-player game.

We hope you can see from just this simple example that creating a good GDD requires a lot more effort than you would think for even a simple game like checkers.

Another exercise you may want to try is to write a better version yourself and then invite your friends to pick it to pieces. Or try writing a GDD for a different simple game such as tic-tac-toe.

Just one big hint to make it better and shorter: Include LOTS of pictures. A picture of the board and the starting position would not only be clearer but would save dozens or hundreds of words of explanation.

What you don't want to be is in a situation where someone in charge tells you, after you've shown them some work you spent hours on, "That's not it, but I'll know it when I see it." You'll go through hours and hours of rework, and you will never get those hours back.

This isn't iteration (normally a good thing) but needless wheel-spinning. Keep an eye out for it. We talk a bit more about this in Chapter 24.

6.5.2 Overscoping

This is what seasoned professionals call a "rookie mistake." Overscoping is simply trying to do too much with the time and resources you have available. It's a very natural inclination to want to cram in as many features, characters, levels, weapons, and so forth as you possibly can, but at some point you have to stop. Sometimes overscoping happens because one team member keeps piling on desired features, but in a team setting, sometimes the collective enthusiasm of the group gets carried away with them.

We, your authors, have always found this to be true.

The best games we've played have always followed this rule.

One of us (Mike) has for years been teaching a course called *Intro to Game Production*, which is all about how actual games get made in the game industry. At the start of the course, student teams are assembled so as to balance out skills

> "Make games with a small number of features that work well and fit together seamlessly."
>
> SPYROS GIANNOPOULOS
> *Software Engineer &*
> *Game Industry Veteran*

and experience on each team. Each team is then charged with the task of coming up with a "pitch," a polished slideshow and presentation that tries to make the case to a potential publisher for a great new game.

> "As an instructor, I constantly had students propose ideas that I had seen fail in the past. My response to these proposals was always the same, 'I wouldn't do that if I were you, as this thing and that thing will inevitably occur.' Being new to development and unproven in battle, some students argued that they could do it, at which point I'd say 'You can try it but you must present a failure recovery plan before attempting it.' As predicted, 9 out of 10 students encountered the predicted issues, but amazingly 1 out of 10 proved me wrong! Their inexperience and dogged determination to succeed powered them forward, enabling them to bring something new and innovative to their project. It's for this reason I believe the perfect game team composition is 25% newbies who bring creativity and raw determination, 25% old farts such as myself who bring wisdom and sound development practices, and the remaining 50% being seasoned developers who know how to get things done."
>
> MICHAEL McCOY, Jr.
> *Designer and Lecturer, Boss Fight Entertainment*

Then, actual game industry professionals (the *clients*) are brought in to listen to the pitches. The other one of us (Adrian) has participated in several of these. After hearing the pitches, these industry folk go off in a huddle and decide which one of them wants to work with which team.

For the rest of the semester, each team then has to answer to the game industry client who chose to work with them and keep *the client* happy.

Without fail, the first thing every client does, in every single semester, is to greatly reduce the scope of the project, usually to crestfallen looks from the students. There has never been an exception to this.

That's why we call overscoping a rookie mistake, although even professionals get caught up in it (see sidebar). By the time you leave game school and have been burned a few times trying to do far too much with the time available, you will become very gun-shy about overscoping.

"Usually, a game is designed with every feature imaginable, plus the kitchen sink. Throughout development, this laundry list is pared down to better correlate with staffing, budget, and time. Adaptability is your greatest ally, as game creation will naturally undergo many adjustments. Change is the necessary ingredient to create a quality product, so embrace it!"

TIM SCHLIE
Sound Designer

6.5.3 The Project Hog

You may have had the misfortune of working with someone like this. The project hog wants to do everything on his terms, and on his terms only. (It's usually a *him*.) He thinks everyone else on the team is incapable of turning in work that he deems to be up to his high standards. He shuts the rest of the team out, not giving meaningful tasks to the others but keeping them for himself. What happens next is that the other members of the team shut down emotionally, and motivation and team morale go into the tank. This is a project headed for failure.

Then, very late in the project, the team melts down altogether. The members who were excluded complain about how they've been kept from contributing. Worse, the project hog complains about how he's been doing all the work, and why isn't anyone helping, and why is it all on him? He usually can't see how he's been the root cause of it all.

No one likes working under these conditions.

The project hog is often the same person we've been calling the lone wolf.

We can learn two things from this. First, if you are not the project hog and you've been prevented from making important contributions on a project, you need to make the appropriate people aware of the situation *early*. By "early" we mean as soon as you see this project-hog pattern unfolding. Don't wait until the last minute when the project is on the verge of collapse.

Who is the appropriate person? Normally, you start with the team's "producer," the person whose job it is to coordinate and schedule work so that the project comes in on time.

It might be the case that the producer is the project hog, and that's even worse. If so, you'll need to make an end run, very discreetly, around the project hog and speak privately with the hog's boss. This has to be handled delicately, and it will be one of the most uncomfortable conversations you will ever have.

The other thing has to do with the project hog himself. Sooner or later, this will catch up to him. The team will implode, the project will fail—or at least disappoint—and recriminations will go flying everywhere. The project hog will tend to blame everyone else, not immediately seeing the true source of the problem—himself. The hog needs an epiphany here.

This is no way to make a great game, and the project hog, sooner or later, is going to have to come to some self-understanding, learning how to share the workload and allowing the game to be a truly collaborative effort. Either that, or go the lone wolf route.

Are you a lone wolf? A project hog? Do you see yourself like this? If so, take steps to develop some self-awareness.

6.5.4 Procrastination

Another natural thing to do is put things off until they reach the crisis stage, then suddenly you are under the gun to get the work done. You might tell yourself, "I work better under pressure" or "I work better when on a deadline," but you are kidding yourself.

We already suggested the book *Getting Things Done* as an excellent way to help you overcome this situation. The sidebar about the Pomodoro Method gives another. The writer of the text you are reading, right here and right now, is making use of it.

THE POMODORO METHOD

Pomodoro Technique Illustrated: The Easy Way to Do More in Less Time is a book by Staffan Noteberg that centers around a popular tomato-shaped kitchen timer ("pomodoro" is Italian for tomato). The trick is to dial in some time interval (25 minutes, for example) and then during that time stay absolutely focused on the task at hand. For this to work you must promise yourself that you will permit no distractions whatsoever, no using your cell phone, no checking email, no web surfing, no texting, nothing. Turn everything else off.

Yes, you are playing tricks on yourself, yet somehow, this works. When the timer goes off, you give yourself a well-earned (short) break, until it's time to start the next cycle. Also, you don't need a tomato-shaped timer; any timer will do. You might find, though, that a tomato-shaped timer assumes a new importance in your life as you make use of it.

There are plenty of books and resources on the web, including TED Talks and YouTube clips, about overcoming procrastination. Most of them boil down to tricking yourself into action. Try some out and adopt whatever works best for you.

CHAPTER 7

The Roles in Building a Game

A S WE HAVE BEEN saying, making games is a team effort. Each member of the team has certain roles that are expected because of their discipline, regardless of who the person is fulfilling the role. On a large team, several persons may fulfil a given role. This is maybe even more the case in companies where there is an overlap between the disciplines and where one person plays several roles. This is typically the case at smaller studios.

In this chapter, we discuss what sorts of roles these are. We then discuss the phases or stages (we'll use these terms synonymously) a typical game development project goes through. As we will see, different roles are brought on at different times during project development. Moreover, how the workday unfolds for the people in the various roles will itself change as the project moves through the phases.

First we talk about the roles on the game development team.

7.1 ROLES ON THE TEAM

It should always be kept in mind that every company will vary somewhat from the following outline, so use it more as a guide than as a carved-in-stone truth. That said, the general tasks and roles are similar across companies.

7.1.1 The Designer

We start with the designer, because it is usually the designer that gets the project going at a studio. This is not counting the role of the publishers and managers, of course, who really start the process by making the decision that a game of a particular genre, on a particular platform, will even be produced in the first place. The designer might be called the senior designer, lead designer, or just designer, depending on the scale of the company and the project.

Initially, the designer is informed by management about the game. It is now the designer's role to come up with a concept design (also called a design concept). Either term will do since the main point of this is to come up with the Concept Document. This document can also be called various things, but here we will call it the Concept Document.

The Concept Document is the creative attempt to meet the publisher's requirements and to carefully outline the proposal. It is basically a one-page overview of the vision for the game. It will be studied and discussed by the other leads, producers, and management before going back to the publisher for approval. Even though it is quite short, every word and picture matters, and there is usually quite a lot of agonizing by the designers over every little aspect of it.

If the publisher approves the Concept Document, the designer then expands the document into a draft Game Design Document (GDD). This will go through several expansion cycles, evolving from the one-page concept to a 6-, 12-, 30-, or even 40+-page document depending on the anticipated size of the project. On very large projects, the GDD could run to several hundred pages. Some studios prefer to maintain the GDD (and the Technical Design Document, or TDD) as a "wiki," one accessible only internally to the team. This may help in managing all those frequent updates.

Each expansion is closely scrutinized by the other leads, producers, and management. When they are happy with it, it is then passed on to the publisher for approval.

It is during this process that the leads from the other disciplines begin to add their own input to the GDD, with sections added on, for example, for technical issues, art styles, audio, voiceover (VO), music, and preliminary schedule estimates. They may also be writing their own documentation (e.g., TDD, art style guides, art bible, character bible) to supplement the main GDD. These other documents are used internally to make sure everyone working on the game is working consistently toward the same end.

The GDD remains the responsibility of the designer or lead designer throughout the process, and indeed throughout the entire production cycle. Apart from keeping the GDD up to date with any changes, the designer needs to make sure the original vision for the product is being maintained every step of the way.

The maintenance of the overarching vision of the game is a key designer responsibility.

Once the draft GDD has been fully approved, the rest of the team is brought on board. The timing of this varies greatly depending on the scale of the project and the scheduled ship date. Shorter projects tend to get people coming on board earlier; the risk with doing this is that, until final publisher approval is obtained, any work they do might end up getting changed or thrown away.

Ideally, the designers now switch from mainly writing documentation to prototyping game production. We say ideally because not all production schedules have enough time for this stage to be properly carried out and instead jump directly to preproduction or, worse, straight to production! (See the second half of this chapter.) It should also be noted that sometimes a prototype is produced simultaneously with the draft GDD and is a "proof-of-concept" requirement the publisher imposes as a requirement for continuing the project.

WHY PROTOTYPE?

We cannot recommend highly enough the practicality of carrying out prototyping and preproduction, even for a limited period. It invariably saves time in the later stages of final production when there is never enough time. It does this by proving or, maybe more importantly, *disproving* the concepts outlined in the GDD while there is still time to fix them.

Sometimes the prototype need not be anything more than "pencil and paper." Yes, depending on what sort of game mechanic the prototype is intended to model, it may be possible to test the mechanic with a cheap, disposable pencil-and-paper version.

The more game design you do, the more we think you will come to appreciate the power of pencil and paper.

The game is now usually split into sections or "levels," and possibly into different elements of game mechanics, which may involve multiple designers. Using a game editor or level editor tool, the designer begins laying out each level, placing objects, characters, and terrain in order to build the intended game experience. At this stage they will often be using proxy art (variously referred to as designer art, programmer art, or placeholder art) and proxy sound and VO (voice-over). These assets gradually get replaced as the correct assets are produced.

PROGRAMMER ART

If you didn't already know this, "programmer art" is basically a term of ridicule. Everyone knows programmers can't draw a straight line (except on a computer), and their sense of color and picture composition is hopeless, right?

No matter. Early in most modern game projects that aren't purely text-based, there has to be a visual component, and so in most games these days, something, *anything*, has to be put up on screen as early in the production process as possible.

If the game is a sequel, or there is other artwork lying around that can be put to use, then the solution is simple. But if not, it is perfectly OK for programmers to slap something together and use it as a proxy or "placeholder." The real art will get put in later. The reason this works is that many of the aesthetic decisions won't be finalized until much later, but the programmers need to get going on the code *now*.

However, on occasion, the programmers manage to produce something decent, and it may even survive to the finished game. Even if it doesn't, there is another, better reason to support the efforts of programmers to create some art. It lets them develop a better understanding of what artists have to go through to make their contributions to games.

Remember, it is the designer's or programmer's role not to create wonderful art, but to get something in there that works and move on. Otherwise, you end up spending too much time on art when you should be spending that time on design. There is also the risk that if you make it too good, it will get left in. Many games have shipped with programmer art because replacing it got deprioritized and time ran out.

(This isn't always a bad thing. We know of one designer who was called upon to make zombie noises for VO. Not only were those sounds good enough to leave in the final game, he was able to land another VO gig at another studio for a different zombie game!)

Depending on the company, during production and final production, the designer's role can encompass a wide range of tasks. The obvious ones are keeping the GDD up to date and completing and testing each of the levels and playing the game overall. Assuming QA (quality assurance) is done by someone else, most testing carried out at this phase is to ensure game balance, but the job of finding, reporting, and possibly fixing bugs often falls on designers, as they are usually the ones who play the game the most and know what it ought to be doing.

Designers may also be responsible for finding and implementing sound effects (SFX), creating or helping with recording VO, writing scripts, and writing background stories. On larger projects the writing tasks may be given over to a professional game writer, who, nowadays, is sometimes called the narrative designer.

The lead designer is also responsible for liaising with the other leads and the producer to make sure the schedule is being maintained. They may also have to speak with the client/publisher and even undertake demonstrations and press interviews.

7.1.2 The Engineer

In the game industry, the term "engineer" generally refers to those people who are known everywhere else as "programmers," the people who studied computer science and know how to write code. Of course, at studios that also work with hardware devices there can be other kinds of engineers, like mechanical and electronics engineers.

After a few years, engineers can become lead engineers. Note that becoming a lead anything is separate from promotion. An engineer's promotion might be to something called the senior engineer. That engineer could conceivably become a lead engineer some years prior to getting this promotion.

The lead engineer is the person brought in as a consultant very early on during a project, ideally during the concept phase. At this time the lead engineer works to figure out potential programming risks, decide what tools to use and possibly what game engine should be used, and provide an overview of probable programming scheduling and staffing needs. Another job of the lead engineer is to assess risk: the possibility that some fancy artificial intelligence (AI), control scheme, or shader just can't be made to work. Risk covers all that and much else, but you get the idea.

The other engineers are not generally brought onto a project until after the draft GDD has been approved.

An exception might be made where a brand-new game engine, or specific new tools, are going to be required, in which case additional engineers could begin working on these while the designer is still working on the draft GDD. Taking this step is one way the team can minimize some of the engineering risks.

Once the draft GDD has been approved, engineers are gradually added to the project to start programming the various aspects of the game. Overall, the engineers are responsible for getting the game actually up and running on the required platforms. Nowadays, although download times and footprints are important, there is generally less concern about the actual size of a game unless it has to fit onto a particular-sized game cartridge or recording medium, like a DVD. Also, in the case of console games and mobile games, there are other technical matters (such as the amount of random-access memory, or RAM, available on the console) that the engineers absolutely need to pay attention to. Engineers are also responsible for ensuring that bugs are fixed and that frame rates are high.

"One of the most important things I have learned about bugs."

"FIND and FIX your bugs early. A bug caught in the design phase takes a few minutes to fix."

"During implementation it can take up to an hour or more. At the end of the project a fix could take days."

SPYROS GIANNOPOULOS
Software Engineer & Game Industry Veteran

HARDWARE LIMITS

These days, engineers spend considerably less time trying to squeeze code down to the smallest possible amount of RAM, at least for PC games.

But for game consoles, and especially for mobile devices, engineers do still have to worry about hardware constraints, like the amount of available memory, that must be respected. If the game can't be loaded into the finite memory of a console or mobile device, it won't run.

Depending on the size of the project and company, the work may be more or less specialized into different sections of the game, for example, AI, audio, system mechanics, graphics, "heads-up display" (HUD), and user interface (UI).

7.1.3 The Artist

Like the designer, the role of the artist can vary considerably depending on the stage of the project.

Right from the start, the concept artist will be involved in drawing draft concepts based on the concept documentation. This could involve creating entirely new characters, new worlds, and so forth, or simply providing color and art style guides. Depending on how well developed the draft GDD is, this may also involve HUD designs or level layout concepts. All of these will be submitted to the client and licensor for approval, along with the draft GDD.

There may be a need for a demo cut scene or play-through, especially if a prototype is not readily available.

The lead (or leads, if there is both a lead artist and a lead animator) will also be involved in preliminary scheduling and staffing calculations.

Once the draft GDD has been approved, the main art team becomes involved. Art covers everything that makes a game look the way it does: the intro, the cut scenes, the HUD, the characters, the lighting, the objects, the score tables, the rewards, the option screens, and so forth and so on. While nowadays everyone thinks of 3D and big special effects or movie cut scenes, there is still an awful lot of 2D art to be done.

At some point there will be a requirement to produce marketing materials and screenshots. Depending on exactly what is required, this may sometimes be covered by the designer, but certainly not always, in which case this task will fall to the art department.

Ideally, toward the end of the project, all designer and programmer art, all that placeholder stuff, has been replaced by fantastic cool artistic art, and the artists are busy polishing it. However, see the sidebar.

IF ONLY THEY WOULD MAKE UP THEIR MINDS

Probably because everyone has an opinion, and because these opinions often differ, it is almost always the case that the art, particularly that for the user interface, is where the most changes take place during production. This can be very disheartening to artists, as a lot of their work gets discarded or changed. This is where having that humble lack of ego really comes in handy.

7.1.4 The Producer

Whatever the actual personnel setup eventually becomes, the producer role is involved right from the very beginning.

The producer role can be held by different people at different times, depending on the company. For example, in a small company, the owner might initially play the role of the producer before handing part of that work off. A large company could have "executive producers" who do the initial work before delegating to those beneath them on the company hierarchy. Or, because executive producers are often responsible for multiple products, the initial work is done by a producer or senior producer and then passed up to the executive producers for approval.

Even before the project moves to the concept stage, the producer works closely with leads from each discipline (not even necessarily those who might be on the final project) to produce a "cost analysis" for a proposed project. This includes how many and what type of staff members will be needed and how long the project will take. This allows studio executives to determine the overall cost, which is then used to make an initial bid to the publisher for the studio to work on the project.

If the initial bid is accepted, the producer will then be involved in all stages of the concept development process and may need to negotiate with the client over features and requests in order to agree on a final budget and project scope.

Once all that has been decided, the producer now takes on the full role of ensuring the project comes in on time, on budget, and of the required quality. If you're getting the sense that the producer (and having the *right* producer) is critical to the success of the project, you're right.

The producer is the key point-of-contact person between the client/licensor and the development studio. The producer must report progress, often on a weekly basis, including problems as they arise and their solutions. The producer needs the courage to be up front about problems as they arise and needs to be resourceful enough and creative enough to put solutions into play that everyone can live with.

Producers must fight against feature creep from both the client/licensor and from their own team. They act as a buffer between the team and the client/licensor and often handle demonstrations and the press.

If you think you want to be a producer eventually, expect to spend at least three years on the job before you will be trusted with something like responsibility for an entire game. Even then, your first promotion into this role will likely be as an associate producer.

DREAD FEATURE CREEP

Everyone loves a lot of features in their games, and game developers are no exception. As a project gets rolling, team members will suggest all sorts of new ideas for features that would be cool to include in the game. It's only natural, and it's called *feature creep*.

The problem is this: Every added feature takes someone's time and costs some amount of money, both of which are in finite supply. Every time a new feature is proposed, the producer must consider whether it can be included or not, and most of the time the answer will be no. Or a conditional yes: "if we add that, we will need to cut this" or "if we add that, then it will cost more/take longer."

The best time to decide on the feature set is during the earliest phases of a project. The later a new, cool idea is suggested, the costlier and riskier including it becomes. The producer is put in the difficult position of having to disappoint the team member who suggested it and the others who supported it.

Sometimes the producer has no choice but to cave. If it is the client or licensor who suggested the new feature, the producer either has to stand firm or ask what other feature the client is willing to give up, or will there be additional money and time added to the schedule. This is not an easy conversation to have.

Seasoned developers have learned to fear the creep.

The producer must play the game at all stages of development to ensure that the targeted level quality is maintained and to provide feedback to the team on what needs to be improved.

A producer's road is a difficult and lonely one. The producer must act in the interest of both the client and the team. She must continually balance between the pressures to improve quality and increase scope while not allowing the time to completion to stretch out or the size of the team to continually expand to meet demands. Ideally the producer is also looking out for the welfare of her team, keeping "crunch time" to a minimum, providing perks, and keeping morale up.

The producer, besides needing substantial technical and organizational skills, must be very much a "people person."

Finally, while the producer has a really important role in providing opinions and critique, she has to remember that she is not the designer or the artist or the engineer. The producer needs the maturity to step aside and actually let these talented people do their jobs, running interference for the team when they need to.

WEARING MULTIPLE HATS

It is often necessary in smaller companies for producers to wear two hats, for example, producer + designer, but it should never be forgotten that the two disciplines of production and design are often at odds with one another. For that reason, we recommend always making the producer a separate person on a project if at all possible.

7.1.5 Sound Designer, Music Composer

Although sound designer and composer are very different roles played by different professionals, we will cover both sound design and music in the same section. The main reason for this is that, while they are both essential parts of today's games, they both suffer from the same problems, namely that, except in large studios, sound and music are often among the last features to be implemented.

BUDGETS FOR SOUND AND MUSIC

If sound and music are so important, why don't more game companies have their own sound studios?

It is all a matter of budget. Sound production studios are expensive, require special soundproofing and construction, and take up a lot of space. Unless the game company is producing multiple games, there is no year-round need for sound production facilities or sound engineers, so they would sit idle for much of the year. Not good for budgets. True, this could be mitigated by hiring out the sound engineer and recording studio, but then you run the risk that, right when you need it for your project, it has already been scheduled for something else.

The game designers probably have an idea of what they expect to hear, both in terms of sound effects and the ever-changing moods they want the music to invoke. A well-prepared GDD will include detailed information about all this.

Sound effects and music will definitely be budgeted for by the producer in terms of cost and by the engineer in terms of memory and storage, but because most studios do not have in-house music or sound studios, these tasks are frequently contracted out. We know from experience that this is a rich source of communication problems and misunderstandings. These in turn affect turnaround times, and these unfortunately often lead to late implementations. None of this good for the game.

These problems can sometimes be mitigated if a studio has found a reliable sound designer and composer/musician and goes back to them on subsequent projects. This is one reason why breaking into this particular aspect of the game industry is so difficult. Not only are there a lot of people who can do sound or music (or claim they can), but the unfortunate reality is that the really good ones are already on the short list of preferred people at all the studios that are delighted with their work.

As a result, the really good ones start to find themselves in high demand, and so a studio might not always find it possible to get the people they want so dearly to work with.

In small studios, it can be even worse. Their production budgets may not even stretch to hiring a professional sound designer or musician, and so the job of finding and often implementing sound and music usually falls to the designer, or sometimes the producer. While it is true that large numbers of sound libraries are available, at varying costs, going through them is time consuming, and often the exact sound is just not available, so a close match has to be accepted. Also, the designer runs the risk of selecting music or SFX about to show up in some other game. As you know, the game forums can be pretty brutal about using me-too material. Do a web search for "Wilhelm Scream" to see what we mean.

Similarly, there are libraries of music, and there are many musical pieces that can be used free of licensing and royalties. Again, the problem is the time needed to find just the right piece, or even a close enough piece, subject to that me-too risk just mentioned.

Thankfully, many publishers recognize the problem and often provide assets of their own. This is particularly true if the product is licensed from a movie where the licensor is able to provide original music and sound effects from the film.

This brings us to VO.

These are even more complex than sound or music and suffer not only from all the problems outlined previously but also from the fact that the actors themselves have their own schedules to maintain. Voiceovers do not come in libraries, unless you count things like grunts and groans. They have to be recorded fresh for each project in a studio.

Prior to doing VOs, unless you are lucky enough that the licensor provides the actors, the producer or the lead designer will need to conduct auditions to cast the voice actors that will be used. Unless someone in your studio is an expert at providing voice direction, the producer will also need to retain a professional director who can get the best out of the actors in terms of mood, cadence, and expression for each line of dialogue.

It is no wonder that the budgets of large AAA games are as high as they are when all this is factored in. It is also no wonder that small indie studios cannot expect to compete with these types of games if you compare them on the basis of VO quality.

7.1.6 Writer and Narrative Designer

Depending on the project, the background story and in-game narrative could be absolutely central to the experience, or they could be of little consequence.

WRITERS VERSUS NARRATIVE DESIGNERS

What is the difference between a writer and a narrative designer?

While there are lots of differences between the two, we will simplify things and define a "writer" as someone who writes the overarching background story, which could include characterizations, while a "narrative designer" writes the in-game narrative, that is, what is spoken by the characters or read by the player.

The writer might only be involved during the early stages of production to create the overall story for the game. At this stage, it is far too soon for the writer to actually write all the dialogue; instead, the writer creates the story in more broadly drawn terms, more like an outline or "treatment." During actual production, the narrative designer is then tasked with the job of writing the actual dialogue and making sure it appears in the game in all the right places. This can only happen during actual development, and the narrative designer needs to keep on top of all the continually changing gameplay to keep these in sync.

In theory, the importance, or lack thereof, of the story and narrative could change from project to project, but in general, studios that go for large overarching stories and lots of in-game narrative tend to want to continue to make games of that type. They can therefore employ writers and narrative designers full time. Other studios treat these roles similarly to sound or music production and contract this work out or make it the responsibility of the designer.

While the background concept of a story is often known, and may even be roughly drafted in advance of the project, usually the overall story is not written out in full until between the concept phase and the preproduction phase. An obvious exception is where the game is based on an existing book or movie and where the role of the writer is more to reshape the story into an experience that will fit well within the game.

The writer is therefore involved early in the process and, although he will be continually consulted and may need to adjust the story as a result of changes made during production, his input is needed less and less frequently as production moves along.

It is unusual to change the overarching story once it has been pinned down, because doing so can be enormously disruptive to the work the artists are doing with the characters and the story world. If you've ever run into "plot holes" or "continuity errors" while playing a story-based game, those were likely the result of tampering with the story too late in the process.

That said, the writer needs to be flexible and available because those dual demons of game production, budget and time, can make it necessary to cut levels, scenes, or characters, which in turn may require a storyline change.

The narrative designer, on the other hand, has a pretty constant workload all the way through production. She may not be on the project from the beginning, but she will generally be on board once full production starts. Often rewrites, updates, and additions are made to the narrative as the game takes shape, and these will keep the narrative designer busy right up until the game is shipped. But wholesale changes to the overarching story are best kept to a minimum or avoided altogether.

7.1.7 Quality Assurance

Quality assurance is usually just referred to as QA.

QA is, without doubt, one of the least appreciated roles in the game industry, except by those who have done it or those who have had the privilege to work with a *good* QA department.

BREAKING INTO THE INDUSTRY

It used to be that QA was the easy route into the game industry if you could not get hired for the position you really wanted. You would take a position in QA while gaining experience and looking for an opportunity to shift into production.

This is becoming less and less true for two reasons. First, QA is becoming more professional, and good QA requires talented people who actually want to do QA. Second, a lot of QA is now outsourced, often to Asia, so there is no direct hiring link between QA teams and game studios.

Having experienced good and bad QA, and both in-house teams (located in the same building) and off-site teams (located anywhere else), there is no doubt that a good in-house QA team is worth every penny they are paid. Their primary role is to find bugs, often ones that would never be found otherwise. Good QA people, however, also have a deep love and knowledge of games and are able to suggest improvements in the HUD and game balance, even art, lighting, and sound, especially early on when changes are cheaper to implement.

Good QA requires a distinct mindset and is not for everyone. While it may sound great—after all, you get paid to play games all day; what wouldn't be great?—several things should be kept in mind about working in QA:

- You do not get to choose what games you play.

- The games you play are incomplete and broken.

- You have to be really methodical in your approach to playing so you can detail everything that you did in order to relocate and repeat any bug you discover.

- You need to be able to communicate what you did to engineers, artists, and designers—in language they understand—so they can replicate the bug.

- When the bug has been fixed, you need to go through the exact same steps you went through the first time to prove that the bug has indeed been fixed.

- You may not even be tasked with playing the entire game; you may only be required to continually play one or two levels...over and over again.

A DAY IN THE LIFE OF A QA TESTER

We know of two QA staffers who were once tasked with doing nothing but going through every level, not playing it, but just running into walls to find missing collisions. They did this for months! We wonder if they spent their off hours running into real walls out of sheer frustration.

If there is no specific QA group, then it generally falls to the designer, producer, and sometimes the leads to fill this role.

The earlier QA becomes involved in a project, the better, but in practice QA people are often not brought in until around the alpha milestone (see the second half of this chapter). They remain on the project until it ships.

The nature of QA work also evolves as game development progresses. Early on, QA will be involved in making sure that the cool new game mechanic is, in fact, *fun to play*. It's good to find this out early! Members of the QA team also do some bug finding for those things that get done early, like the core mechanics, the control scheme, the HUD, and interface screens, even basic things like starting a new game or loading and saving an existing one.

Later on, it's all about finding bugs and making sure they get fixed. As the project moves closer to the ship date, it's about finding that last critical bug and testing for "completeness," making sure everything that's supposed to be in the finished game is in fact in there.

A final note on QA.

If you play games to any degree, you will no doubt have come across bugs, art glitches, typos, even crashes! So, you may ask, "Why didn't QA find this?" or "Why was this not fixed?"

Well, it really is a matter of statistics and time.

First the statistics:

Even if you have a big QA team, say, 50 people, working full-time testing the game, they cannot possibly catch everything that a couple of hundred thousand players will be able to discover on Day One of release.

Say those 50 people spent three months doing QA. That adds up to approximately 36,000 person-hours of game play in which to both find bugs and test fixes.

Let us now assume that the game ships and is moderately successful. Say it sells 100,000 copies (which is not that many compared to most AAA titles, which sell in the millions). So after only a week of being played by the public, even if players play for only five hours each in that week, the game will have accrued 500,000 person-hours of play. Needless to say, the public will have done many things that could not even have been attempted by QA. So it really shouldn't be surprising that the playing public finds bugs that were not found by QA.

HOW MUCH QA DO YOU NEED?

Yes, 50 people make for a large QA team. Remember, a lot of game studios do not have that many people in the entire company, but big AAA products may have several hundred people in QA. That will not be the norm for small and medium-sized studios.

This is all about in-house QA. Another way QA increasingly gets done is to contract it out to third-party firms that specialize exclusively in QA, many of which are located in Asian countries.

Another recent trend is having the game-playing public do some of the testing. A smaller studio could offer a free version of the game in exchange for doing free beta testing on it. This can be perilous for the small studio, since it could result in some people pirating the game. If you want to be a beta tester, expect to get checked out and approved beforehand.

A final way for the smaller studio to get in more QA is to offer "presale" versions of the game. Here, you buy a not-yet-ready version of the game well ahead of time. You buy the game at a substantial discount, and you're promised the finished version when it's ready. In exchange, you're expected to do "beta testing" of the game and report back via the web what you find out.

If you sign up to be a beta tester, please be righteous about it and hold up your end of the bargain.

Second is the time factor.

Every project has a ship date that must be met eventually, or the product never makes money. As this ship date approaches, the amount of time available to fix things that have been found shrinks considerably. As this happens, known bugs start to be graded more and more into the categories of MUST FIX and WILL NOT FIX.

Must-fix bugs are all the known crash bugs and hang-up bugs. A crash bug is one that causes the game to actually crash, something guaranteed to annoy your players. Worse is a bug that crashes the operating system of a player's game console or PC. These are even worse. Also troublesome are hang-up bugs where the game "burps," that is, it stops working for a fraction of a second before starting up again.

These really cannot be allowed to ship with the finished game, and many late nights (the dreaded "crunch time") are spent killing as many of these bugs as possible.

The will-not-fix (WNF) bugs are all the others. These generally take a lot of time to deal with yet show up infrequently. In many cases they only show up sporadically on oddball or ancient machine setups. (Consoles are another matter.) Sometimes fixing the bug could involve rewriting code that is already working. This could in turn introduce more bugs, and nobody wants that at this stage. Making changes this late in production to code that was believed to be reliable is a surefire way to long and agonizing nights on the job.

Given the twin factors of statistics and time, it is inevitable that all games will ship with some bugs. The hope is that QA will catch the really bad ones. At least nowadays, with direct digital downloading, it is far easier to issue patches than it used to be, which is why it has become so popular with the major studios.

7.2 THE PHASES OF GAME DEVELOPMENT

We now turn our attention to the phases of game development followed by most studios. We will explain some of the terms like "alpha" and "beta" that we mentioned in the previous section.

Most companies follow the general production pattern outlined in what follows, although the length of time in each phase and the actual timing of involvement by the different roles can vary considerably, with some individuals performing in multiple roles along the way. Many game schools follow this pattern on student team projects, if only to help you get used to the setup.

The phases, more or less, are as follows. At the end of each we indicate the most important people involved during that phase.

7.2.1 Concept Phase

The concept phase covers that period of work before the project is actually approved. This usually means that the team (which is only a skeleton team at this point) is investigating and developing concepts (ideas) for a new game or a sequel. They might be doing this with the full expectation that the concept will get approved eventually. For example, in the case of a large studio where work on a new game or a sequel to an existing one is ramping up, this is merely the first part of the process.

It can also be "on spec," where a skeleton team of experienced people is put together to come up with a new idea and develop it sufficiently for approval, with the hopes of pitching it successfully, either internally within the studio or to an external publisher. We note, however, that this rarely happens outside of small or totally independent studios. It really is not that often that a team can come up with a new idea in a large, in-house studio. The people involved are more likely to be asked to come up with an idea based on an existing game or an upcoming movie.

Sometimes the concept phase comes as the result of a request for proposal (RFP). This is the situation where a major game company (say, Nintendo) sends out the broad outlines for a new game to a highly select list of developers. If the developer is interested, it will put together a well-developed concept in the hopes that the major company likes it well enough to go forward with a development contract.

RFPs are not open; they are only sent to developers who are well known to—and well regarded by—the major company. Getting onto this list of select studios is often a major objective for an independent developer, as it can mean a steady supply of work in the years ahead. Maintaining a solid reputation of delivering great games on time and on budget is obviously a big part of this. Note that when we say "independent developer" here, we are not talking about the two-guys-in-a-garage studio, but the kind of studio that is not owned by a major player that survives by taking on contract work for game development from major publishers and studios.

Main involvement: lead designer, writer, producer, managers
Consultancy involvement: lead engineer, lead artist, lead animator

7.2.2 Prototype Phase

If the concept is approved, the developers are asked to show proof that the concept is going to work as approved. This usually means building a "prototype" that demonstrates the key mechanics described in the concept.

A prototype is not the full game, not by a long shot. It is simply built to show that the cool-sounding mechanics are actually fun to play. It might or might not use the same game engine that the full game will use. A prototype could be built using GameMaker Studio 2*, for example, whereas the final game could be getting built with Unity or UE4. It might or might not have particularly complete art assets. A prototype for a franchise game might include character assets to show the client how their intellectual property will look in the new game. For this purpose, it's OK to use assets from an earlier game as placeholders, even though everyone understands that newer assets will be created for the new game.

A prototype might also be constructed as a "proof of concept" for some tricky algorithm or game mechanic. Or one might be constructed to demonstrate the idea of the game to clients or marketing folks. A prototypes, in short, can be constructed for just about any purpose if, by doing so, it brings clarity to some novel aspect of the design.

An important thing to keep in mind about prototypes is that they are intended to be built using as few resources as possible and "thrown away" afterwards. They are generally built simply to get a key idea across. They cost time and resources to develop, which will have to come out of the overall budget for the project. Nevertheless, they still have immense value if they succeed in demonstrating that key idea to all concerned.

Main involvement: lead designer, engineer, producer

Consultancy involvement: lead engineer, lead artist, lead animator, managers

7.2.3 The Preproduction Phase

Once the concept is approved, the development team enters the phase called "preproduction". During this phase, all the details from the approved Concept Document get fully fleshed out, that is, as fully as possible. The outputs from this phase are the GDD and the TDD. These represent the first major milestones on the way to the completed game. Note that during preproduction the team is not yet up to full strength. Most of the work gets done by a core team of mostly senior people.

If the project is very large, there may be additional milestones partway through preproduction, as a way of monitoring progress.

Once all this is ready, the team is ready to transition to the production phase. Note that this doesn't necessarily happen all at once. On large projects, those portions from preproduction that have won approval can have production work started on them even as other parts are still getting refined during preproduction.

Besides the GDD and the TDD, it is also during the preproduction phase that a lot of other vital project materials get generated. The most important of these is the "Project Plan," sometimes known as the "Game Plan." This is an *exhaustive* list of absolutely everything that needs

---

* GameMaker Studio 2 is made by YoYo Games, located at https://www.yoyogames.com/gamemaker.

to be done, who is going to do it, and when, down to the final traffic cone and belt buckle. It can consist of thousands of lines of entries in a giant spreadsheet or represented using some other production tracking tool. This is the main planning tool that will be used by the producer during production, and setting one up and keeping it current are absolutely critical to success.

Of course, millions of things can go wrong during production, and so the Game Plan is a so-called "living document." This means that it will be subject to constant tweaking and revision as the project moves forward, but the producer should keep it up to date and rely on it to guide all the work the team is doing. If the project is large enough, this work might be entrusted to an associate producer.

The key reason for this can be expressed in two words: NO SURPRISES! During the production phase, work from all the disciplines should get cranked out on a reliable and regular basis. Things do not always go according to plan, and a clever producer will already have built-in buffers to try to stay ahead of the chaos.

Main involvement: lead designer, writer, lead engineer, lead artist, lead animator, producer
Consultancy involvement: managers

"Schedule in time for the unknowns."
"Schedule extra time for the unexpected: major bugs, late features and other unknowns. Doubling your workers rarely halves the time it takes to finish."

SPYROS GIANNOPOULOS
Software Engineer & Game Industry Veteran

7.2.4 The Production Phase

The production phase is where most of the work on the game gets done. One of the things the senior people need to determine during preproduction are the "staffing needs": how many artists, programmers, designers, writers, sound designers, and so forth are going to be needed, what they are going to be working on, and for how long. The team must be assembled and in place, ready to go, when production starts up.

By far, the production phase takes up most of the time on any project. To monitor progress (and to keep those progress payments coming in), the work is arranged as a series of "milestones." There are at least three or four such milestones, which normally look something like this:

- *First Playable*: This is the point where the game is at least minimally playable, even if only for a few minutes. How much of the game needs to be there to qualify as meeting First Playable will vary considerably depending on the development company or the client. Maybe not all the planned game play will be in place, but the "cool new game mechanic" should be. The basic process of launching, loading, playing, visiting option screens, and saving and exiting are all in place and working, even if none of the option screens do anything yet.

Virtually none of the planned art assets will be in place. "Placeholder" and "programmer" art assets are used instead, or possibly art from an older game if this is a sequel. Most of the things seen on the screen might be just big cubes textured with "test pattern" textures. The HUD and many of the UI elements are missing or don't do much. The control scheme "sorta" works.

Another way to deliver a First Playable is the "vertical slice." A vertical slice is intended to show the final look and demonstrate gameplay, but it only plays for a minute or two. In a vertical slice, every final feature must be represented, even though nothing else that contributes to the couple of minutes of play will have been completed yet. We note that not everyone in the industry likes the idea of vertical slices, but it is one way to show off a game that is still under development.

- *Alpha*: The major gameplay features that need to be in the game are now all implemented. The art assets are perhaps 40% to 50% done. The game runs correctly (or mostly correctly) on the target platform in debug mode.

  The alpha stage is a good stage to playtest key features to make any necessary adjustments before going much further. Everyone involved has to feel comfortable with the way the game plays.

  At this point, any player or tester picking up the game should start to get a solid feel for the complete game experience originally conceived in the Concept Document.

- *Code Complete*, also known as *Feature Complete*: The game is now at the point where all features are in place. Since a feature needs to have code written for it, and since code is written to implement features, this means that *every single feature* that is going to end up in the complete game has to have its code completely finished.

  And by "completely finished" we mean that the code has been written, QA has tested it to death to make sure it doesn't break, and the code has been fully integrated into the rest of the game code. It doesn't count if a programmer stays up late to put the code in but the rest of the testing and integration hasn't happened yet. All the code has to survive QA testing for it to be considered "complete."

  This is a critical milestone because it acts as a kind of lock-down. *No one* should be permitted to monkey with the features after this, not even the big boss, because to do so jeopardizes the integrity of the whole game. Well, let's correct this. The big boss, or the client, *can* add features, but it is going to cost.

- *Beta*: By now, all code and art assets are complete. Only serious bugs after this will be addressed. At this point, some bugs may be treated as WNF.

  Nothing can be added after beta: not assets, code, or features, *except* to fix a critical bug. No producer, sane or otherwise, wants this rule to be violated, *ever*, though it can't always be avoided.

By the time the game is at beta, the production team size is gradually reduced as the game becomes more complete and the remaining bugs get fixed. People are pulled off the project to reduce costs. The people who remain at this stage could be in any role depending entirely on what the project still needs at this point. The people taken off the project will get assigned to other teams that are just beginning to ramp up, or they might have to scout around for something new to work on.

At this point, the project may colloquially be referred to as *DONE*. It's a nice place to be.

While that is going on, the QA team will be ramping up on ruthless bug detection, so the development team is not out of the woods yet.

- *Code Release Candidate (CRC)*: At this point the game development team, the producer, and the client all believe the game is "perfect." But not so fast! This is the point where the QA department now <u>really</u> goes to town on the game, making absolutely sure absolutely everything that was promised is in there and that it doesn't break, even under a variety of test conditions and on a motley set of varying machine configurations, especially for PC and mobile games.

  At this point, the project may colloquially be referred to as *DONE DE DONE*.

- *Gold Master*: This CRC is the CRC that really is the CRC. Any cleanups, bug fixes, and polishing that needed to be done have now been done. The crew in QA is a contented lot, and the client has signed off on the whole project.

  The project may colloquially be referred to as *DONE DE DONE…DONE!*

  The dev team can now ship the game, write up the all-important postmortem document, and have itself a lavishly funded ship party. After that, they go home and catch up on their sleep. We'll have more to say about the postmortem in Chapter 21.

In a nutshell, these are basically the milestones that game development teams follow. The terminology and steps vary from studio to studio, but not by much. This is a proven way to work.

Main involvement: all leads, producer(s), designers, narrative designers, level designers, engineers, sound, music, artists, QA (usually from alpha but ideally as early as possible)

Consultancy involvement: managers

7.3 WRAPPING UP

This is pretty much how development in the game industry is done, from the tiniest studio to the largest AAA behemoths. The size of the company isn't as important as the size of the team, however.

On small teams, people wear a lot of different hats. On larger teams, the workloads become more specialized, so you will see fewer occasions where the programmers get to crank out some artwork.

On very large teams, you'll start to see more hierarchy and specialization. The idea of having "leads"—art lead, engineering lead, for example—only makes sense when there are a bunch of people to lead, say, when the production team grows to more than a half-dozen people or so. All of this depends on the company and the company's idea of how to run things.

On very large teams, you'll also start to see people with "assistant" or "associate" in their title, like associate producer. You also start to see specialization. An artist might now be a texture artist, 3D animator, rigger, or lighting designer. Engineers may specialize in graphics, AI, networking, or back-room server operations.

Many hands make light work…yeah, right.

CHAPTER 8

Year Two

8.1 BACK TO SCHOOL

We hope you had a relaxing and productive summer. But now it's time to start your second year, your sophomore year. (If you are in a two-year program, this will be more like starting your "third year" in a conventional four-year program.)

No doubt you've worked through those first-year heebie-jeebies and general noob-ness, and now you are a sophomore. Your school may call it something else, as the word "sophomore" is very close to the word "sophomoric," and this is no accident. It is at about this time that you get a little too cocky for your own good, because you know more than those lowly first-year students. You haven't really hit the point where you realize that you don't know as much as you think you do. Sorry.

UNKNOWN UNKNOWNS

Donald Rumsfeld was the U.S. Secretary of Defense during the presidency of George W. Bush. In 2002, speaking about military intelligence, he made the following statement:

> "Reports that say that something hasn't happened are always interesting to me, because as we know, there are known knowns; there are things we know we know. We also know there are known unknowns; that is to say we know there are some things we do not know. But there are also unknown unknowns—the ones we don't know we don't know. And if one looks throughout the history of our country and other free countries, it is the latter category that tend to be the difficult ones."

> (Wikipedia 2018)

He took a lot of ridicule over that, but he was actually making very deep sense. There are things going on out there that an intelligence agency may suspect are going on, and the agency can take steps to find them out. But there are other things going on (terrorist plotting, for example) that an intelligence agency has no awareness of whatsoever. These are the "unknown unknowns," and they are the most dangerous. The same is true in life. You really don't know what you don't know. Wisdom, as the ancient Greek philosopher Socrates pointed out a long time ago, begins when you develop a keen respect for the limits of your knowledge and develop some humility over that fact. It's OK to say "I don't know."

During this year you are going to start really working to master your specialty areas. You've gotten much of the basics out of the way, and now it is time to go deeper. In this chapter we'll look at what sorts of things you can expect to be learning, plus our own unique take on those other things you could be learning on top of that.

We'll break these out according to specialties.

8.1.1 Game Design

In some of the programs we're most familiar with, everyone studies game design along with their specialty areas like computer science or visual arts. During your second year you can expect to be a member of many more teams, making many more games.

By now, you should be getting very familiar with one or two of the major 3D game engines in popular use: Unity and, increasingly, Epic's Unreal Engine 4 (UE4). You probably already got started on one of these during Year One. At least we hope so.

What can we say? Just plan on getting very, very familiar with them.

The Unity engine can be downloaded at https://unity3d.com/.

UE4 can be downloaded at https://www.unrealengine.com/what-is-unreal-engine-4.

Your program probably has at least one course called Game Design, and you probably took it during Year One. But getting good at "design" (the D-word) is a lifelong, ongoing process. Do you think of yourself as a *great* designer? Do you *want* to be a great designer? Do you have what it takes?

We're not just talking about designing games in particular, but the whole mysterious design process itself. The many conflicting challenges a designer faces was aptly described by iconoclastic architect and designer Christopher Alexander, who explains the design process for a tea kettle. Yes, a tea kettle. Even for something as mundane as that, there is much for the designer to consider:

> "Let us look again at just what kind of difficulty the designer faces. Take, for example, the design of a simple kettle. He has to invent a kettle, which fits the context of its use. It must not be too small. It must not be hard to pick up when it is hot. It must not be easy to let go of by mistake. It must not be hard to store in the kitchen. It must not be hard to get water out of. It must pour cleanly. It must not let the water in it cool too quickly. The material it is made out of must not cost too much. It must be able to withstand the temperature of boiling water. It must not be too hard to clean on the outside. It must not be a shape which is too hard to machine. It must not be a shape which is unsuitable for whatever reasonably-priced metal it is made of. It must not be too hard to assemble, because this costs man-hours of labor. It must not corrode in steamy kitchens. Its inside must not be too difficult to keep free of scale. It must not be hard to fill with water. It must not be uneconomical to heat small quantities of water in, when it is not full. It must not appeal to such a minority that it cannot be manufactured in a appropriate way because of its small demand. It must not be so tricky to hold that accidents occur when children or invalids try to use it. It must not be able to boil dry and burn without warning. It must not be unstable on the stove while it is boiling."

ALEXANDER 1964

One thing we observe at work with the great designers (and again, not just of games) is their "habit of mind" where they read a lot and find everything interesting. After all, anything and everything is interesting to at least some people. Then, when something comes along that requires more in-depth knowledge, they dive in and (partially) master the subject matter. Then, when it comes to actually designing, they have what is needed to tackle the design challenge—from a multiplicity of angles, as with the tea kettle designer—to turn out something brilliant.

Say the challenge is to build a game involving dinosaurs. Our designers will go to town learning plenty about dinosaurs. Maybe they were keenly interested in dinosaurs when they were ten, and this challenge inspired her to reawaken her childhood passion. But a lot has happened in the world of paleontology since then. For example, many paleontologists now believe that some dinosaurs had feathers, since we now know from DNA analysis that birds descended from dinosaurs. Now there's a handy bit of information that could well find its way into the game.

Note that our designer doesn't need to be a full-on Ph.D.-level paleontologist to gain this knowledge and put it to use. She simply needs to do *just enough* research to get the process started.

And you can do this, too. Follow your passions. (For one of us, it was skateboarding, even though we're hopeless at it in real life; for the other it was military history. For both of us, though, these passions came in handy later on.) Some little bit of knowledge rattling around your head may be just the thing you need when trying to dream up ideas. You never know what little tidbit of knowledge you've picked up will lead to a breakthrough idea.

So even though you might not be taking any courses with the D-word in their titles this year, you can still be feeding your brain with the knowledge you need to be a better designer, no matter what your specialty area is. We've put a bunch of useful design resources in the appendix.

8.1.2 Computer Science

Most colleges and universities that offer computer science as a major generally follow the recommended curriculum set by the Association for Computer Machinery (ACM), perhaps the oldest professional association devoted to all things computational. Its name says something about its age, as the ACM was founded back when computers were vast piles of rack cabinets stuffed with vacuum tubes and blinking lights. Playing with them must have been fascinating, and hence its name.

THE ASSOCIATION FOR COMPUTER MACHINERY

The ACM, at www.acm.org, hosts a truly vast library of papers, books, and much else having to do with software, going all the way back to its origins in 1947. Your school library probably has access to this repository, and you may occasionally want to tap into it. Ask your librarian!

You can also access it by becoming a member of the ACM. Student memberships are reasonably affordable considering all you get.

The Institute of Electrical and Electronics Engineers, or IEEE (www.ieee.org/index.html), is another professional association that maintains a vast library of highly technical information. This includes, in addition to their original work in telecommunications, ever increasing content about computer systems and computer science. They offer student activities and memberships as well.

Not only are these organizations super-useful resources, but having a student membership in them looks good on a résumé.

These days, of course, we realize that software seems much more important in the grand scheme of things than the actual hardware it runs on. When was the last time you heard somebody make a big deal about which flavor of Intel™ chip was in their laptop? True, we're more likely to get excited about what your new NVIDIA™ graphics card is capable of.

But software is the main dish, and this is going to be what you'll be concentrating on this year. You may have already taken some of these courses already, or maybe you'll postpone them to a future year, but we'll go over the most common ones now.

Data Structures. This one is essential. Here, you learn about stacks, queues, lists, hashmaps, trees, and a lot of other interesting ways to model the world as bits and bytes. While you're taking this course, you'll be asked to write code to actually implement these fundamental data structures.

Every programming language in common use today, however, has a number of "libraries" to support these vital data structures, or these data structures might even be part of the language itself. Python, for example, has built-in lists, delimited by the [ ] characters, and dictionaries (called "dicts") expressed with the { } characters. Dictionaries are also known as hashmaps.

So, since all these things have already been built, you may be asking yourself, why do I even have to learn how to code them?

The main reason, if we had to guess, is that by doing these, you are programming your brain to think more like a computer. This seems backwards, but it's really not. It's all a part of that procedural literacy we discussed earlier.

As you become more accomplished as a programmer, you will be challenged to solve intricate problems in the real world that will require you to map that real world onto data structures that a computer can actually work with. Your skill and ability to create such mappings—and get them working quickly and correctly—will be a most valuable asset. So put aside your misgivings about having to learn about these things and embrace them for what they can do for you instead. After that, use the libraries!

Algorithms. This is what programmers do: turn caffeine into algorithms.

The algorithms course will be about designing code that has a fighting chance of executing very rapidly and very accurately. You could probably "solve" the game of chess using the logic programming language Prolog, but don't expect to get an answer within the remaining lifetime of the universe.

Games need to finish their algorithmic business at "frame rate" (these days a normal target for nonmobile games is at least 60 frames per second, or fps), and your code can't take too long to do what it needs to do frame by frame. The algorithms course will teach you how to do this. Besides, its so-called "Big-O notation" is rather cool once you grok what it is telling you about how efficient your code is.

Programming Languages. Many CS programs have a course like this one, where you study several weird (and possibly obsolete) programming languages, just to show you that some very brilliant people devised some very clever ways to work on particular kinds of programming problems.

We already mentioned one of them, Prolog, a language that works with logical expressions and solves them using the rules of deductive logic. As we saw, you could solve chess this way, but not in your, or the universe's, lifetime. Another language you might run into is LISP (or its variant, Scheme), the original language for AI dating all the way back to 1958. It doesn't look like anything else out there. Then there's Scala, a rather neat language based on Java that its devoted fans consider a lot better than Java. You can build some serious systems with it. You might also get to play with languages like Erlang or Haskell, or maybe something more obscure or experimental.

Operating Systems. Yes, like MacOS, Linux, or Windows. In the old days (and one of us is old enough to have done this), you would be expected to actually write a primitive operating system, one that can manage a file system, accept keyboard input and pump ASCII character output to a "terminal" (you don't see those much anymore), and launch and shut down programs stored on the file system—all that and more.

These days what we expect from a modern operating system like Windows or MacOS is far beyond what a student or student team could hope to create in a semester, but in this course you will gain an understanding of what goes on deep down inside any operating system. For more advanced kinds of programming, this knowledge is essential.

In terms of the programming homework, since you won't be building an actual OS, you will instead probably be working primarily on three things: process synchronization, shell scripts, and device drivers.

Process Synchronization. This course will cover how to get large complex applications to make maximum use of system resources, exploiting all the "cores" in a multicore environment, for example, and arranging work to maximize "throughput," the amount of work the application can complete in some unit of time. Does this sound like something a game engine has to deal with?

Shell Scripting. This is the business of bolting together large suites of applications to create a cohesive process—the sort of things that people who construct large back-room server operations have to deal with. In the game industry, this sort of knowledge is invaluable for automating and streamlining workflow processes so that the artists, programmers, and designers waste as little time as possible during production. It's also needed for those massive servers that handle MMOGs for thousands of players at the same time, not to mention the servers set up to support the game's community of fans.

Device Drivers. These are those very low-level pieces of code that allow hardware devices, like video cards and audio devices, to work seamlessly within an operating system. The code that allows your latest NVIDIA card to operate is the device driver, and device drivers are among the hardest programs to write and get working correctly. For one thing, a device driver should *never, ever* crash, although they do from time to time in the real world. Also, the coding is done at an incredibly low level, what programmers call "close to the metal," making this work doubly challenging.

Even if you never go on to work at these deeper levels, you will come away from the course with a deeper appreciation of what goes on under the hood and develop a more accurate sense of "what is possible" on a given computer. On the other hand, if you discover you are really good at this, you may well become a member of the programming priesthood in your organization, the person that more junior programmers come to with the really tough problems.

Artificial Intelligence. AI courses come in two flavors: traditional academic AI (also called Good Old-Fashioned Artificial Intelligence, or GOFAI) and AI for Games. There is only partial overlap between the two. A course in AI for Games is about the algorithms most useful for computer games, like path-finding (the A* algorithm), techniques for strategy games ("influence maps"), and, of course, behaviors for non-player characters (the "behavior tree").

If your school offers both, go for the AI for Games version, assuming your school allows you to count it toward a Computer Science degree. If you have room in your schedule, you might even want to take both.

In addition to the above, your school may offer other computer science classes that you may find interesting and that are appropriate for you to take at this stage of your academic career.

8.1.3 Visual Arts

During your second year, you'll continue to skill up in your chosen area while getting exposed to a lot of art materials.

Art History. The history of art through the centuries is simply fascinating, and anyone can benefit by studying it. Certainly, wannabe artists should be studying it, but anyone who loves art should find a course like this delightful. Even programmers.

Consider the game *Bioshock,* developed by 2K Boston and 2K Australia and published by 2K Games. Here's a game that was a love letter to the historic art movement known as Art Deco. Anyone familiar with this movement can see how beautifully crafted the locale of the game, the underwater city of Rapture, was. It looks as good as it does because the artists researched Art Deco deeply, so much so that the game bursts with lavishly and faithfully constructed interiors, down to the doorknobs and faucets.

Life Drawing. This is a class where you draw actual people using only pencils and charcoal on sketchpad paper, trying to draw them as accurately as possible. This is surprisingly difficult to do well.

It's possible your school doesn't offer a course like this; many don't. You may, however, be able to find a course like this at a local art college, art museum, or "art center" that offers art courses.

Why do we recommend this? There are a lot of artists who have developed great skills with Photoshop, Maya, Mudbox®, Houdini®, and ZBrush® but who cannot actually *draw.* Being able to depict the human form in a lifelike way greatly helps you, especially when you are called upon to create "concept art."

CONCEPT ART

Concept art is the means by which a preliminary idea for a world or character or game object gets turned into a visual representation for all involved with the project to see. This is usually done at the earliest stages of development (often even prior to the preproduction phase). Concept art helps convey the vision of the project and gives participants a frame of reference on which to base subsequent design thinking. Concept art can range from primitive sketches to fairly complete drawings. The key idea here is that concept art is something done early on. This sets the stage for more complete renditions to be created right up until the project is finished.

According to legend, when Walt Disney was interviewing animation artists, he would hand the artist a sketch pad and some drawing implements. He would ask the artist to draw—from memory—a picture of Minnie Mouse or Goofy or some other Disney character, and he would expect the artist to crank out one quickly and accurately and good enough that it could be used on an actual animation cel (a sheet of clear acetate plastic).

Could you do that? If not, there was surely some other starving artist in the crowded waiting room who could. It was that competitive.

We've seen the same thing with artists looking for work in the game industry. Plenty of them can draw all sorts of scaly, tentacled monsters, but ask them to draw a *farmer*, and forget it.

This is why we recommend getting as good as you can at drawing the human form. Once you have that down, you can learn to draw other creatures that will look believable and great. Later on, you might find drawing dogs, cats, or dragons useful, too.

You are, of course, still growing as an artist, and you are probably at the point where you are trying to "find your own voice," that is, you are trying to develop your own personal style, to deliver your personal vision to the world. This takes a good long time, and it will change and evolve over the course of your life. Do everything you can to feed this: learn art history, go to museums, read biographies, and basically study the greats who came before you. Make a lot of crappy artwork in different styles, and then throw them away. Then decide what you want to keep and what to discard, and be ruthless about this.

Now, there is a paradox between that goal and developing yourself as a "commercial" artist. If you get a job with a major studio, you will be expected to create art in a specific style that will be spelled out for you. Typically, this is done with a document (with lots of pictures, drawings, and color palettes) called the style guide or style bible. Remember that story about interviewing at Disney; you face much the same challenge. Being able to do "commercial strength" work is how you get and keep jobs.

But what about *my* vision, you ask? Well, if you are fortunate enough to go your own way in an indie studio or start-up, then you will get closer to calling the shots. This is where your hard work finding your voice pays off. You can take all you've learned and conceptualized to create your own style guide, and with that you can communicate your vision to other artists on the team and in the world.

But what if you don't get to do that? Well, a lot will depend on your focus and energy and fortunes in life, but you can still do this. Bill Watterson, the creator of *Calvin and Hobbes*, arguably the world's greatest comic strip ever, was able to retire from the daily grind, take the money, and pursue fine-arts painting in Washington State on his own terms. This is an extreme example, but nothing keeps you from pursuing your own artistic visions with passion when away from work.

If you are truly an artist, you are already doing this anyway.

2D Animation. Also called sprite animation, this is a distinctly different skill from 3D animation, posing a different sort of challenge. Here you create those little square or rectangular blocks of pixels and get them to move. This can be done the hard way, pixel by pixel, or by using tricks like animating full 2D or 3D models at the skeletal level, then "flattening" them, making them blockier, into 2D sprites. You'll be getting better at Adobe Illustrator® and Adobe Photoshop (or a free alternative like GIMP) and also working with purpose-built sprite animation tools like Pyxel Edit®. Pyxel Edit is very affordable and is available through the Humble Bundle™ store.

Beginning, Intermediate, Advanced 3D Animation. These are heavyweight courses, with typically two or three levels offered since there is so much to learn. Most likely you'll be learning Maya or 3D Studio®, the industry leaders. You might use Blender, the free alternative instead, but that is rather less desirable if you intend to become a professional animator. But Blender has been used by indie and hobby developers who can't afford the professional tools.

Expect to spend many hours getting into the myriad fine points of the art of animation and the intricacies of these software packages. This is not easy work, but you want to get to where you can amaze people with your skills.

Other Art Courses. Art schools are idiosyncratic, and some of the other courses that might be offered can differ widely from school to school. Regardless, you will no doubt find courses in at least some of these major topic areas:

- Graphic design

- Typography

- Design studios (of various kinds)

- Communication theory

- Art history (e.g., Western, other art traditions, 20th century)

- Color theory

- Prototype design

- Research methods

- Programming for artists

- Other "computer art" courses

- Human/computer interaction

- User experience design

- Digital design aesthetics

Sound Design. Courses in a sound design program will necessarily cover, at a minimum, topics like these, and many more:

- The physiology of hearing

- Acoustics

- Music cognition

- Audio fundamentals for recording

- Audio mixing and mastering

- Sound design

- Ear training

- Creative music production

- The music business (e.g., copyright, licensing, publishing)

- Game audio production

- Courses involving various audio tools (e.g., Abelton Live®, Max®, ProTools®)

Music Composition. A music composition program will have some overlap with the courses in sound design, except that the emphasis is obviously much more on the composition side of things and less on production and recording. Composing music begins with music theory, possibly quite a lot of it, so expect courses like the following:

- Music theory 101, 201, 301 (harmony, chords and scales, etc.)

- Music Theory and Composition 1, 2, 3, 4

- Music History (classical, blues, jazz, rock, world)

- Composition involving software tools like Abelton Live and Sibelius®

- Instrumentation, orchestration, arranging

- Music for film, music for games

- Song writing, lyric writing

- Experimental music, developing your artistry, and so forth

Writing Courses. Writing programs usually start off with courses like English Composition and maybe something with a name like Reading Critically. You would have handled these in your first year, or maybe even via AP credit, and you definitely want to get these fundamentals out of the way so you can get to the fun stuff. Naturally, as you think about the kind of writer you want to be, make your selections accordingly. After that, you can expect an array of choices for writing in all its manifestations, in courses like:

- Nonfiction Writing

- Writing for the Arts

- Promotional Writing

- Business and Professional Writing

- Creative Nonfiction

- News Writing and Editing

- Writing for Digital Media

- Magazine Journalism

- Science Fiction

- Fantasy

- Poetry

- Playwriting

- Screenwriting

- Writing for Games

For all the items listed above, follow the recommendations and requirements of your particular program. The preceding lists are not meant to be exhaustive, merely representative. They also span many of the courses you will be taking in your junior and senior years, and so we won't be repeating these lists in later chapters.

CHAPTER 9

Becoming a Professional

9.1 ACT PROFESSIONALLY, EVEN IN SCHOOL

Woody Allen once said, "Eighty percent of success is showing up."

BRAINYQUOTE 2017

He was on to something. If you seek to work as a game developer, in whatever capacity, you are seeking to become a respected professional in this industry.

Now, doctors, accountants, and lawyers are also professionals, and society shows them considerable respect (well, maybe not so much the lawyers). If you are smart enough and dedicated enough to become a medical doctor, we hope you will give up on making games and head over to medical school. You'll be doing more for the world even as the game industry loses a great talent.

A professional game developer is a lot like a professional filmmaker or musician. They get respect from some quarters and disdain from others, but that's show biz.

When we speak about professionalism here, we are speaking about acting in all the ways that help the teams you are on make great games, further your career, and maybe even let you make lots and lots of money (that's show biz, too).

Technically, you are a professional if you get paid for the work you do. It's a terrific feeling, getting that first paycheck for doing something you love. You are crossing that chasm between amateur and professional, and there is no feeling quite like it.

But what does being a true professional entail? We've lined up a number of key ideas. First…

Do Everything You Promised to Do.

This is the main one. To it we would add "on time and under budget," so…

Do Everything You Promised to Do, on Time and on Budget.

This will quickly become impossible if you say "yes" to every request that comes your way. There is simply not enough time to do everything you want to do in life, and so you need to exercise the ability to say no when it is warranted. This is that problem of overscoping we discussed a while back.

Of course, say yes to the daily things that make up your job. Many companies in the industry practice some sort of "agile" development process (like Scrum, see Chapter 6). You need to meet the agile process halfway. Through a process of negotiation between you and your producer, you arrive at the amount of work you need to finish within each upcoming sprint. Once you agree on this, you get to work, and you *make sure you get it done by the deadline*. It's that simple.

At least it's that simple in an ideal world. In the world we inhabit, however, any number of things can go wrong. If they are not going seriously wrong, the solution is pretty straightforward: Stay late for a few evenings until you get things back on track. But you can only do so much of this.

Respect Others' Time.

The workplace can be a distracting place. It can be noisy, phones can be ringing, emails can be piling up. This has actually reached crisis proportions in many organizations. According to a study conducted by CareerBuilder.com, a job search website, top killers of productivity include cellphones, texting, surfing the net, and spending time on social media. Those are only the technological ones. See the sidebar for the link.

You can choose to not be a part of the problem by honoring the fact that the people you work with are also under the gun.

PRODUCTIVITY KILLERS

The killers of office productivity include tempting technological ones like social media but also things like background noise and coworkers who stop by for a visit. Read more about it here:

www.businessnewsdaily.com/8098-distractions-kiling-productivity.html

MULTITASKING

Lots of tech-savvy on-the-go types claim they can multitask, that is, keep a dozen eggs in the air at the same time. But don't expect multitasking to save you. We know from studies in cognitive science that every time you do a "context switch," that is, swapping out one task to begin another, it comes at a cost. A review of several research papers can be found at the American Psychological Association website (APA 2006).

A programmer, for example, working deep inside some difficult code, gets a phone call about…nothing in particular, maybe a reminder to pick up milk on the way home. Doesn't matter, that interruption could cause that programmer to get derailed for a good half-hour before she gets her concentration back. Yes, a context switch can be that expensive.

Sorry, but the research just doesn't support the idea that multitasking is productive. Every time you "context switch," you need to spend some time moving off the current task and adjusting your mind to the task you just switched to. It might take only a few seconds or it might take several minutes. It adds up, and before you know it you may have lost as much as an hour a day being so productive while multitasking.

What works far better is to perform tasks serially. Pick one task, work on it to completion (or to a reasonable place to stop working on it for the day), then pick the next task and work on it. Rinse and repeat.

If you combine this way of working with *The One Thing* (see sidebar below) and *The Pomodoro Method*, you'll be unstoppable and the envy of your workmates.

While on the job, you will constantly be getting stuck over some fine point about scripting the game or using some advanced feature in your art software. This happens to everyone. The natural thing to do is to go seek out your local guru and ask her how to do it.

This is not the best way to go about it. The more professional way to act: Find out on your own!

The web is vast, and you can often find the answer online because very likely someone else has already encountered your issue and was kind enough to tell the rest of us. You might even find a helpful tutorial on YouTube. It is far better that you make every effort to solve your problems on your own this way instead of always running for help. Even better, you just boosted your skill level. Even better than that, maybe you share the link with your coworkers so they can learn, too (at a time and place where you are not disrupting them, of course).

If and only after a reasonable amount of searching and researching the problem you encountered turns up *nada* on the web, then you might be able to impress the guru with having discovered a problem no one has seen before.

What if you are really, truly stuck? What to do next depends in part on the corporate culture. The more senior a person is, the more valuable that person's time is, and even the most patient of individuals have their limits. Very often, your company, or the individual in question, has set up policies for these sorts of situations. For example, they may have a policy of "if my office door is closed, don't bother me." Or they may post the equivalent of professor's "office hours" to mark the times when it is OK to visit. If you can't see the person right away, put the problem aside and turn your attention to something else you can work on.

Do the Hardest Thing First.

Even if you don't think of yourself as a morning person, there is little question that for most people the best time to tackle the toughest task of the day is at the start of the day. This is when your brain has the greatest amount of its essential fuel, glucose, available to it, you are well rested, your mind has defragged itself via last night's dreams, and you haven't fogged your mind yet with other issues. Maybe you just had your first cup of coffee, too.

Do the hardest thing first. Sounds simple, doesn't it? Yet there is a very natural human tendency to work around the big issue, to deal with lots of smaller things first "to get them out of the way." This seems entirely reasonable. Who wants all that clutter hanging around before you get started on the main event?

THE ONE THING

The One Thing by Gary Keller is a terrific little productivity booster that will change the way you approach each workday (Keller and Papasan 2013).

We're not going to rehash the book here (please read it yourself), except to reproduce his key idea. Every day, ask yourself, *"What is the one thing I can be doing about_____, such that by doing it everything else will be easier or unnecessary?"*

But this is backwards, even though it may take a while to fully appreciate it. When you make the hardest thing you work on the first thing you work on, something wonderful happens. Not only do you get that terrific feeling of accomplishment, you also discover that the rest of the day is a comparative breeze. Plus, you are working on the less important tasks at the time when your brain starts running low on fuel.

You'll be amazed at how everything else falls into place once you adopt this habit.

Keep It Positive, No Matter What.

It's been called positive mental attitude (PMA), and you want it.

Now, we think the whole idea of PMA is a bit oversold. It's the answer to all of life's problems, right? Not quite. There is far more to success and happiness than PMA, but it is an essential ingredient.

Keeping it positive is pretty easy when things are going well (unless you are the grumpy type) but much harder to maintain when things get tough. This is one area where we see how true professionals behave.

We know how a lot of this works from the way people like soldiers and first responders are trained. It's all in the training. This is why soldiers are put through grueling boot camp before being allowed into battle, and firefighters practice on staged, yet very real, fires.

So how do you toughen up? In part you've already been doing this, by surviving game school and maybe a few rounds of crunch time. But there are helpful habits you can get into long before that soul-crushing crisis that will leave you better prepared when the time comes.

Your Health Is #1.

First is your physical health. We can't possibly advise you about how you should go about maintaining your physical health. It's your life and your responsibility, and besides, we didn't go to medical school…we made games.

Health comes before everything else. Without good health, all the rest of what you do slides into the toilet. While you are young, you can load up on processed foods and sugary soft drinks without maybe too much ill effect, but over time these will bring you down. Actually, lousy processed foods and beverages are damaging you right now; you just won't notice their damaging effects till later in life.

But the stereotype of the overweight gamer, chomping down chips and soda and not putting in any exercise, has some truth to it. Look around you. Look at yourself.

HEALTHY EMPLOYEES ARE GOOD BUSINESS

There is a good reason why a lot of the top companies have gyms, pay for wellness classes, bring in masseurs during stress times, and on and on. They recognize that having a healthy workforce is good for their business. So, if it good for them, just maybe it is good for you, too.

This isn't simply driven by greed, even if it is healthy for the bottom line. *Everybody* benefits from good health.

We started off this book by observing that video games are simply another branch of the entertainment industry, of show biz. Look at the top people in show business. They are generally remarkably fit, watch their diets, and take care of themselves. Not all of them, but most. The ones with staying power certainly do.

Now, there have sure been a lot of sad cases in the entertainment industry. Comedians John Candy and Chris Farley died young. James Garofalo, who played Tony Soprano, died young. There are other ways of checking out, too, notably drug abuse and alcoholism. It's tough to steer a clear path through all the temptations that come with massive success, and no one is necessarily immune, but good habits and clear thinking are a start.

Serenity, Now!

Staying cool under pressure is what it's all about, and the mark of the true professional.

Ever wonder why celebrities often take up martial arts, meditation, yoga, or tai chi? Strengthening the body and sharpening the mind are the goals here. An actor working on a movie might begin the day at 4 AM for makeup and wardrobe, work till 8 or 9 at night (and often later), and do this five or six days a week for the duration of principal photography. After that, they rest for a bit, but not for too long.

This looks and sounds a lot like crunch time, and you really can't keep that up for long periods without a solid reserve of physical and mental stamina. Add to that the pressures of maintaining your close relationships or your family. Your ability to weather the storm depends on keeping a cool head.

Consider, therefore, the practice called "mindfulness meditation." One of us regularly practices this, and it is immensely helpful, in ways that are not at all obvious. Mindfulness meditation is "easy": just sit in the correct posture for 20 or 30 or 45 minutes, breathe regularly, and empty the mind of thought. The scare quotes around the "easy" are intentional. This is far harder than it looks (try it!), but the rewards can be amazing. Just don't expect instantaneous results; it takes years to really get the hang of it and experience the benefits.

The other one of us does not practice "mindfulness meditation" but follows the old adage of "when you feel the stress, stop, count to 10, and take deep breaths." This works, too. Proper breathing is important.

Learning how to keep your cool during periods of crisis helps mark you as a true professional, one whom everyone will hold in high regard and will want to work with. What can be better for your career than that?

9.2 YOUR RÉSUMÉ AND YOUR PORTFOLIO (AGAIN)

We've covered this a lot elsewhere in this book, so we're not going to say much here.

The main thing is to maintain these important materials as you go through your career, even if you've been employed reasonably steadily and aren't currently on the job market.

We recommend doing this because memories are faulty. Every three months or so, revisit these documents and update them with your latest work experience and work examples. This shouldn't take long, maybe an hour or two. This is much better than scratching your head after not doing this for a couple of years, trying to remember all the great things you've accomplished.

9.3 PRACTICE MAKES PERFECT

Professionalism isn't something you are born with. You won't be the consummate professional on the day you start getting paid for your work. You will make mistakes and screw things up. Everybody, repeat *everybody*, does. You may think this won't apply to you, but it will.

Professionals, however, admit their mistakes and seek solutions while endeavoring not to make the same mistake again. And if they are really good, they won't make that mistake ever again.

BODY LANGUAGE

There is a TED Talk by Amy Cuddy called *Your Body Language Shapes Who You Are*: http://www.ted.com/talks/amy_cuddy_your_body_language_shapes_who_you_are.
It isn't about what you think it is.

The secret isn't really a secret: just keep banging away at it until you arrive. Or, to put it crudely, fake it till you make it. More precisely, it's work at it until you have it mastered.

Ever wonder how people at the top got to be at the top? They didn't start there; they began at the beginning and just kept at it. There is an old saying in the music business: "He worked ten years to become an overnight success." That's closer to the reality of it.

You might get there sooner than that, or later, or maybe not at all. Luck has a lot to do with it. Our lives are governed by chance more than most of us would like, but it's inescapable. With luck, maybe you'll create that game that captures everyone's attention and you become rich overnight, or maybe you won't. Either way, that's unlikely to happen without your holding up your end of the bargain.

CHAPTER 10

San Francisco (and LA) Bound

10.1 THE GAME DEVELOPER CONFERENCE

If there is a mecca for game developers, it's the annual Game Developer Conference (GDC), which takes place around March of every year in San Francisco at the massive Moscone Convention Center. With more than 20,000 visitors, the GDC takes over nearly the entire multibuilding complex these days.

Going to the GDC is simply flat-out exciting and inspirational. You'll see many of the stars of the industry. There will be new things to look at and try out on the trade show floor. At the end of it you'll be both exhausted and exhilarated.

This is not a cheap conference by any means: not only the conference itself, but also, unless you already live in the Bay Area, the airfare and staying at the expensive hotels in San Francisco. But you should try as hard as you can to get to at least one of these during your career. And, from our point of view, do it, if at all possible, during your senior year.

If you go, leave some space in your luggage for all the swag you'll be bringing back. Also, make sure you have a supply of decent business cards. There won't be much to say on these except your name and what you do ("Artificial Intelligence Programmer," for example). If you've started a studio with some other people, even if you haven't set up a corporation yet, by all means have cards for that.

The GDC splits out in various ways into different areas and activities. It takes place over a five-day workweek. The main action takes place on Wednesday, Thursday, and Friday. That's when the trade show floor is open (on the ground level), while the in-depth industry talks and roundtables take place throughout the Moscone complex.

The trade show floor will feature all the established game industry companies and a lot of new ones. Microsoft®, Nintendo®, and Sony® will all be there. Activision/Blizzard®, Electronic Arts®, and Ubisoft® will all be there. There will also be a lot of new, or relatively new, outfits: studios, controller manufacturers, middleware software companies, and a whole lot more.

10.2 BRING BUSINESS CARDS AND RÉSUMÉS…

Don't be surprised if the major outfits don't pay much attention to you, and don't let it get to you. The smaller companies are much more likely to greet you enthusiastically. Walk around. Meet people. Have conversations. Collect business cards. Leave them business cards, and maybe a résumé if they ask for one. Keep a notebook with you.

And be sure to snatch up however much free swag as you can carry.

What is more interesting on the ground floor are all the little curtained-off booths in the back. This is where you will find company recruiters taking job applications. This can be for both full-time and internship/co-op positions. The game companies know that lots of students descend on the GDC every year, and this is a good way for them to collect a lot of applications all in one place at relatively low cost.

You may also see on your travels to the back area other spots where private meetings are held. You are not invited to them, so don't go poking your nose in those places. It's unprofessional and could get you ejected. Without a refund.

If you want to meet with company recruiters while at the GDC, one effective strategy is to contact the companies you are interested in well in advance. Tell them you'll be at the GDC and ask if you can set up an appointment. Do this only if you are serious about following through. If the company thinks there is any chance there might be a good fit between you and the company, they may well agree to this. Needless to say, if you do score an interview slot, be sure to show up.

A basic pass to the GDC gets you onto the trade show floor. You need a more powerful and expensive pass (the Mega Pass) to attend the talks. The talks are, to us anyway, a key reason to be at the GDC. This is where you get to hear presentations on all sorts of game development matters. These are given by top industry people and cover not only programming, design, and art topics, but also business and marketing, intellectual property law, employment law, and much more.

The talks are scheduled as follows. Monday and Tuesday are the various workshops, which can last a half day, a day, or the whole two days. These are crash courses in some area of game development, and we can tell you that these are also worth your time. You'll need to register early for these as they fill up quickly.

Along with the workshops there are talks about game design, legal issues like copyright law, market analysis, writing for games, artificial intelligence, and much else.

Wednesday, Thursday, and Friday are devoted to hour-long talks, and there will be a couple hundred of these scattered throughout the conference. There are always several talks going on at the same time, so there is no hope of catching them all.

The good news about getting the Mega Pass is that, in addition to being able to attend these talks, you can later view most of them online on the GDC Vault. One of these passes gives you a year's access to the entire GDC Vault for that year and all previous years, provided they were recorded in the first place. This is incredibly valuable, and if you don't make use of the Vault, you're missing out on what is probably the most useful benefit of all.

10.3 PAYING FOR THE GDC

As we said, this is no cheap affair, and you may want to seek out ways to help defray the costs.

One way is to become a "student volunteer." You apply, and if you get accepted, you don't have to pay for the Expo Pass. The competition for this is fierce, so don't be surprised if your excellent application doesn't make the cut. If you do get one, not only are you lucky, but, assuming you don't screw up, you'll make it onto the much shorter list of students who may be invited back the following year. It is easier for them to work with people who have proven themselves reliable, after all.

While there, you'll be a student ambassador of sorts. This is another way of saying, a gofer. You'll primarily be telling people how to get to various places and providing general assistance. You'll get chances to roam the trade show floor and drop off your résumé to interested companies. Everyone understands that's one of the main reasons you're there.

Unfortunately, the student volunteer pass doesn't get you into the talks or give you access to the GDC Vault.

10.4 SENSORY OVERLOAD

Your first GDC can be pretty overwhelming. You're not going to be able to take it all in, but that's fine. Whatever you choose to do while there will be valuable one way or another. Just be sure to get enough sleep (2 or 3 hours a night should do it) and stay hydrated.

10.5 DON'T FORGET THE PARTIES—NETWORKING

No discussion of the GDC would be complete without mentioning the parties. Yes, there are parties, and plenty of them. This is why you'll be totally exhausted by the end of the conference. The parties take place all over San Francisco, although mostly near the Moscone

Center. Some parties are easy to get into; others are pretty exclusive and hard to sniff out. Depending on your chutzpah and personal charm, you may be able to snag an invite or two. This is easier if you are over 21 and of legal drinking age.

CHUTZPAH

"Chutzpah" is an old Yiddish word meaning more or less the same thing as "hue-vos" or "cojones." It means having brass balls. Chutzpah is murdering your mother and father and then throwing yourself on the mercy of the court because you're an orphan.

Want a classic example of chutzpah? Check out this story about how Steven Spielberg broke into the movie business. You can read about it here:

http://www.internships.com/eyeoftheintern/news/famous-interns/steven-spielberg/

Having plenty of chutzpah is part of moving your career forward in the entertainment industry. Don't be afraid to get out there and make contacts, even though it puts you far outside your comfort zone.

One party you can definitely attend is the one given by the International Game Developers Association (IGDA). The IGDA also operates a booth at the conference, and you're welcome to stop by and visit. You may be able to snag a handsome IGDA T-shirt while there (get there early, though, as they run out quickly). Their party is another great way to meet people and network. You do need to be a student member, though.

Other parties are much tougher to get into. Many of them you can just forget about at this stage of your career. For the others, this is where your ability to market yourself really pays off. Don't be put off by the idea of "selling out." You are not selling out. You are making others aware (with all due modesty on your part) that you're in this game and have some valuable skills and talents to offer. Besides, "selling out" is a lot harder than it looks; first you have to become hugely successful.

10.6 THE E3 TRADE SHOW!

The E3 is a very different affair than the GDC. While the GDC is focused on the folks who do game development, the E3 is all about the media and the press. The E3 is where you find the major announcements for upcoming game releases. New consoles are usually announced there, too. While you do hear about upcoming releases at the GDC, this is much less common because it's not the best place for game companies to score maximum media coverage.

We mentioned "the press." Until quite recently, attendance at the E3 was restricted to media entities like television networks, newspapers and magazines, and those web-based media outlets like IGN and Kotaku. But as the Internet exploded, anyone could launch a game-oriented blog or YouTube channel and start reviewing games. The people doing this were able to argue—successfully—that they were members of the press, too.

After a few years of this, it became an open secret that to get into E3, all you had to do was have some sort of web presence and apply for a media pass.

Finally, the E3 organizers grew weary of this, and E3 is now open to the public—for a price.

We don't think E3 is as useful as GDC for the budding game developer, but it sure is fun. It is also *loud*. Think of the loudest arcade you've ever been to and multiply that by 100.*

10.7 OTHER CONFERENCES AND TRADE SHOWS

Where to begin? There are the major conferences, like GDC Paris and others of that magnitude. There are a host of regional conferences and conventions, many of which you've probably heard of, like PAX and PAX East.

We'll mention just one here, the Montreal International Game Summit, or MIGS.

The MIGS is much smaller in scope than GDC, which makes interacting with the other attendees (and often the speakers) much easier.

It is, not surprisingly, a Canadian-centric conference. Why not? Ubisoft is right there, and Montreal is a major game development hub that employs over 4,000 people working at Ubisoft and other, smaller studios.

As an aside, for students in the U.S., one thing to keep in the back of your mind is that the nation of Canada is keenly interested in building up its own supply of high-tech companies and people, and getting a job there, if you have some hard skills like computer programming, may be easier than you think. You could even apply for citizenship. You need to enjoy long hard winters, so this may be less interesting to you if you aren't already an avid skier or snowboarder.

We like MIGS for lots of reasons, not least of which is that it takes place in Montreal, one of the most cosmopolitan cities in the Western Hemisphere. As part of French-speaking Québec, it has some of the best dining anywhere. Also, the drinking age in Canada is 18, so you can enjoy a fine wine with your dinner (but please enjoy responsibly). At least try the "poutine," French fries (*pommes frites, s'il vous plait*) covered with gravy and melted cheese. Yum!

We certainly advocate eating healthy, but sometimes you just have to make an exception.

---

* Or 40 dB$_{SPL}$ louder, for you sound guys.

CHAPTER 11

Year Three

11.1 LEVELING UP

OK, you've made it to the third year. You're now an upperclassperson or a junior, whatever your school calls it.

Younger students will look up to you for help and maybe ask a lot of questions. It's just win-win all around if you help out. You are less likely to run into many of those students in regular curricular activities, however, since you won't be in too many of the classes at the same time. You are more likely to meet them at your game development club or your local chapter of the IGDA.

By this time, you will have completed most, or all, of your core courses, both in your games program and any other field you are majoring in. This year you'll probably be finishing up these courses, and now it is time to start specializing and deepening your skills.

THE T-SHAPED PERSON

This is an idea you might come across if you spend any time reading business or motivational books and articles.

The idea here is that the horizontal bar at the top of the T represents your skills across a variety of areas (Berger 2010). This is just the thing you need to be effective in game development. A little about programming, a little about art, a little about design, a little about storytelling.

The vertical bar of the T represents your knowledge-in-depth. This is your specialty area: gaining mastery over the one thing you are best at. This is what you will be concentrating on during your junior year.

Note: There are also Π-shaped people and even M-shaped people, but they are relatively rare. Are you one of them?

You've already learned most of the basics about game design and game mechanics. Are you finished learning about game design? Of course not. You'll be studying that for the rest of your career. But the basics are mostly out of the way, and you will be spending much of the coming year working on games.

These are games that go beyond the "student games" you made during your first two years. By now you've developed sharper critical thinking skills, and as a result, your games should show more sophistication and polish. It should be clear to anyone playing the game (especially industry professionals) that you've given careful thought to your design decisions, and you've paid attention to the details.

Your games are probably not quite at that happy state, but now at least you are at a point where you can usually recognize just what those things are that you are not happy with. These critical skills are something you'll continue to improve the more you make games and put them out there for people to play.

11.2 DON'T BE SO CRITICAL (?)

Let's talk about that word "critical." We hear about critical thinking, being overly critical, film criticism, critical theory (if you're an academic), and so forth.

Getting criticism for your work, whether positive or negative, is going to be good for you, provided the criticism comes from people who know what they are talking about. Not all criticism is created equal, and it pays to pay attention only to people who have something worthwhile to offer. Trolls and haters are not worth bothering with, although telling the difference between them and legitimate critics is not always easy.* Even if someone is not a professional in the industry, if they are in your target audience, then their criticism may be valid. If someone is a hater, find out why they hate your game before ruling them out. They may actually have a point.

In the art world there is the "critique," a formal process whereby accomplished artists, reviewers, and (yes) art critics evaluate student art projects. They point out, in a very thorough and fine-grained way, what works and what doesn't, and why. This is an especially important process toward getting a Master of Fine Arts degree. It can also be soul-crushing (especially when you turn in subpar work), but you need to suck it up.

This is not only in the arts. Software developers have their own soul-crushing ritual called the code review. Here, senior programming folk go through your code, often line by line, and ask many pointed questions about why you did the things you did. They will point

---

* And you've probably discovered by now they are not worth wasting time on, whether on Reddit, Facebook, or YouTube.

out possible points where the code might fail, where there are security holes, where it will execute inefficiently and wreck the frame rate, where it won't scale up. You need to take the criticism seriously, especially when you turn in subpar work.

Any discipline you are attempting to master will be populated by others who have been at it a lot longer than you have and who know more than you do. They are not your enemy. Where you want to be is in a place where they see your potential and genuinely want to help you.

There are a couple of things to keep in mind when confronting criticism.

A properly delivered critique or code review is all about "it," not "you." "It" is your game, or whatever work you contributed to the game. *"It" is not you.* A very difficult life skill to master is to be able to decouple yourself from your work. This is much harder than it looks since there is a powerful natural human tendency to let your creations get all bound up emotionally with your personal identity.

A properly delivered critique or code review will keep things at that level. "You" should not be getting personally attacked, only your work. But until you get the hang of decoupling yourself from your work, you'll feel like you're under siege. In fact, it's not uncommon for people (especially students) to think they've heard the critics attack them personally, even though, if you had recorded the whole thing and played it back later, you'd realize that they didn't attack *you* at all.

So get used to it. This is one of the most valuable ways there is to get better at whatever it is that you do. Plus, the critics you are dealing with now may well become your allies later on.

Once you get into the game industry, your work will be subjected to a lot of criticism from all sorts of people. While it would be nice to think that those doing the criticizing know what they are talking about, sadly that is not always the case. For example, a well-known children's game was criticized in one game magazine along the lines of *"well, it might be great for my seven-year-old but it is just too easy."* Hmmm, maybe if the critic in question had done his homework, he would have seen that the game was in fact designed for six- to ten-year-olds.

11.3 MASTERING THE TOOLS

By now, you've gotten pretty adept at the tools. At the time of this writing most of you have been using 3D game engines like Unity or UE4 for a while. You may have gotten a lot of design time in with 2D game engines like GameMaker, RPGMaker®, or Construct 2. If you're an artist, you've been working on mastery in Photoshop, Maya, perhaps Mudbox® or Houdini™, and other useful tools.

"If there is any advice I can impart to younger artist, when you're not working, dedicate some of your down time to improving your workflow and art processes. These can be simple things such as speeding up your texturing process or learning new modeling tools. Your knowledge of what's on the horizon of art and tech can make you an invaluable asset.

In this day and age of YouTube, Pinterest, Gnomon, CGSociety, and so on and so on, there are lots of opportunities to hone your abilities, improve your knowledge, find mentorship, join online social groups and forums. This can be key for your growth within your discipline, growth as an individual and it will help you create relationships with peers that can help you moving forward. Do not rely on your current employer to train you up for your next task, be proactive in your learning when you have downtime."

ABDUL BROWN

3D/2D Artist, Occasional Concept Artist, Occasional Animator, and Occasional Problem Solver

No doubt you've noticed that working with these tools is now a lot easier, and you can flow through work much more rapidly and accurately. You've learned what most of those tiny little buttons do. You've learned a pile of handy shortcuts, workarounds, and tricks. You are gaining mastery over the tools, exactly where you want to be.

This is the year where you are simply going to get better and better at these. You are now entering a phase where you've gotten past the learning curve (not that you ever really finish) and can now just hammer away at it toward your objectives.

Because you are gaining mastery, you can push the boundaries of what your games can be far beyond what you could do when you first started out. That's the whole point, right?

11.4 THIRD-YEAR COURSES

We covered most of the possible courses in Chapter 8. All we are going to say here is that during your third year you should be finishing up the core courses in your major(s) and now get to sample those other upper-level courses every department offers. These usually have prerequisites, those lower-level courses you must take first.

For game courses, your school will likely offer courses with names like these:

- Level Design

- Game Production

- Game Entrepreneurship

- Game Architecture

- Artificial Intelligence for Games

- User Experience Design

- Social Impact of Games

- Other relevant film or media courses

Your computer science department will likely offer courses with names like the following. Take whichever ones appeal the most to you and that don't violate your distribution requirements.

This is just a partial list of what might be available:

- Network Architecture
- Software Engineering
- Graph Theory (here, a graph doesn't mean what you think it means)
- Computability and Complexity
- Machine Learning
- Network Programming
- Cryptography and Network Security
- Computational Social Processes
- Computational Finance
- Introduction to Artificial Intelligence
- Parallel Programming
- Data Science
- Data and Society
- Database Systems
- Database Mining
- Distributed Computing
- Advanced Computer Graphics
- Data Visualization
- Numerical Computing
- Computer Vision
- Computational Linear Algebra
- Robotics

Here's just a sample of what you might find over in the Arts Department:

- Digital Filmmaking
- Art for Interactive Media
- Art History
- Basic Drawing

- Digital Imaging

- Graphic Storytelling

- Sculpture

- Advanced Digital 3-D Projects

- Multimedia Performance Systems

- Documentary Video Production

- 3D Visual Effects

- 3D Animation

- Art, Community, and Technology

- Inflatable Sculpture

- Living Art

- Life Drawing and Anatomy

- Hactivism

- Exploring Movement and Sound

- Writing and Directing for Video

But don't stop there. Explore what the other departments are up to. You just might get some new ideas for a game.…

11.5 MAKING CONTACTS

If you've been active in extracurricular activities at your school (e.g., game club, game jams, IGDA, game conferences, guest speakers), you've gotten to know people. Perhaps you've set up a LinkedIn account (recommended!) and perhaps also maintain a decent Facebook presence.

What about other social media like Twitter, Snapchat, or Instagram? Here you have to balance the enormous time you can potentially waste on these (and on Facebook) against what you can potentially gain by creating and maintaining a network of contacts.

In our opinion, LinkedIn is your best bet, followed by a carefully managed Facebook presence.

After building contact lists for a while on your favorite social media, you may find things getting unmanageable. You can simply leave things as they are, letting these sites manage your contacts, and that is probably fine. But you may eventually want to centralize your contacts in one place, if for no other reason than that it's under your control. A spreadsheet might be all you need.

11.6 LANDING AN INTERNSHIP

Now that you are finishing up Year Three and looking forward to an interesting summer, plan on landing an internship.

We already covered some of this in Chapter 10 and will get into it some more in Chapter 12, so we will only touch on a few other points here.

First, now that you're going to be a senior next academic year, the stakes are higher, but your ability to land an internship is stronger than last year. How well you do depends on a number of factors, only one of which is whether you have something to offer that someone wants.

The competition for internship slots is intense, so you have to look more attractive than the next person. Having solid skills goes without saying. Marketing yourself is another matter.

Now, before you get all bothered by the idea of marketing (and, we confess, we like to make fun of marketing, too), all we want to do here is to get you thinking about how you can make yourself visible, highly visible, to potential employers. If you don't, the next guy will. Guess who gets the job?

There is nothing immoral or unethical about singing your own praises as long as you are honest about it. Certainly, you should not claim credit for work that is not yours. Eventually, you are likely to get caught, and that will really put a dent in your reputation.

But there is nothing wrong with selling yourself, and in fact, you do that anyway when you send out applications or participate in a phone interview. In essence, a potential employer is testing to see if they want to "buy your brand" (that is, *you*). You, in turn, are trying to sell them on why you are their best choice. Really, marketing is little more than that: bringing a buyer who wants to buy together with a seller who wants to sell. If both agree on the product and the price is right, the sale can go through.

As we pointed out earlier, you want to get going with all this in January, but not usually earlier, unless the company itself has put an early internship recruitment program in place. We cover this in the next chapter.

CHAPTER 12

Internships and Co-ops

12.1 REMEMBER THAT PORTFOLIO THING?

We've been urging you all along to start, and then maintain, a portfolio of your best work. Now is the time to put your portfolio to good use, and that will be for securing yourself a coveted summer internship at a game studio. In this discussion we'll also talk about so-called co-ops (cooperative programs), where your college or university works with several corporations (not necessarily nearby) who will have you on their staff for a fixed period of time. Once that ends, you go back to school until you eventually graduate.

An internship, however, is typically for the summer months, although there are no hard and fast rules that it has to be that way. A co-op is more likely to take place during the spring or fall, and sometimes you work for an even longer stretch of time: combining spring + summer or summer + fall.

Your college or university ought to have some resources for this, although since video game development programs are relatively new, they may not be able to help you as much as you would like. Expect to have to do a lot of the scouting work yourself. You want to start early and work hard to make a favorable impression.

Internships (and some co-ops) come in two varieties: paid and unpaid. In the case of co-ops, your unpaid co-op will almost certainly be counted toward academic credit. This is usually only the case when there is a long-standing relationship between the school and the corporation since the school is going to want a clear and honest way of determining your grade. Because programs vary so much, however, you should investigate this before proceeding. Unpaid co-ops without the prospect of getting academic credit at the end are, most likely, illegal. As far as we know, it is against the law for a for-profit company to hire people and not pay them. (Volunteering for a nonprofit is another matter.)

Although we want to remind you that WE ARE NOT LAWYERS.

We should point out that companies within the industry sometimes refer to internships as co-ops and vice versa.

Be sure to check the expectations for what you are applying for. It would be very bad to discover later on that you applied for something, expecting it to last a few weeks, when it is actually supposed to last several months, or you were expecting academic credit or pay and didn't get it.

12.2 FINDING AN INTERNSHIP

If your college does not have a well-established system for placing interns with companies, then a good place to start is people you already know in the game industry. Indicate to them that you're interested in spending the summer with them. How readily you can do this, of course, depends on the nature of your relationship. Networking is important here, which is why we advocate hanging out at your local IGDA chapter meetings and going to talks.

This may not be a practical way to go, in which case you'll simply need to start researching companies and sending them your résumé and portfolio. It's perfectly OK, in most cases, to put your portfolio on the web; just make sure you have its URL posted very prominently in the materials you send.

One big thing to check if you do post your work on a website is to make sure it opens correctly in all three major browsers (Explorer, Chrome, and Firefox), as well as Safari on the Mac. There is no guarantee as to which browser your prospective employer will use, and they will certainly not bother trying them all if the first one they try doesn't work. Also, as we saw earlier, do not expect them to try out any executable files you have included. No one working at a studio will trust launching an unknown piece of software, even if it passes an antivirus scan. There is simply too much at stake, and so they will almost certainly not look at them.

If you really want to show off your game play, create a video clip for it instead. Try to keep it under five minutes, ideally under three. Try to make it as professional looking as you can, and don't be afraid of doing a little editing and postproduction. Don't waste time talking about option screens and the like; just get into the action and emphasize the novel features of your game. You can use voiceover if you need to, but please work out in advance what you want to say—or even script it—when you go to record. No one likes listening to a rambling, disconnected speech. Keep it focused, and emphasize the key points.

Of course, you'll have your own personal list of favorite studios you'd like to work at, like Blizzard Entertainment®, Valve, Bethesda Softworks®, and Bioware®. Needless to say, everyone else has these studios on their short lists. No surprise here: It is close to impossible to get an internship there unless you are both brilliant and lucky.

Another way to find out opportunities is to talk to others (mostly other upperclasspeople) who have already done it. This is one valuable fringe benefit of being active in your local game development club.

If these don't lead to anything, you'll need to cast a wider net. A great place to start is with this mostly definitive list of game studios at this frequently updated Wikipedia page (Wikipedia 2018):

https://en.wikipedia.org/wiki/List_of_video_game_developers

This immense article is frequently updated, and there is no way you would want to try to contact all of them, or even most of them. Worse, there are plenty of other small studios that aren't even listed. But you will want to go through the list, trying to find ones that might be a close fit for the kinds of games you want to work on.

Many of these will be small, or even tiny, studios, perhaps only one or two people, and they won't have anything for you. If something looks promising, click through and see if anything is possible. Visit their website and look for a link like "Jobs" or "Careers."

If you do visit a studio's site and there are job postings there, they will usually be for jobs to be filled by people who already have some industry experience. Oops, that rules you out. But no need to give up that quickly. Not every opening is necessarily posted, and if you have some skill or talent they might be interested in, they might create an internship just for you. Admittedly, the odds of this happening are pretty low, but they are *not* zero. Ask politely, and it could pay off.

While visiting a company's site, check out what they do, and see if there is any possibility of a match. Since you are still in school and don't have an industry track record, you can't afford to be picky. It won't kill you to work on a game or genre you are less familiar with or less fond of if you can get some valuable industry experience that way.

All of this should be started as early in January as possible. Recall, however, that there is no point in contacting companies in December. You can certainly begin researching companies in December (a good use of your time during the winter break), but don't start actually contacting companies until January.

One reason for this is that most corporate environments wind down toward the end of the year, owing to the holidays and vacations. Even game studios, if slammed with work around then, won't really be considering internships at the end of the year.

Another reason is that most corporations end their fiscal year on December 31, and hiring is pretty much off the table, except for must-fill emergency hires.

All this changes in January, when everyone gets back to work.

12.3 MAKING A GOOD IMPRESSION

Now let's get into the actual pitch you'll be making to the companies you are interested in. There are basically three key items to include:

- A cover letter

- Your résumé

- Your portfolio

Let's discuss each in turn.

The Cover Letter. This is the basic means by which you introduce yourself to the company. It should be short, a single page in length, never longer.

What you want to do here is supply a brief introduction. (`"I'm a second-year student at _____ majoring in both Game Design and _____."`)

Then you indicate what position you are seeking. Some mention could be made about your future plans, although this is of much less consequence in a cover letter for a summer internship. (`"I am applying for your summer internship position in _____ in your _____ division."`)

Keep to the point. Obviously, there are only so many ways of saying these things, and so you could use "boilerplate" from typical cover letters, but that won't be the case for the all-important next paragraph, where you sing the (fact-based) praises of yourself, and here you want to put in your best writing. Do emphasize your strong points, but don't make it sound boastful; it's in poor taste, and the unlucky person stuck with reading the stack of applications has heard it all before. But you do want to make sure the reader can get a clear idea of your skills and unique offerings.

Don't waste people's time, either. The person reading this reads a lot of them and wants to get through them as quickly as possible. Make your point quickly. You want to say the best things you can say about yourself in a single, tightly worded paragraph.

After that, move to the closing, something like `"I appreciate this opportunity to apply for this position and look forward to your response."` Be sure you include all the ways you can be contacted: phone, e-mail address, and possibly LinkedIn.

JOB HUNTING USING SOCIAL NETWORKS

We think social media are best used in ways for which they were originally invented: keeping up with your friends, with all that implies. We think they are less useful for job hunting, except indirectly when a friend tells you about a job; there is one exception: LinkedIn.

We are not talking here about sites like GlassDoor or Monster®, which are job search and job matching services, but sites that let you manage your networks of friends and associates. For this, LinkedIn is the one that nearly everyone in the industry uses, and so we suggest that you do, too.

Sign off with something like "Best regards." We like that better than "Warm regards" (too intimate), "Regards" (not enthusiastic), "Hopefully" (sounds like you're begging), or "Very truly yours" (old-fashioned and corny).

Aside from these tips, we're not going to provide a canned letter beyond the hints we dropped earlier. You can find plenty of sample letters on the web.

Just be sure the spelling is perfect, the grammar is 100% correct, and your writing is exquisite. You don't want to bore the reader. Also make sure the cover letter is in your own voice and not something you just copy-pasted from the web. You may want to let someone you know who is experienced in these matters review it carefully for possible improvements.

Finally, expect to make strategic changes to your cover letter (besides changing the addressee information at the top). You will probably want to tune the personal paragraph to meet the particular requirements of the company you are applying to. The letter should never sound canned and generic but like it was written especially for the party to whom it is addressed. This is more work on your part, but every little bit helps.

One final point: If the information about the internship you are acting on supplies the name of an actual person, be sure you contact that person directly (and get their address right) and no other. A misdirected application is unlikely to make it to that person otherwise.

If the company is big enough to have a human resources (HR) department, then you should send your materials there. You can usually find a name by looking for the company's contact information on their website. Companies too small to have their own HR department will still usually list a contact person.

Your Résumé. If you are still in college, you won't have much of a résumé yet, but there is nonetheless plenty to say about yourself. The main things to cover are any prior job experience (like a counselor at a summer camp), the courses you have taken in your majors, any game jams or competitions you have been involved in, any awards or prizes you have won, your overall GPA, and the things you pursue on the side (especially community or charity work).

We're not going to go through the whole résumé construction business here. All the usual advice about résumé writing applies, and there are plenty of books and websites you can turn to. You can start this process by using the services provided by your college; this will be an office with a name like Career Advising Center.

Your Portfolio. By now you're already tired of us carrying on about this, but your portfolio is critically important, probably more so than your résumé at this stage of your career.

You want to show you can do the work and do it well. It's that simple. Before you start on a barrage of mailings, or e-mailings, or ZIP file uploads, make another pass over your portfolio and give it another tweak. As with the résumé, it will be helpful to ask someone experienced with these matters to go over it, item by item, with you. Your school should have resources you can access for this.

Be ruthless about dropping all your marginal work. We hope that there is enough left that you won't feel embarrassed by it. The person reviewing your application is probably reviewing dozens or hundreds of them, and she will not go hunting to find the occasional gold nugget buried in the mud, so only include the nuggets. Seriously, two or three great pieces are worth way more than a dozen mediocre ones. Also, unless the company has specifically asked for an example of something, do not worry too much that your style or work is not similar to what the company does. The person looking at it is usually experienced and talented enough to recognize potential.

Regardless of the position you are applying for, be more focused on the content than you think you have to be. If your strength is in 3D modeling, does it really make sense to include a piece of poetry that you wrote in high school or a mediocre chiptune that you composed? Leave these sorts of things out unless they offer a nice window into your soul.

As always, less is more. You want to demonstrate that you can bring a project to a finished, polished, ready-to-ship state. If you include just one game that you made by yourself and that has all these qualities, it may be all you need.

Once you have everything together, put your materials aside for a day or two, and then look at them again with fresh eyes. It's best to do this early in the day, when your eyes are really fresh. You'll be surprised at how many potential gaffes you can uncover this way.

And now that you are ready to blast away, blast away!

12.4 PERSISTENCE PAYS

Now comes the hard part: the waiting. You probably won't hear anything, from anybody, for two or three weeks. Don't lose heart! As we said, the people reviewing internship applications are probably buried with work, and they likely have other job responsibilities as well. Do not expect immediate responses.

It is an unfortunate reality of modern corporate America that many companies simply don't make the effort to get back to job applicants, whether the news is good or bad. Not all companies are guilty of this, and it's certainly not confined to the game industry.

The classier companies are good at getting back, so that even if you don't get the gig, they will send you a consoling e-mail (maybe a physical letter, but that's dying out). Here is a chance for some character building. It will bother you immensely, especially on the first one you get, but you need to get over it. And you will. After a couple of days, you'll be back in action.

If the news is positive, congratulations! You don't have the gig yet, though, because what happens next will likely be phone interviews, possibly followed by the all-important, all-day, in-person interview. This is the structure typically followed for full-time hires. Since you are seeking an internship, however, things may not get this formal, but do expect to have to go through additional vetting on your way to landing the spot.

How long to wait? How long is a piece of string? To be honest, we would not bother with follow-ups for an internship or co-op. If the company wants you, they will contact you. Continually poking at them is more likely to annoy them. We would almost extend this to applying for full-time jobs, too, unless it is one you really want. In that case, we suggest you wait at least four weeks and then send a very polite, short e-mail. And that's it.

12.5 ON THE JOB

Let's assume that you've landed a coveted internship, and now you have to act professionally. We talked about professionalism in Chapter 9. You might want to reread that part.

First of all, recognize that you are there to *learn*. You really don't know everything, and maybe not anything that is relevant to what that particular studio does. Seriously. Try not to be "that guy" who knows more than the professionals you will be partnered with. Nobody likes a smart-ass. That's one sure way to wear out your welcome and sideline your future prospects with that studio. (Of course, there is a teensy chance you do know more than the professional. If so, bite your tongue and go along anyway, OK?) Generally speaking, a little humility goes far here.

If you're fortunate, you'll get to work alongside experienced industry folk and, in most cases, people who genuinely want to see you become successful. But, as they say, you have to give in order to get. Since you are the most junior person on the team, you will likely be given the least exciting or critical pieces to work on. This only makes sense; no one is going to bet the game on an untried entity like yourself.

Whatever it is you are given to do, learn as much as you can from it. Bring the task to a successful close, and don't be afraid to ask for help if you get genuinely stuck. When you're done, tackle the next task with equal energy. By the time the summer is over, you'll be amazed at what you have accomplished.

Always bear in mind that they are watching you: not only your job performance, but also how well you get along with the team and contribute in positive ways to a great game. No one expects you to perform miracles at this point, but management, in the form of the team's leads and producers, will want to know if you have the right stuff to be offered a permanent spot once you graduate. Don't blow it.

One note about the dark side of internships, though. Your internship should involve your actually learning useful skills for game development. That is the central reason for doing an internship in the first place. While you won't be given the most desirable work to do, neither should you be stuck doing purely clerical work or making coffee. You have every right to be given meaningful work that helps you advance your skills.

Now, you may end up doing QA, which we talked about in Chapter 7. This is not exactly glamorous work, but it is necessary to playtest and debug games, and you may be called upon to do exactly that. It's OK if you are, since QA has long been the bottom-of-the-food-chain job in this industry, and you *are* learning some valuable skills.

What is *not* OK is getting stuck doing work that has nothing to do with learning how to build games. While this sort of abuse is relatively uncommon, be aware that it sometimes does happen.

If you are unlucky enough to find yourself in this position, then the first person to talk to would be your lead. Phrase it in such a way that you continue to show interest in the project and the company. For example, you might say, "I seem to be doing a lot of tasks that are not directly related to my learning game industry skills. I was wondering if that was likely to change soon?" Or, "I seem to be doing a lot of things that are not increasing my industry skills. Am I missing something, or will that change once I have learned the basics?"

You will need to adjust the wording to match the company and people you are working with. Some like formality, others are way more relaxed; another skill that you will need to acquire is judging how to phrase difficult questions to match your environment.

Then, depending on the answer, you can make a decision as to what to do about it. If it really looks like you are being used as cheap labor, try to talk to your professor or career services people at your school for advice. For one thing, your college would not want to recommend this company again. For another, they have more clout than you.

What you definitely do not want to do is get into a major argument with anyone at the company. Word would get out throughout the industry in no time; yes, the industry is still that small, and you would be digging a hole for yourself with other prospective employers. At the very worst, just grin and bear it. It is only for a few months at most, and you will still be able to put down on your résumé that you worked for WXYZ Studio as an intern. That's worth something.

12.6 INTELLECTUAL PROPERTY

On the first day of your internship you'll be taken around to various individuals, including someone from the HR department if the studio is large enough to have one or, if not, the person who does HR tasks for the studio. That person will collect all sorts of personal information from you, all required by law and company policy.

One document you will most certainly be required to sign is a nondisclosure agreement (NDA). This may be drawn up only for the particular project you will be joining, or it may be a more general NDA covering any and all company secrets, including games under development.

It is critically important that you know what you are agreeing to. First off, you are probably over 18 and are legally an adult, so you really are binding yourself to the terms of the agreement, which, after all, is an enforceable legal contract. All that scary language about "damages" and "penalties" applies to _you_.

Basically, you are agreeing not to divulge anything to an outside party about the game you are working on. By that we mean _anything_: the game play, the story, the characters, the platforms, the game engine, and so forth and so on, to _anyone including your partner and especially your friends_. It can also be broader than that, for example, requiring that you not divulge internal production processes (which are a competitive advantage that the company wants to protect).

Read the NDA carefully several times to make sure you understand it, and then sign it. You won't get the job if you refuse, so do not bother making a fuss about "your rights." Here, you don't have any! If you feel that strongly about NDAs, then walk away now, because they will be a part of your life as long as you are in the game industry.

After that, make absolutely sure you honor the terms of the agreement. This is often harder than it looks. There is a great temptation to carry on about the game in online game forums, for example, but that is a serious career-killing mistake. We know of cases where exactly this has happened, and the consequences were ugly and severe, leading, not surprisingly, to the guy getting fired. Don't be that guy.

A more insidious problem has to do with people like game "journalists" who are trying to smoke out a story about a game in production, and you, as the innocent young person, might be someone they home in on.

Here you need some serious street smarts. If someone approaches you and tries to pump you for information about your project, no matter how casually or how roundabout, your Spidey sense should start tingling. There are unscrupulous people out there who think nothing of trying to exploit you that way. They will get the story, and you will get hurt. While a slip-up on your part is perhaps more defensible than blabbing on a forum, you do not want to be the person in the room getting chewed out…and then fired.

Welcome to the real world.

12.7 GETTING INVITED BACK

If you've done everyone right and kept everyone happy, you stand an excellent chance of getting invited back, possibly for another summer internship (if you are going to be a junior) or full-time employment (if you are going to be a senior). If so, give yourself a pat on the back.

Don't forget, though, that the conditions of the NDA still apply, so be very canny about talking about your experiences once you return to school. All this is simply a part of acting professionally, and there is nothing better you can be doing for your career than to have others around you begin to respect you as a professional.

Keep in mind also that conditions are constantly changing in this industry, and a promise to get invited back might not materialize owing to cutbacks, cancellations, or closures. No matter; what you have gained from all this is an all-important entry to add to your résumé: working at a real studio on a real game. You might even make it into the end credits.

CHAPTER 13

Year Four

O K, SO YOU'RE ABOUT to go into your final year of game school. Pat yourself on the back for not bailing out and switching to accounting or cyber security* or nursing.

13.1 WE'RE GOING TO KEEP HOUNDING YOU ABOUT YOUR PORTFOLIO

Spend some quality time with your portfolio. If you can, look over the portfolios from past years, and after you stop cringing, once again pat yourself on the back for all the great progress you've made since then.

Just get into the habit of editing your portfolio ruthlessly and at regular intervals.

13.2 THE SCHOOL YEAR

---

* Actually, if you're already majoring in Computer Science and have a devious mind, then a career in cyber security is worth a thought. We read somewhere that there are 27 jobs for each cyber security expert out there, so jobs are p-l-e-n-t-i-f-u-l. You're a gamer, so you just might have that "devious mind" part covered. But you also need to have that frightening "I can hack anything" talent going for you as well.

Your fourth year will be qualitatively different from the first three. By now, you've gotten most or all of your required courses out of the way. Your skills are beginning to feel like mastery. You can take something on, and the work just flows. You don't have to keep stopping and restarting over the simple stuff.

In Year Four you're likely to discover that this just gets easier, even though you're now doing work far more sophisticated than when you started out. Enjoy the feeling that mastery brings.

During Year Four, with the required courses out of the way, what is left to take will fall into a few categories. Let's go over these now.

13.3 DISTRIBUTION REQUIREMENTS

Some of your remaining courses will be those pesky "distribution requirements" you've been putting off. Now is the time to take Astronomy or Rocks for Jocks. These are those easy science requirements that everyone has to take at any accredited institution of higher learning. Now you're in a position to enjoy them and the lighter workloads they bring. Don't blame your school for making you take these; the various "accreditation boards"—the people who decide whether an institution is a legitimate institute of higher education—are the ones who require this. And taking these are good for you.

Especially astronomy. Although you won't necessarily have to work hard at it, we think it's worth making the extra effort. Astronomy is amazing! It is awe-inspiring and can help you pick up a more cosmic perspective that can really get your creative juices going. One of us was fortunate enough to take such a course with a fairly famous astronomer (no, it wasn't Carl Sagan), and every class was a performance. *Nobody* skipped his lectures. (And that same one of us actually got to meet Carl Sagan some years later.) The other also took astronomy in high school and had a blast. Hmm, wonder why we recommend astronomy. ☺

This is not to slam, Rocks for Jocks, that is, Earth Science or Geology or whatever your school calls it. Those are good, too.

Just get these done. See the section below about degree clearance.

13.4 SOCIAL SCIENCES

We believe it is a very good idea to take a communication course or two while at university. Communication courses don't seem to get respect at many schools, but we think this is a mistake. You are going to need to communicate effectively if you want to flourish in this industry. It means you can effectively share your ideas with others and persuade them of their brilliance and value.

We especially recommend taking a course along the way that involves public speaking. You have probably heard that old bit that people are more afraid of public speaking than of dying. Well, if you put an actual gun to someone's head, she will do some public speaking readily enough, but this is another one of those life skills that is going to turn out to be more important than you think.

13.5 THE SENIOR PROJECT

The second category of courses is usually called the capstone, senior project, senior thesis, or similar. These are one- or two-semester-long courses where you get to flex all the skills you've picked up on a substantial, nontrivial project. We'll just simply call this the senior project.

These are usually team-based in the case of game development projects. If you are in some sort of dual major, you may also be doing a senior project in the other major that is more likely to be solo in nature.

Whether team- or solo-based, you generally won't be attending full-time classes for it, although this varies depending on your particular program. Your program may be set up with classes only some of the time, for example, only during the first part of the semester or only once a week. You will be given more independence to work on your project outside of class time. In fact, nearly all of the work gets done outside of class time.

What you will be asked to do periodically is to show evidence of progress and submit reports about that progress. You may be meeting with a faculty adviser (whether team or solo) every week or every other week. Obviously you'll need to be long over your earlier habits of procrastination and poor time management. At this point your adviser will expect you to have the discipline and time management skills in place to do the work without needing constant supervision.

Whichever sort of senior project you end up on, make good use of the opportunity to integrate the many skills you've acquired along the way. Up to now, you may have gotten the feeling that what you have been learning is a bunch of disconnected topics, and to some extent they are. The senior project is where you get to connect them up. Magic can happen.

Of course, you're interested in developing games, and the good news here is that you've been learning to tie together your skills all along. You're lucky: Game development is one of those terrific multidisciplinary fields where you get to work in many different areas at once, safe in the knowledge that you are wiring up your brain for greatness later on.

13.5.1 Game Development

This senior project is probably going to be your last shot at building something you can be proud to include in your portfolio. Again, team size and project duration depend on your particular program. Of one semester versus two semesters, we definitely prefer the two-semester format: It gives you far more time to build a quality, well-polished, and well-balanced game. Plus, the team can work on it over the holiday break (although less than you might hope for).

13.5.2 Arts and Music

In an art or music program the senior project entails creating a major work that can withstand evaluation by professional artists, that ritual called the "critique," or "crit" for short, that we discussed in Chapter 11.

One requirement for a major art project like this usually asks you to prepare a fairly lengthy statement about the work: your inspirations and motivations that led you to the work you created, the issues and challenges you encountered, and how you solved them. This written portion isn't so much to "explain" the work (since great art shouldn't need the artist to explain it) but more to demonstrate to your professors how your creative process works and how you used it to work through the problems and challenges you encountered. You might prefer to write an art "manifesto," your world view and its relationship to your art.

The critique, then, is when you have to endure that withering and soul-destroying blast by people who know what they are talking about. By now you've learned a lot about what you can get away with when submitting work to your professors. Art is all about breaking the rules, after all, but you have to master the rules first. All the faculty members you encounter in art school know this.

The real fun comes when outside reviewers examine your work. This is quite commonplace for students going for their Master's in Fine Arts, but your school might be well connected enough that you will encounter outside reviewers at the undergraduate level as well.

We said earlier the process is "soul-destroying," but it doesn't have to be. First off, you get a semester or two to get quality feedback, coaching, and suggestions from your instructors as you go along. By the end of the process, there shouldn't be too many surprises left, at least until the outside reviewers get into the act.

While listening to total strangers (especially established artists you admire and respect) tearing apart your work can be deeply painful, don't forget that they are criticizing *it*, not *you*.[*] Get used to it, and get over it. Your work will get critiqued throughout your professional career. Getting angry or defensive does you no good. And it's *very* unprofessional.

13.5.3 Science and Engineering

The senior project for computer science or engineering students operates somewhat differently.

Here you need to apply your skills and talents to work on some unsolved problem or challenge by doing original work toward a solution. Depending on your co-major, this may involve designing a new app, creating or improving some obscure algorithm, creating a 3D-printed prototype design model for a new product, or constructing an interesting interface device out of an Arduino® board and some hardware.

As with the senior project in art or music, you are expected to integrate all your skills and talents to come up with something new and original. The project may be something you decide on, or it may be thrust upon you by the faculty member you sign up with. Very often, at the beginning of the project you negotiate what the project is and the scope of work you're expected to put into it.

This is something you should be clear on even if the faculty member doesn't explicitly ask for it. We've talked about the dangers of overscoping and feature creep, and the same advice applies here. It is only natural for faculty members to want to get as much work out of you as they can, and it is only natural for you to do as little work as you can. A good faculty adviser will be aware of this tendency and be mature enough to not let you melt down through overwork, but *do* expect to work very hard on the project you both mutually agreed on at the start.

So be very clear on the deliverables from the outset and use that information to let you manage your work over the time you have available.

---

[*] Of course, you may occasionally run into some particularly successful artist who has grown smug and arrogant and who not only hates your work but also hates you for creating it. This is really going to sting, but, once again, stiffen your spine and your upper lip, and endure it. As we said earlier, in the world of business, such folks are called "difficult persons," and entire books have been written on how to deal with them.

Another thing, if you haven't already learned this, is to *make use of the resources available to you.* You stand on the shoulders of giants. A little bit of research at the start of the project can steer you much more rapidly to a solution if for no other reason than you can avoid making the mistakes others have made before you. Your school library spends a lot of money making advanced texts and academic journal articles available, yet it continues to amaze us how little use the library gets. Yes, there is also plenty online (and you should use those resources, too), but online resources, the ones you don't pay for at least, can take you only so far.

If you are making something in software, you can learn about the libraries, software development kits, and application programming interfaces that can greatly simplify the work you need to do in actually building your application. Learn what these can do for you. If you are using Python to write some software, maybe you can build your brilliant project out of the many Python libraries and get away with writing only a couple dozen lines of code (just kidding).

Most of all, ask questions!

13.6 INDEPENDENT STUDIES

You may also be able to do original work via an independent study. This is usually worth the same number of credits as a conventional course but doesn't involve regular class hours or any sort of standard set of "deliverables," that is, some set of intended course outcomes. It is very similar to the senior project but smaller in scope and generally optional.

As with the senior project, you might get to work on a project of your own choosing or on a project already under way with a faculty member. If you have something interesting in mind, you can often shop around for a faculty member interested in signing you on. Other times you will work on a massive existing project, one that runs over several semesters. Depending on your program, you won't always be able to do this, so ask around.

Again, as with the senior project you will be largely independent and self-directed. You will likely meet with the faculty adviser on a weekly or biweekly basis, perhaps only for an hour or so. The rest of the time you are on your own.

What sorts of things can be the subject of an independent study? Generally, it can be about anything reasonable as long as it can be shown to have academic value. This usually means that there is a research component, so look at existing work in the area to avoid repeating something that has already been done. Your faculty adviser will normally steer you toward the body of knowledge you need to study before work gets under way. That's the "study" part of independent study.

The other aspect of this is your doing new and original work to advance what is already known. Perhaps you want to develop a new shader using a new algorithm. That could work. So could improving an existing shader by developing a more efficient algorithm.

This approach works in all areas. One of us had an art student create art assets for a cathedral to appear in a game, specifically the gargoyles that appear on many large cathedrals, especially in Europe. Since the development team wanted things to be historically accurate, this student's independent study required preparing an historical overview of how gargoyle designs have changed over the centuries and in different geographical regions. Why is this a good thing to undertake? Our favorite go-to example is the first *Bioshock* game.

Signing up for an independent study or two during your academic career is another fine way to build up your portfolio. It has the added benefit of maybe giving you something interesting to talk about during a job interview.

13.7 ELECTIVES

If you have any slots left in your schedule, you can take some electives. Find something in the catalog that strikes your fancy, and learn something new. Don't pass up the opportunity to perhaps get an idea for a game from it.

13.8 DEGREE CLEARANCE

Before you get very far into your fourth year, be sure to review your transcript to make sure you are on track to graduate on schedule. How you are able to review your transcript varies across institutions, but after you log into your school's system, you should be able to not only see your grades but also get indications as to what degree requirements have been met and which ones you still need to complete. This printout may not be entirely accurate: It may correctly list the courses and grades, but it might be misleading as to whether you have really met the requirements for graduation.

This is not something to mess with. You want to speak to a human being who is in a position to make the correct determination. If it seems like there are distribution requirements you still haven't met, and won't be meeting in the year ahead, you'll want to get those resolved soon. Did you fulfill a four-credit slot with a three-credit course at some other institution? Then you may still need to scare up one credit somehow. Is there some pesky one-credit phys-ed course you haven't gotten around to yet? Are there some social science or humanities course you haven't taken yet to fulfill "distribution requirements"? Use those remaining elective slots to sign up for the courses you actually need.

If you are unclear about your status here, by all means talk to someone in the know. Your institution no doubt has someone who can speak authoritatively about degree clearance and give you the correct advice. Ideally, you'll speak to someone who has "signature authority" to make this determination and make it official.

If you find you need to do this, get it in writing! Or at least in a series of e-mails that you can keep on hand in case of disputes later on. The last thing you want to have happen is for your graduation to be held up over something avoidable. This will be far more unpleasant if you put off dealing with this until the spring semester, by which time the problem becomes much harder to fix.

13.9 GAME FESTIVALS AND COMPETITIONS

We hope you've been making some games you can be proud of, whether solo or part of a team. Submit them to the various local, regional, and even national game festivals and contests held all over the place. You might just win. As the New York State Lottery used to remind us, *you never know!*

We understand that there is a natural reluctance to show off your work in public. Why, people might not like your game! It can be scary. We get it, because we've been there.

But this is just part of getting along in life. When you get to the point where people actually start paying you real money for your skills, you'll be showing your work to all sorts of people all the time. Might as well start now.

It takes a bit of courage to make the leap, so we encourage you to get over your fears. What's the worst that can happen? People laugh at your game? Pitiless ridicule and scorn? Uninvited trolling? Well, sure, all that is possible, but people aren't usually that cruel (except when they hide behind anonymity on the Internet) (except when they are being "difficult people") (except when they've risen so high they dismiss the ones coming up) (…).

OK, let's back up a bit. Perhaps your game is really and truly wretched, something you just can't bring yourself to take pride in. If it's that bad, take a pass. Otherwise, what's the harm in submitting it?

The main value in getting your game out there is that you get a chance to get at least three kinds of high-quality feedback. First, you can get some carefully thought-through critique by industry professionals, and just a few sentences from them can be as important as anything you experience in class.

Second, you'll get some less carefully thought-through (and less diplomatic) feedback from other contestants, but if they offer constructive criticism given from their vantage point, then perhaps it will pay to listen.

Finally, you get feedback from the players. When you hear "players" here, think "customers," because these are the people who may one day actually buy your games. This feedback will be all over the map, and so take it with many grains of salt. But listening to customers is key to commercial success, like it or not.

And who knows, you might actually win. This gives you something very nice to put on the résumé and the portfolio. It also gives you something to talk about during a job interview. Winning a game competition is one of the best things that can happen for your career at this point. Unfortunately, you actually have to win first.

THE IGNORANCE TAX

Note: Neither of us plays the lottery. As people who learned how to work out probabilities, a useful game design skill, we know a sucker bet when we see one.

13.10 JOB HUNTING

As we discussed earlier, there's almost no point in looking for a gig in the fall semester. Almost no one looks at résumés or considers hiring during the holiday season. As we saw, most companies won't bother doing any hiring this late in the year. There are exceptions, of course. A major project may be ramping up, and the studio needs people—now. Or there is a sudden vacancy for a key person that opened up that needs action—now. It is highly unlikely, though, that this desperate need is for an inexperienced college graduate fresh out of school. So for the most part, apart from research into companies, you can wait on your job search until the start of the new year.

So since you want something to do to help pay back those student loans, begin your job search in January. If you've been fortunate enough to work as an intern or co-op at a studio, and they really liked your work, you could be invited back for a full-time job. This will certainly simplify your life.

13.11 GETTING READY TO GET OUT

You're going to be ridiculously busy, not only getting all your courses and projects done and out of the way but also worrying about getting all the graduation paperwork filed on time, and maybe packing up your apartment or dorm room.

It's pretty exhilarating, though, as you contemplate what the next chapter of your life is going to look like. The main thing is not to melt down along the way.

Ride it out. You're going to hit a stretch where it seems like work will never end, you're not getting a lot of sleep, and you're not really having any fun. This lasts for only a finite period of time, and you will survive it, even if it doesn't feel that way at the time.

Get used to the discomfort. People who always take the comfortable path in life don't accomplish very much in the long run.

It'll all be over soon.

CHAPTER 14

Graduation Day

14.1 FINALLY…

This is going to be the shortest chapter in this book.

As you wind down from all that insane project work in your final spring semester, it's time to get ready for graduation. There's a lot of paperwork to file and perhaps some last-minute meetings with professors and administrators to make sure you have everything in place. But you didn't have many of these because you had the wisdom and foresight to not let things reach crisis proportions, right?

Graduating college is one of those Big Transitions that life deals you, and you might as well enjoy the ride. You might be surprised at how emotional you're going to get over this. Nothing to be ashamed of. You'll be parting company with people you've gotten to be friends with. You'll promise to keep in touch. Maybe you will. But time and distance have a way of eroding friendships, unless you take the initiative to keep them alive. Facebook and LinkedIn can help.

You'll be spending a week or two after class ends getting ready for the big day. You'll probably have to start dismantling your dorm room or apartment, getting ready to move. If you have a job lined up, and we hope you do, you'll need to think about making the move and maybe getting settled in a new city. It's all pretty exciting. Years from now, you're really going to enjoy reliving these moments.

14.2 THE BIG DAY

It's up to you whether to go to your graduation ceremonies or not. Or to any of those award dinners and whatnot that dot the academic calendar in May. Your parents may have other ideas. If they're traveling in, they'll want you to "take the walk." After all, they probably helped pay for it.

14.3 AFTERWARDS

Now is the time for some well-earned downtime. First, if you already have a job lined up, we hope you've arranged to start it maybe four to six weeks after graduation to give yourself time to decompress and get yourself ready for the next stage of your life.

If your funds and student loans are in decent shape, you could consider backpacking in Europe or South America or somewhere. It's a big, beautiful world out there, and this is one of the sweetest times in your life to enjoy it. Get one of those books with titles like *Europe on X Dollars a Day*, and plan something out. Stay at inexpensive youth hostels, and do a lot of backpacking. You'll meet a lot of interesting people along the way. You've earned it.

If you are still looking for a job in the industry, read ahead to the next chapter.

And that's it…the shortest chapter in this book.

CHAPTER 15

Transitions

15.1 BEING A PROFESSIONAL, THIS TIME FOR REAL

We talked about what it takes to be a professional in Chapter 9. We hope you've had a chance to put some of those ideas to good use during an internship or co-op.

But now you've graduated, and it is time to venture out into the big, bad world. Actually, it's not bad at all; it's wonderful. Your adventure is only beginning. That's why your graduation ceremony is called "Commencement."

So let's commence.

15.2 BE FLEXIBLE IN ALL THINGS

Game studios are scattered far and wide here on Earth, but there is still a tendency for large numbers of studios to clump around certain urban areas and not others. In the United States, the major cities for game development on the West Coast are Los Angeles and San Francisco, and their many nearby towns, with Seattle thrown into the mix. Elsewhere in the U.S. are cities like Boston, Austin, and New York City. Several mid-sized cities are also on the list, usually because they boast at least one major studio. These include Bethesda,

Maryland, and Troy, New York. Canada has Montreal (home of Ubisoft), Toronto, and Vancouver.

If you didn't grow up in one of these cities, you should get used to the idea of having to move to one after you graduate. This is fun, because those cities are vibrant and hip and attractive for young twenty-somethings to spend a few years in. These will be years you'll remember.

Thus, when seeking out new employment, plan on having to move.

"The advice I like to always give students it to be open minded and be willing to move. Those who are willing to move for work stay in the games industry longer and are more successful! You'll have many more opportunities if you are open to new experiences and willing to go to new places."

ROBERTA TAM
Lead Game Artist at King

Also plan on maybe taking a job with a studio that makes games that are not necessarily in your favorite genre. You will still get a lot out of it, and once you can get your name into the credits of a shipped game, you will have many more options when it comes time to jump ship. In the game industry, as with much high-tech, it's entirely expected that you will jump from job to job early in your career, and no one is surprised by that. Just make sure it's you jumping off, not your boss kicking you out.

You might not get the position you wanted when you are first hired, either. We mentioned earlier that you might not get to be a programmer or designer at your first job, despite your qualifications, and you might have to serve time doing QA. No matter, you can move beyond that if you can show your employers how much more you are capable of.

"The game industry is most definitely unpredictable. Developers must be able to morph into the correctly shaped pegs to fill the current holes. In small companies, a developer may be a designer on Monday, scripter on Tuesday and Wednesday, mockup/place holder artist on Thursday, and sound designer on Friday. The rapid iteration and constant change of game schools prepare graduates to transform to meet these challenges and enjoy the variety of work."

MICHAEL McCOY, JR.,
Designer and Lecturer, Boss Fight Entertainment

Regardless of what position you land, what city you move to, or what sorts of games you work on, you can still use the opportunity to sharpen your skills and acquire new ones.

15.3 MANAGING EXPECTATIONS

Simple rule: If you don't expect too much, you will not be disappointed.

15.3.1 Salary

An old misconception about the game industry is that everyone owns a Ferrari.

Well, while it is true that some people own Ferraris and have made a lot of money, this is not the case for the vast majority in the industry.

That is not to say that you cannot make a comfortable living, and in general the video game industry pays more than the average salary for the given location.

The main exception is programming, where shortages often drive many high-tech industries to offer higher salaries to encourage recruitment. By contrast, the game industry can rely on the fact that people actually want to program games rather than business software, and unless you are exceptional, the game industry can get away with not having to match salaries to the same extent.

For artists and animators, the main competition is from the film industry, although salaries are difficult to compare directly between the two because artists perform somewhat different roles in these two industries. There is a growing demand for web designers, but in general web design doesn't currently pay as well as video games.

As for game designers, designing games pretty much puts you in the game industry. After all, despite a growth in gamification, what would a bank want with a game designer?

GAMIFICATION

From Wikipedia: "Gamification is the application of game-design elements and game principles in non-game contexts. Gamification commonly employs game design elements which are used in non-game contexts to improve user engagement, organizational productivity, flow, learning, crowdsourcing, employee recruitment and evaluation, ease of use, usefulness of systems, physical exercise, traffic violations, voter apathy, and more." (Wikipedia 2017)

Gamification is not without its critics, however, as you'll see later in the same Wikipedia article.

So with all that said, what can you expect in the way of salary?

First off, there is no norm. Every company has its own costs to meet, which vary considerably depending on the location of the company. They also have their own gaps to fill in their staff roster, which may boost offers for a short time.

At the time of this writing:

Straight out of college, an engineer can probably expect between $35K and $45K, an artist or designer can probably expect between $30K and $35K. These figures will be higher in major cities, but then again, your cost of living there will also be higher.

One thing to be fully aware of is that, straight out of college, you have almost no wiggle room when it comes to salary or other compensation. Even though your prospective employer will probably ask you at some stage what you expect to earn, they already know what they are prepared to pay you.

SHOW ME THE MONEY

Do some research <u>before</u> the interviews or application so you do not give some outrageous figure, and way too low is just as bad as way too high. This question is more a test of your having done some research than it is a salary negotiation.

In addition to salary, almost all companies provide full medical benefits, including vision and dental. Some offer bonuses based on sales of the games you worked on, while others offer straight annual bonuses. It is unlikely that straight out of college you will be given share options, but if they ever offer them, grab them with both hands.

Smaller companies tend to pay less than larger companies, and top AAA companies pay more. Of course, getting into those is harder, too.

After five years these figures will probably have doubled and, as your experience and position rise, so does compensation. One thing that is true in the game industry is that it is very merit based. If you are good/brilliant, you will get paid more and will have more opportunities. It is not difficult to earn six figures, especially if you are good. On the other hand, if you are just not cutting it, you will probably be cut.

15.3.2 Promotion

We keep saying this because it is true: There is no norm.

It will be based on the company structure and your skills, but it will probably be at least two years before you are given a lead position, longer for a lead position on a major AAA project.

You will get title changes unrelated to "lead" positions. For example, when you are first hired you may be a "junior designer." After a year to eighteen months you might be promoted to "designer." After three to five years (this really varies by company) you might become a "senior designer." Each of these changes usually brings with it additional compensation.

We talk more about getting promoted in Chapter 22.

15.3.3 Job Security

There is none.

In my (Adrian's) twenty-five years I have lost count of the number of companies that have gone down, with the associated fallout of job losses. These were not just small, poorly organized companies, but also large, apparently secure, companies.

The positive side is that I have also seen countless new companies spring up and grow. Even some of those that had fallen have risen like phoenixes from the ashes.

Even if the entire company does not go down, a failed project, a project that is cut, or a failure to sign up a new project can lead to painful cutbacks and layoffs.

This is not to say that you cannot remain with a company for a long time. We know several people who have remained at the same place for ten or more years, and even some who have never been through a layoff or downsizing.

But, rather like those Ferraris, these are the exception rather than the rule. If you set your expectation to around five years, then you will probably be OK. If it lasts longer, yay!

15.3.4 Vacation

Most companies offer fairly standard vacation packages, that is, starting with two weeks' vacation plus up to nine or ten of the major holidays. After five years you will probably get extra vacation days (three weeks) and again after ten years (four weeks). There are also standard special days off for the death of a close family member and maternity leave.

Of course, your ability to actually take any vacation days will almost certainly be covered by part of your contract that says you can't take time off if the project needs to be finished.

Good old "crunch."

15.4 DIFFERENCES BETWEEN COMPANIES

15.4.1 Discipline Orientation

Companies, particularly small to medium-size companies, typically take on the values and mindsets of their owners/managers/founders. Most of these people have been in the industry themselves and worked their way up. They therefore usually have a background in one of the three main areas of game production: design, art, or engineering. For this reason, a studio can be categorized as being design-, art-, or engineering-oriented.

What this means is that every studio has a built-in bias toward the way their games are made, which games are made, how problems get resolved, and what are considered the most important aspects of the production of a game built around that orientation.

This is important to keep in mind, not just when you go about considering which companies you may want to work at, but also what to expect when you work there. If you are an artist working in an engineering-oriented studio, for example, you cannot let the fact that others sometimes tend to overlook your artistic passion get to you. This is an extreme, of course; successful companies cannot be totally driven by only one discipline. They would not stay successful for very long if they were. Game production remains a true team effort, but understanding the biases within a company makes it easier to get less frustrated. It is yet another part of being professional.

15.4.2 Size and Number of Employees

Just as there are differences between small teams and large teams, there are differences between the way things work in small companies (fewer than twenty people) and large companies (over fifty people), and those in between.

Fifty may not seem like that many people to start classifying a company as large, but once you expand above that number, a whole new layer of management is required just to run the place. This is one reason why many companies stop expanding at around fifty people. They do not want to take on the added managerial layer, preferring instead to keep management size low and production teams high as a proportion of the company.

Another reason is that once a company exceeds fifty people in size, a number of federal labor and health care laws kick in that can be very expensive for a company to comply with.

In a small company it is almost guaranteed that everyone knows everyone else. This aids production and staff allocation because people's strengths and weaknesses are known by everyone as well. The company is able to maintain a "family" atmosphere, especially if they are good about things like outings, company picnics, and holiday parties.

In particular, getting hired in a small company will largely be a matter of your personality, maybe even more than your skill set. Most of all, a small operation will want to know that you can fit into the rest of the family. Of course, if you don't have the needed skill set, you won't even be considered, but even great skills will not carry the day if your personality is seen as likely to clash with the people already there.

In a small company, the owners/founders are often still heavily involved in all the decisions relating to the company. They may still take an active part in the production process, at least in the producer/executive producer roles. In a design-oriented company, the owners and founders are often the ones who have the final say on what the ultimate design will be.

If the company is building a game under contract to a publisher, the publisher ultimately gets to call the shots, but expect that within the day-to-day operations of the development team, the owners/founders will have plenty to say. The collaboration and discussions that won the studio the contract in the first place is why the owners and founders are in the best position to persuade the publisher about great design ideas and to work out suitable compromises.

In a large company, it becomes increasingly difficult for everyone to know everyone else; instead, you tend to know the people in the same department, or in the same discipline, or working on the same project. The "family" atmosphere largely disappears from the company as a whole and is transferred downwards into the department, the discipline, or the team. This isn't quite as dire as it sounds. As you (and others) move around from project to project, you will have opportunities to collaborate with new people. Only at the very largest studios (and very much like large animation studios) are you likely to stay glued to your seat doing the same thing day after day.

The bigger the company is, the greater the visibility gap between those at the bottom and those at the top. It can seem more and more that executive decisions are taken without considering their impacts on the teams and without consulting the teams beforehand.

Being hired into a large company is more about having the right skill set and meeting established job specifications and less about a candidate's personality. It's still important to fit in with the prospective team members. For this reason, interviews are often set up to include meetings with at least the leads from that team, so they can get a sense of whether or not they can work with you. This happens only after you've made it past the first few hurdles: meeting the job specs as the Human Resources (HR) department understands them, then getting past a series of phone interviews.

The number of projects and the size of the teams themselves may also change as the company grows, although this is a function of why the company grew in the first place. Some companies expand so they can take on more projects while keeping team sizes down to, say, around twenty people. Other companies expand so they can take on bigger projects so the size of the production teams grows as the company grows, allowing them to work on bigger titles.

In a large company, unless it has a large number of small teams, there is therefore more likely to be greater specialization. It may be the case that, for example, the engineering discipline is split into AI programmers, audio programmers, game mechanics programmers, graphics programmers, and so forth, whereas in a small company people are much more likely to wear multiple hats within their discipline.

Large companies might have the capability to bring work in-house that in a smaller studio would be contracted out. They may have a recording studio, a full-time audio engineer, an in-house QA department, a tools team, and an HR department.

Smaller companies, on the other hand, tend to contract out sound and music or get the designers or engineers to do it. The functions of HR are carried out by managers, who are also often the project producers. In addition, QA is also conducted by a team or contracted out.

It should be noted that just because a company is bigger does not automatically mean it is better, or more respected, or gets to work on better projects, or that it even earns larger profits. It is just bigger. It is really down to your personality whether working in a big company or a small company is for you. Of course, you may not have a choice when it's your first job, and you may have to try working at both before you know.

One thing about working for a company once you get out of school, as opposed to trying to start your own studio, is that you get to learn on someone else's dime. You will learn quite a lot more about the reality of making and marketing games once you actually land an industry job. After a few years of this (and after paying off those student loans) you may feel that you are at the point where you can go off on your own, something we discuss in Chapter 26.

15.4.3 Indie versus Owned

While digital distribution and app stores are beginning to make inroads, it is still pretty true that the bulk of the game industry comprises two major segments: the production studios and the publishing companies.

This leads to two types of production studios, independent (indie) and owned (also referred to as in-house studios). When we speak of "independent" in this context, we mean studios that successfully get contracted to work on game development projects, not just two guys in a garage.

A publisher will contract with a production studio to make the game that the publisher wants to release. This may or may not be a licensed product (an intellectual property like Batman® or Lego®), so there may or may not be a licensor involved on top of that. The term "intellectual property" is often shortened to IP.

Sometimes a licensor may deal directly with a production studio to produce a game based on its licensed product. In this case, the licensor is effectively taking on the role of publisher, so we are going to treat them the same way.

15.4.3.1 Indie Studios

Independent studios either contract out their services or sell their own intellectual property (games), or a combination of both, to publishers. Publishers here are experts in marketing and distribution, making sure the product is on the shelves or available on digital distribution systems like Steam®. They are responsible for making sure word gets out to the various industry people who need to know: bloggers and vloggers, game reviewers, industry trade publications, and the like.

These are the sorts of things that indie studios are either not equipped to do or would rather not have to bother with, so they can concentrate on making games. Hence, we have publishers in the game industry. They perform a variety of different functions that *aren't* designing and developing games. They will have definite opinions about what they want to see in the game they are contracting out, however, and they have the clout, because they have the checkbook, to make these stick.

The main advantage of being an independent is that, because it is not tied to a single license or a single publisher, the studio has a lot more say in what games it prefers to work on. This, however, is a mixed blessing: you have the freedom to make what you want, but you have to hope that the game you want to make is one that plenty of other players will want to pay for and play.

The major disadvantage of being independent is that the studio has to constantly seek new contracts. This takes time and effort on the part of its staff that is not directed toward actual game production, which is where the profit is made. This activity is usually done by the owners, founders, and other senior people in the company. This is why they seek to get onto approved vendor lists for the major studios or console manufacturers so they can bid on those coveted requests for proposals.

A second disadvantage for the indie is competition. Indie studios generally have a lot more direct competition with other studios to win contracts in the first place.

15.4.3.2 Owned Studios

An owned studio is a production studio that is owned/controlled by a publishing company or "holding" company. Activision is a good example of such an arrangement. Within Activision are a host of separate studios that are mostly autonomous and have their own "cultures" while still operating within the overall framework and policies of Activision.

The parent company decides what products each of the owned studios will make, and those studios have little or no choice in the matter. Of course, smart management will make every reasonable effort to match up a new project with whichever owned studio is best able and most suited to develop it.

The main advantage of being an in-house studio is that the studio does not need to be spending as much time on seeking work; it can concentrate more of its effort on producing a great product. Another advantage is that the parent company may be able to move resources around among its studios to meet staffing needs as production schedules evolve.

In the case of publishing companies that own multiple studios, this may not always be the situation. Some publishers encourage competition between their own studios, each bidding on new projects as they come in. In general, though, the effort needed to procure a continual supply of work is still less for an owned studio than for an indie.

A final advantage is that the publishing company generally has more money on tap and a very vested interest in not letting the product or the studio fail, at least as long as the studio is producing quality work on time and within budget. A failing studio is at risk, though, of having its plug pulled and the work taken away, resulting in a round of layoffs and corporate reshuffling.

15.4.4 Private versus Shareholder

The big difference between a privately owned company and a publicly owned company lies in the legal requirements placed on each. A publicly owned (or publicly traded) company is required by law to maximize shareholder equity. That is, the primary responsibility of the managers of the company is not to the players (customers), its management, or its employees, but to the shareholders, the actual owners of the company.

In a privately held company, the owners get to call the shots, but even here there are plenty of legal requirements they have to meet. Also, the owners usually get paid last, after the expenses, payroll, taxes, and all the rest are paid. It's tough owning a small business. Ask anyone who owns one.

Maintaining the well-being of the company is obviously a major factor in being responsible to shareholders, but so is keeping risks and costs low and profits high. This can lead to excess conservatism and playing it safe, hence, sequels to already successful titles and licensing films, books, and so forth, rather than going for "out there" new products and ideas. We tend to get the latter from the indie studios, and that's a very healthy thing for the industry overall.

THE ART FILM MODEL

The game industry has yet to fully embrace the model used by the film industry for helping to bring about those marvelous little creations that aren't blockbusters but that richly deserve to be made. The major studios have "art house" divisions for just this purpose. Fox has Fox Searchlight, Universal has Focus Features, Sony has Sony Pictures Classics, and so forth.

The idea is to take some of those piles of money from blockbuster profits and use them to fund small-scale projects that revolve around really worthwhile stories. Many of these are "actor bait," stories whose characters are so compelling that A-list actors will line up to audition for the parts. They usually work on a special arrangement, getting paid "SAG minimum" (SAG is the Screen Actors Guild), far less than they normally earn, in exchange for a piece of the profits "at the back end" if the film makes money. Some of the great films made this way include *District 9* (Columbia/TriStar), *Napoleon Dynamite* (Fox Searchlight), *Slumdog Millionaire* (Fox Searchlight), and *The Grand Budapest Hotel* (Fox Searchlight).

Another arrangement is where a major studio funds a worthwhile production by a smaller independent production company and handles the subsequent distribution. The recent Oscar®-winning films *Moonlight* and *La La Land* are examples

Without these intelligent business arrangements, many really worthwhile films would never light up a screen. We'd love to see this happen in the game industry, too. This is one way the industry can stay vital and innovative.

Electronic Arts™ has begun to do some of this in recent years under the name EA Originals,* with games like *Fe* and *Sea of Solitude*. It will be interesting to see how this develops, and we wish them great success.

Some of the other major publishers run what are sometimes called budget studios or budget lines, but for now we have to count on the more innovative indie studios to carry the day. The list of hits produced by the indies is impressive: *Braid* (Number None), *Bastion* (Supergiant Games), *Undertale* (Toby Fox), *The Binding of Isaac* (Edmund McMillen and Florian Himsl), *Don't Starve* (Klei Entertainment), *Journey* (thatgamecompany), *Antechamber* (Alexander Bruce), *Super Meat Boy* (Edmund McMillen), *Owlboy* (D-Pad Studio), and many others.

From an employee's perspective, working for a publicly owned company has the advantage of being generally more secure, although total job security doesn't exist in most high-tech industries. Public companies may be better equipped to develop projects with much larger budgets, have better marketing and sales forces, and can exercise more clout with licensors. Major owners of intellectual property like Disney are simply going to go to the major studios first with a new project and aren't likely to listen to proposals from the little guys. The little guys can sometimes pick up the crumbs, as it were, by doing the less popular or older platform versions of the major blockbuster that the AAA studio is doing, or by "porting" a major title developed by someone else to a different platform.

The downside is that bigger budgets lead to more scrutiny and more pressure to succeed, and the result is often less risk taking and experimentation.

There are far fewer opportunities to create a brand-new original IP. It is much more the case, as Adrian notes, that *"The games industry is not about making games; it is about making money from people buying your games."*

From the employee's perspective, that is, *your* perspective, working for a privately owned (and probably smaller) company is generally much less secure, but you are more likely to be able to work on something completely new and original.

---

* https://www.ea.com/ea-originals

CHAPTER 16

The Hiring Process

16.1 CORPORATE CULTURE

We touched on corporate culture in the previous chapter, how studios come to favor engineering, art, or design based on what the studio owners and founders believe to be the most important factor. There is more to corporate culture than that, however, so let's explore a little more deeply.

According to QuickBase, an online learning site, "An organization's culture is the systematic way employees, leaders, and work groups behave and interact with each other. Company culture is collectively composed of values, beliefs, norms, language, symbols, and habits" (QuickBase 2014). The article goes on discuss the six cultural dimensions devised by social psychologist Geert Hofstede. Hofstede is widely regarded as the world's leading authority on organizational cultures.

As cited in QuickBase, Hofstede lists six primary dimensions of corporate culture:

1. Means- vs. goal-oriented

2. Internally vs. externally driven

3. Easygoing vs. strict work discipline

4. Local vs. professional

5. Open vs. closed system

6. Employee- vs. work-centered

These are pretty self-explanatory but deserve additional comment with regard to the game industry. We suggest checking the link for more details if you are curious. Obviously, these are not binary dimensions. All vary along a continuum, and it's doubtful that any company is totally pinned to either extreme on any of these.

16.1.1 Means- versus Goal-Oriented

This orientation is about *how* work gets done versus *what* work gets done. For a typical game studio, in our experience, goal-oriented wins out. Developing a great game and getting it out the door on time and on budget is the key driver that keeps everybody focused and busy. At the same time, productivity depends heavily on having a solid "production pipeline" in place. To keep the plumbing analogy going, a good pipeline allows all the code, art assets, documentation, reports, and all the other "work product" created in the course of building a game to flow freely throughout the organization. A solid pipeline doesn't guarantee success, but a bad one virtually guarantees failure.

Thus, in even the most goal-oriented studio, some people, primarily the engineers and the IT folk, have to worry about clearing the blockages out of the pipe and keeping them out. This is means-oriented, and while the work is not glamorous or fun, it needs to be done. What we've seen often is that, no matter how important good tools are, there never seems to be enough time to actually build them. Then, after enough headaches and too much "crunch time" have built up, the need for new (or improved) tools is elevated to a top priority. This realization usually happens during the so-called postmortem (Chapter 21) and only after the team has experienced a lot of pain.

Incidentally, if you are an engineer and like to build "tools," those specialized pieces of software (like level editors and log file analyzers) that are part of any good pipeline, please bring that up during job interviews, especially when talking to team members. There never seem to be enough tool builders around, and that may help to put you on the short list.

16.1.2 Internally versus Externally Driven

This refers to the degree to which a company has a customer or (in this case) client focus. An internally focused studio takes the attitude of "we know best," whereas an externally driven studio listens to its customers and clients.

This is a bit of an oversimplification. Since nearly all companies beyond the one- or two-person team has to sell actual games to actual players, nearly every company will be largely externally driven. But who are the customers? If the team is building a game under contract to a publisher, the immediate customer is the publisher, the outfit you need to keep happy. They, in turn, want to sell games, and it is essential for them to do all the marketing research needed to truly understand the target audience.

At the same time, game development itself involves a large and arcane set of skills, which is why publishers generally don't build games in-house. In this sense, teams are internally focused, acting as the true experts in getting the game built. The producer on the team is the person to keep all this in balance, making sure the game is built to satisfy an externally driven need while also making sure the publisher knows (or can be persuaded) why the team makes the design decisions they do.

16.1.3 Easygoing versus Strict Work Discipline

This one is also pretty obvious, but the actual effect on the typical team member's workday is a bit subtler.

Team members are quite rightly regarded as professionals, which means they are mature enough to get work done on their own. We talked about this in Chapter 9. Human nature being what it is, though, usually some amount of supervision is necessary.

At very large studios, people are generally put into narrow and well-defined subspecialties, for example, texture artist versus 3D rigger or AI engineer versus shader designer. If the studio is using Scrum (Chapter 6), then everyone gets a list of things that must be accomplished within each two- or three-week sprint. Scrum appears to be an effective compromise between easygoing and strict that has worked well for the game industry.

16.1.4 Local versus Professional

This dimension refers to how members of the organization relate to one another. In a local orientation, team members relate to their peers, and over time the relationship tends to become more like a family. As a result, there can be pressure to think, look, and act the same as everyone else. In a professional orientation, team members relate more to their chosen profession. For example, an AI programmer may tend to associate more with other AI programmers and take pride in knowing the latest advances in the AI field.

16.1.5 Open versus Closed System

This dimension is basically a measure of how open and approachable everyone is (management, in particular). This especially applies to new people joining the company. To newbies, an open system is more welcoming and helpful than a closed system. In a closed-system organization, there is more of a tendency to just cut you loose, to allow you to sink or swim on your own.

16.1.6 Employee- versus Work-Centered

Also pretty obvious: To what extent does the company care about the health, well-being, and satisfaction of the people who work there? In a work-centered culture, the work comes first, and there is less sympathy for the personal needs and problems of those who do the work. In this industry, which is relentlessly driven by time and budgets, some amount of work-centrism is inevitable. But companies do differ widely in how thoroughly they support their employees.

When scouting around for employment, you may want to sniff around for information about what sorts of cultures can be found in the companies you are interested in. This is pretty hard information to come by unless you have access to former or current employees, and even then you may not get the whole story.

But decide for yourself what kind of company you would best fit in at, and let that guide your search.

16.2 THE CHARACTERISTICS EMPLOYERS SEEK

As a hiring manager, and as someone heavily involved in the vetting of candidates, one of us (Adrian) has worked with many people on hiring the perfect person. They all agreed that certain characteristics were highly sought after, regardless of the role the person was applying for.

The characteristics were as follows:

- A passion for video games

- Strong communication skills

- A team player mindset

- Positive mental attitude

- Flexible and adaptable mental attitude

- Ability to own up to one's mistakes

- Strong self-motivation

- Effective organizational skills

- An attention to detail

- Confidence in abilities

- Open to constructive feedback

- A college degree in a relevant subject

Let's go through each of these to see why they are important.

16.2.1 A Passion for Video Games

Producing video games is very different from simply playing them. Very different!

Simply liking games is not enough. You need the passion! It is your passion that gets you through the boredom and frustration and the low points of game production that will inevitably occur.

Whether you are a designer, an artist, or an engineer, you will be spending your <u>entire</u> <u>working day</u> producing video games. If you do not <u>really</u> like video games, with all that entails, why would you choose to make games as your career?

16.2.2 Strong Communication Skills

As we keep saying in this book, producing video games is a team effort. Whatever your role is on that team, it is essential that you be able to communicate with the other members of the team in a clear, concise manner.

A communication may occur in a variety of ways, from a simple e-mail, to another member of the team telling you that you finished your task well, to a conversation at a meeting, up to a major standup presentation in front of clients, marketing agents, publishers, and the heads of your studio.

The types of media used vary considerably, too: e-mail, text, phone, video conferencing, written documentation, Skype, Discord, face-to-face verbal communication, and sometimes even film or television.

A CAUTIONARY TALE

A designer comes up with the design for an animal in their game and they call this animal a horse.

They go to the artists and describe the horse and ask if the artists can draw it. They say "Sure, come back in two weeks." The designer then goes to the engineers and describes the horse and asks if they can program it. They say "Sure, come back in two weeks."

Two weeks go by, and the designer goes to the artists and asks if they have their horse ready. They say "Yes. Here it is." But they have drawn a unicorn!

Now this is not surprising because that is what artists do. They make things look awesome. But of course, a unicorn is not a horse.

So the designer goes to the engineers and asks if they have their horse. They say "Yes. Here it is." But they have programmed a camel! Again this is not surprising because engineers are very practical people and like efficiency, and in many ways a camel is more efficient than a horse. But a camel is not a horse.

So after two weeks of production time the designer has a unicorn and a camel but no horse. It is not the artist's fault, it is not the engineer's fault, it is the designer's fault for failing to communicate correctly what the designer needed.

The preceding discussion does not even begin to include the essential ability to communicate to a given player exactly what it is she is supposed to do and how to do it.

16.2.3 A Team Player Mindset

Almost without exception, video game production involves a team. It may be a small team of a handful of people or a huge team of three hundred or more. Either way, successful teams rely on the individuals on the team to do their part...without disrupting the work of the other team members.

We have more to say about teamwork in Chapters 6 and 19.

16.2.4 Positive Mental Attitude

Making games is hard work. There will be many times when you will be given tasks that place you under a lot of pressure or that you really do not like doing or that will interfere with your life outside of work. Nonetheless, such tasks need to be done, and often you are really the only one who can do it.

Also, things will often go wrong, as a result of your own mistakes or someone else's. It sucks when that happens, but it happens.

When these things happen, the last thing the producer or the rest of the team wants is you constantly complaining. *Don't be that complaining person!* It's a career killer.

Take a positive mental attitude, dig in to that "passion for video games," and get on with it to the best of your ability.

16.2.5 Strong Self-Motivation

The game industry is task-oriented and deadline-driven. Once given a task, you are expected to complete it by a certain time, but, especially as you become more experienced, you will not be constantly monitored.

It is up to you to complete the task on time and to a high standard. Even though you are a member of a team, you are often isolated in your task and need to have the self-motivation and discipline to remain focused on it.

This can be easy when the tasks you have are new, exciting, and something you are really into. Just as often, though, you will have tasks that you have been working on for days or weeks, that are very similar to others you have done, but that are not what you would have chosen for yourself.

Different people motivate themselves in different ways, but however you inspire yourself to carry on, finding the drive to get things done is an essential skill.

16.2.6 Effective Organizational Skills

As mentioned in the previous section, you are responsible for the completion of your own tasks. This includes organizing how and when you will work on them.

The degree of freedom to organize your work will vary with your skill set, experience with the company, and the degree to which your task is interlinked with those of others on the team. The producer and leads will direct your overarching goals to ensure that you are not holding up others on the team. If you are inexperienced or struggling, they may suggest ways to optimize your workload, but they will not be standing over your shoulder all day. They don't have time for that.

Other than giving project-level instructions on naming conventions and file locations, they will not be telling you how and when to save your work or what file structures you should use for your little piece of the game. If you cannot find a piece of work because you messed up your filing system, that will be down to you. If you lose work because you forgot to save it, that will be down to you.

16.2.7 Attention to Detail

Apart from programming, which has its own requirements for attention to detail, all aspects of game production have to fit within a design and a vision that can involve literally thousands of details. Some of these are aesthetic, some are legal, some are practical, but they are *all* important to get correct.

Just a few examples are given below, but there are many, many more, and an attitude of "well, it's close enough" will simply not cut it.

- Art has to look and feel correct, shadows need to fall correctly, and shading must not look out of place.

- Art may have to match and comply with licensor requirements, perhaps right down to the pixel. Requirements for color palettes might be equally demanding. This happens especially when displaying third-party corporate images. This is why art leads compile style guides.

- Characters must not only look like their design but they must also move according to their size and weight based on the physics of the game. Having a 200-ton behemoth dance like a ballerina may look funny (which might be OK if that is the intent or the physics in this game world are different from that on Earth), but wrong-looking physics wrecks believability.

- The design and game play must match the product descriptions agreed upon in the production contract.

- The performance (e.g., the frame rate) of the game also needs to meet the contractually agreed-upon product descriptions.

- QA must provide highly detailed descriptions of how to recreate bugs or issues so they can be fixed and retested.

- Credits and acknowledgements are subject to very specific contractual requirements to prevent lawsuits down the road.

The list of detail-oriented elements in a game is virtually endless.

16.2.8 A Flexible and Adaptable Attitude

The one constant in the game industry is change.

You should expect change to be the norm and be ready to adapt to it.

This could be as simple as moving your desk every time you switch projects so you no longer have that great location with a window but are now stuffed in a corner somewhere. Of course, for some people, being stuffed in a corner away from the distractions of a window may be seen as an improvement!

It may be as complex as having to learn a whole new programming language or art software package or having to design for a new platform.

It may be as disastrous as the project being cancelled or, worse, losing your job.

No matter how small or large or devastating the change is, it will occur. To survive for any length of time in the game industry, you have to be prepared to adapt to circumstances and have the flexibility to change yourself and your work methods to cope with the new.

"One thing I have learned is that change is the only constant and adaptability is key. You may have been assigned a list of tasks as a content person or assigned to a specific role but then the ground shifts and new gaps arise. The more you are able to find solutions or fill those gaps the faster you will move up the ladder. You will find yourself invaluable to any team and sought after.

You need to work on maintaining skills in your expertise, but work equally as hard on your soft skills. Teamwork, communication and collaboration will take you farther than just being a good artist or programmer. This becomes even more apparent the higher you climb.

Once you have the job it is still important to work on developing a strong network. You never know when the guy you worked with 3 years ago may now be your boss, a connection that gets you your next job, or someone you got to know to be part of your team. It truly is still a small industry."

STEVE DERRICK
Chief of Staff, Vicarious Visions

16.2.9 Confidence in Abilities

If you are applying for a position, then make sure you are confident that you will be capable of carrying it out, and then demonstrate that confidence during the interview.

Confidence in your abilities includes the confidence to say that you do not know something or that you have not had experience doing something; but you can then show how you could learn what you need or that you have similar experience that you could adapt to the position you're applying for.

It is usually best to say "I don't know" instead of dancing around the question. This is the proper answer any good scientist will give when asked about something Science (with a capital S) hasn't figured out yet.

This is an excellent habit of mind, we think, even if you haven't been trained as a scientist. It is better than claiming knowledge you don't have. That sort of thing tends to come back later and bite you in the butt.

16.2.10 Openness to Constructive Feedback

Constructive feedback is one of the major ways you can learn from the experience of others.

It will come in many shapes and forms, but however it arrives, you should develop a desire to receive it. We talked about this earlier in the section on senior projects in Chapter 13.

If someone who has been making games for ten years tells you that you could have saved time by writing the code differently, or that the lighting on your background is not quite right and could be improved by applying some other texture, or your level design is way too cluttered or too empty to be fun, then this feedback is helpful to you, both right now and in the future.

One thing to be aware of is the difference between constructive feedback and demeaning criticism! The former is genuinely helpful, while the latter can be annoying at best and demoralizing at worst.

It all hinges around that word "constructive." Constructive feedback comes with useful advice and suggestions on how to improve.

Mere criticism, even if often accompanied by suggestions, is generally not as helpful.

Constructive feedback usually, although not exclusively, comes from within your own team or company and comes from a desire to both improve the product and to help you.

Criticism usually comes from outside your team, often from sources that do not understand some of the restrictions you may be working under.

One of the drawbacks of the industry is that oftentimes, the people who have the final say have their own agendas and opinions about the product and the work done on it.

Recognizing the difference between constructive feedback and criticism is something you will gradually learn. Take advantage of the first and put up with the second so it does not adversely affect your performance. Yes, even the criticism that you actually have to go along with.

16.2.11 A College Degree in a Relevant Subject

While it is technically true, especially for small indie companies or if you are forming your own group, that you can certainly make games without a college degree, if you want to be considered for a position with a major company, you will need one. This wasn't always the case, but it is now.

Unfair though that may be—because companies are overwhelmed by applications—an easy first cut is the college degree paper qualification. No degree, no next step. Think of it as a giant filter, filtering out the unworthy, yes, and sometimes the worthy as well, but that's just the way it is.

So what counts as a relevant subject?

This really depends on what position you want to fill. Obvious ones, though, are Computer Science if you are going to be an engineer, Visual Arts or Animation for artists and animators, and Game Design for designers. That said, there are some overlaps and some not so direct connections, too.

While a rapidly growing number of games are made with Unity or UE4 or using platforms that deliver browser-friendly games in HTML5 like Construct 2, programmers *must* include in their degree C++, which, as of this publication, remains the main programming language for the deep parts of video games. Moreover, C++ is the programming language used for scripting in the mighty UE4.

For these reasons, C++ really is the mainstream programming language for consoles and PCs, and your mastery of it signals to an employer that you've worked hard to master your craft. It is a badge of honor.

Another major programming language you will likely encounter, if you haven't already, is C#, the dominant language used by Unity for game scripting and also the basis for many important "dev kits" used to develop games on the Xbox. And why not? C# was developed at Microsoft.

Although it has "C" in its name, C# more resembles Java than C++, but many in its user base insist it is a much better language than Java. Don't let the fact that Microsoft invented C# put you off; it is increasingly cross-platform (as used in Unity) and supported by an open-source alternative called the Mono Project (www.mono-project.com).

Apart from Fine Arts and Animation degrees, artists should try to also include graphics design, color theory, life drawing, and perhaps courses in film and lighting techniques.

If you want to be a writer for games, then study that craft and do lots of it. Some companies need narrative design, so degrees in Writing, Screenwriting, or Filmmaking may also be acceptable. Having only an English degree by itself won't make you very competitive, so if you have the chance to study game writing in particular, by all means do so. We've put a few relevant titles in the appendix. One thing you can do to skill up here is download Twine, Inklewriter, or some other tool for building "branching narrative" text-based adventures and try your hand at it.

Apart from a specific Game Design degree, design is the one area where your degree can be more diverse. You just have to show in your application or during a job interview that it has relevance to game design. For example, people have become game designers from such areas as architecture, history, journalism, mathematics, physics, and many others. Any training you've received that can get you thinking like a designer could work here.

It all really depends on what the company is looking for. You, the applicant, should ideally be able to show them you have created effective game designs.

That said, artists and designers should always aim to broaden their appeal to a company by developing depth, for example, a designer who has taken an animation course or an artist who has taken a programming course.

Music and sound production come with their own degrees, but music in particular can be freelanced.

16.3 WHAT YOU NEED TO DO TO GET READY

Needless to say, on the day of the interview, be well bathed, well groomed, and, well, inoffensive. Even in a casual industry like the game industry, personal hygiene will be appreciated by the interviewer and your future coworkers.

Don't overdress. You probably don't need that suit and tie. On the other hand, don't underdress. Cutaway jeans and T-shirts may be OK once you have the job, but quality business casual is your best bet for the interview.

In the meantime, your prospective employer will be doing a thing called "due diligence" on you. This can include verifying your school attendance, running a credit check, and inquiring about your previous work record.

There are practical and legal limits as to how far that can go (for example, looking at your criminal record, if you have one, might be a no-no, although with the Internet that rule is getting easier to skirt).

One area of due diligence that most employers these days will chase is your activity on social media, especially Facebook. You've gotten rid of those drunken frat party images, right? Well, they may not be as deleted as you think they are. In any event, it wouldn't hurt to clean up your social media accounts well in advance of going out on your job search.

One last thing: If they should uncover some incongruities about your past, you are probably toast.

16.4 THE INTERVIEW PROCESS

Well before you get an actual in-person interview, you will almost certainly jump through a whole series of hoops.

Your résumé, nowadays nearly always uploaded digitally, has been picked through to see if there is a match between the company's needs and what you bring to the table. That tall metaphorical stack of résumés gets down to a much shorter metaphorical stack of résumés.

Obviously you hope to be in the short pile. Assuming you are, you will get either an e-mail or a phone call to set up your first phone screen. Yay! The process has begun.

Yes, unless you live very locally to the company, your first interview will almost certainly be via phone even if later ones are not. This is, after all, much cheaper for the company than spending money on a plane ticket and hotel to fly you out. You may even undergo a series of interviews over the phone before things move to the next stage.

The phone interviews begin a sort of courtship ritual. They are sounding you out, and you are sounding them out. You might be asked general questions about your education, past experience, and interests. Or they may jump straight in with a technical interview to judge if you know what your résumé says you know. There may be multiple interviews with different people.

> **CAN WE TALK?**
>
> Today, of course, "over the phone" can have them actually taking a look at you via Skype or a video-enabled cell phone. If so, don't be sitting there in your jammies. Dress as if it were an in-person interview.

It's a good idea to bone up on the company you're interviewing with well in advance of this first call. You probably have to some extent: you know what games they have shipped recently and what sorts of games they make generally. You want to be knowledgeable about and interested in the company's activities, so you can ask them about what sorts of projects they might put you on, what it's like to work there, and so forth. Keep in mind that a lot of what they are currently working on is probably shrouded in secrecy, so be respectful and back off if the discussion strays into that area.

Do not bring up the issue of pay and benefits at this time. Those discussions, if they happen at all, will take place much later.

These calls serve a couple of purposes. First, they get to find out exactly just how much you know. Second, they get a sense of your personality and how well you are likely to fit in with the rest of the team.

If you survive this round of interviewing, then you'll be asked for a live, in-person interview. This is done at their headquarters and at their expense if it involves flying you out.

We hope you have had the chance to be at the receiving end of a live job interview once or twice before now. Sure, those other interviews, for internships or summer jobs, were not as intensely important as the one you are about to experience, but they were good practice.

Being nervous is normal, and a skilled interviewer will understand that and not generally hold it against you. Keep in mind, too, that some of the people, especially the more technically inclined people, may be just as nervous as you are. Job interviews are not a normal part of their workday, and this can make them uncomfortable.

Plan on remaining most or all of the day. You will be shuttled back and forth among many people: managers, producers, and team members. Usually someone will be assigned to be your "handler," to greet you when you arrive, show you around, and answer your questions.

You will nearly always be asked to complete an "aptitude test," where you demonstrate your skills. These can get mighty grueling, especially for engineers, who are usually asked to write some code (in C++, no less), find the bugs in some existing code, and in general answer tough questions about algorithms, best coding practices, and the like. The more hardcore the studio, the more hardcore the test.

You artists might be asked to demonstrate your prowess with a tool like Maya or whatever other toolset you say you are good at. They want to see that you are reasonably facile with the tools at hand. As part of this, they might ask you to perform some simple tasks on one of their own in-house tools, ones that you are entirely unfamiliar with, just to see how you reason out the process.

Designers might have to create a design on the fly, including scripts, stories, or level layouts.

You will probably be served lunch, unless by lunchtime they have already decided against you and shuffle you out. Well, why not feed you while you are there? Here is a pro tip, however. You are being observed and evaluated here, too. How are your table manners? Also, how well do you treat the wait staff? Being unpleasant or condescending with the people who cook and serve your food is a major red flag to an employer.

If you get through all this, congratulations! You might be told right then and there that you're hired, or it may take several days. Either way, enjoy the nap on the flight home.

Finally, you get word: you're either in or out. Yes, it is possible that after all this you don't actually land the gig. You probably weren't the only one flown out for the position, but by this stage, there would only be a handful of candidates left.

So whether you ultimately get the position or not, take comfort in the fact that you successfully navigated these treacherous waters and made your way to the elite group at the narrow end of the funnel. The next time will be easier.

16.5 SALARY AND OTHER NEGOTIATIONS

If you have a few years' experience, there may be some wiggle room, but there are rarely negotiations for entry-level posts. They will make you an offer; take it or leave it.

The company owns everything you make while you are there—get used to it.

If you already have some designs or publications under your belt or have written an app, then there should be a section in your contract where you declare these so they are not considered part of the employer's assets.

There will usually be a section in the contract that prohibits you from working on other projects, particularly game-related ones, while employed by the company. This means what it says: You cannot be working on your own games even in your spare time while employed by the company. While it may be difficult to prove, doing so is an infringement of the contract and could lead to trouble.

Again, sometimes there are gray areas, for example, getting paid to lecture on games or writing a book about games. These issues should be brought up during the hiring process so you can find out the relevant company policy. This is also the time to clearly indicate other work you've done that you want to maintain ownership and control of.

In general, you are better off declaring things than not, just to avoid potential legal issues.

CHAPTER 17

Your First Gig

W̲E̲ A̲R̲E̲ N̲O̲T̲ T̲A̲L̲K̲I̲N̲G̲ here about your first gig as an intern, but your first paid, full-time job. If you were lucky enough to get an internship while still in college, then you have a head start on this.

This is the real McCoy.

You graduated college and landed a job, maybe the exact one you wanted, or maybe not, but those two things are the most important successes in your life up to this moment.

That is about to change. Success will now be measured on how you perform on a day-by-day, week-by-week basis. No one cares that you graduated top of the class with honors or scraped by at the bottom. Almost everyone here will also have a degree, so you are not that special.

You have gone from the crème de la crème, college senior, back down to the bottom of the pile. Almost everyone where you work will have more experience in the industry than you do. Most, although maybe not all, will also have more skills than you.

17.1 DAY ONE

Your first day will be odd. You may not even start at the regular time but be asked to come in a little later so the people you need to meet are all ready to get you started properly.

Unless you have been dropped into the deep end because you are starting at a company that is in deep crunch mode and they need all hands on deck, it is highly unlikely you will do much actual work on your first day.

You will almost certainly do the following, although maybe in a different order:

First you will have lots of paperwork to fill out: nondisclosure agreement (NDA), bank and tax forms to get your salary, parking permits, company badge, health plans, pension deduction forms, and no doubt several others. You may have filled some out before your arrival (or be told to take them with you and bring them back later), but it is pretty much guaranteed there will still be plenty more administrative stuff to do. You may be given keys: to a locker, to the office, to your desk, to the filing cabinets. Depending on the company, there may be canteen vouchers or tickets to movie theaters and local events.

Having gotten the admin out of the way, you will almost certainly be shown around the office and the building so you can find your way around. In a small company, that may not take long, but in a large company, it could take a while. You might even manage to get lost.

During this time, you will probably get to meet your project team (or at least some of them) and, depending on the size of the company, several other people as well, all of whom seem to know your name, but you have no clue how to remember all theirs!

This tour is usually done by your lead, one of your fellow workers on the project you are assigned to, or maybe a designated "buddy." ("Buddy" sounds so much nicer than "handler.") The "buddy" is not necessarily from your project but is there to answer your questions, take you on the tour, and generally help you find your feet in the early days. They will tell you about all the cool things the company does when they are not working on games, like the board games group, the bowling league, or the softball team, for example. Well, that's assuming your company has any of those things. Most do because studios have learned that these are great ways to build and maintain team spirit and morale.

Soon it will be time for your team to take you to lunch—yes, it has taken that long, and it is lunchtime already.

At some point you will even get shown your desk! If you are lucky and the company is organized, it may even have a computer on it.

If you are really lucky, the IT department will already have gotten all the software you need up and running and will have given you a temporary password and an e-mail address. You can now start setting up your machine, downloading all the project files, and finding your way around the internal systems and version control setups. This will take you a while. Maybe even the rest of the day.

Usually you can get help from a resident expert who will show you the fine points of the official "version control system," a software system like Git or Perforce that keeps track of every art asset and bit of code created for the project. We hope you used something like Git (or its web-hosting service GitHub) while in college to manage your team projects. They are indispensable! Your studio might use Perforce, a popular choice in the game industry, or perhaps an older system like SVN, and you might not be as familiar with them. Whatever process is in place for version control, you want to make sure you can make effective use of it, as it will definitely be a part of your day-to-day life.

Your first task, once you've gotten your machine up and running, will probably be to simply play the game that you will be working on. This is really important as you need to understand how far along the project is, its style, and how you will fit into its development. Because you are now a *game maker*, you will be able to bring your critical eye to the work you see. But don't go busting anyone's chops yet.

And all of a sudden you realize your first day at work is over. Sensory overload kicks in, and you head home. You didn't get to make awesome art, write devastating code, or design a key level, but you did meet lots of interesting, talented people who you will now be working with.

17.2 MONTH ONE…

Again, depending on the state of your project and the setup at your company, your first week will probably be fairly slow as you gradually learn more of what the project needs are and exactly what your role is going to be.

You may have to play several of the company's games to familiarize yourself with them and then offer suggestions on how to improve them or give a critique of them. Although usually informal, this is actually a kind of test. Your colleagues are sounding you out, trying to find what particular insights you can bring to the table. For example, you may be able to identify, in a very detailed and "fine-grained" way, what is great, good, or not so good about a level in the game, maybe enough to impress the original level designer. You're now starting to talk their language. You are taking another step on that long journey from being a *player* of games to a *maker* of games.

You will start attending meetings, especially if the company runs some form of agile production process like Scrum. As we saw in Chapter 6, one kind of meeting you might be attending regularly is the ten-minute daily scrum meeting.

"Probably the most important thing I've learned in the game business is to cultivate humility. On the one hand, you have to believe in your creative instincts and trust your skills. But it's a medium of working very indirectly. You're trying to get certain emotional experiences for your players by setting up situations, almost like a practical joke. There's a lot that can go wrong.

So, you believe in your ideas and you've thought them through a lot, and you develop a lot of certainty. That's good. But in order for it to pay off, you've got to be committed to testing your work in the fire. You've got to walk in remembering that you could be wrong. You often *will* be, in one way or another. The trick lies less in knowing what to make than discovering what you don't know."

TIM STELLMACH
Veteran Game Designer

Like in your internship, you need to prove that the company made the right decision when they hired you, and your first few weeks will almost certainly feel similar. (See Chapter 12 on internships). In fact, in many organizations you are technically "on probation" for some period of time (somewhere between six weeks and six months is common). This is something you may have agreed to in all that paperwork you filled out on Day One. Probation here means that they can let you go (legally) more easily during this period than later on.

So during this period, you will be given small tasks to complete, and if you do well with those, then the tasks will increase in size and complexity.

That said, there are some subtle differences. Expectations of your abilities will be higher. You will be given more responsibility than when you were an intern, although maybe not all at once. After a few weeks on the job, certainly you should expect to be given quite a lot more things to be responsible for.

You will be expected to work longer on your own with less input and help, although you should still ask if you are not sure. But show the gurus the courtesy of trying to find out the answers on your own first.

You will also be expected to contribute meaningfully to discussions on your project and on issues and problems that crop up and to come up with potential solutions. You will slowly be pulled into brainstorming sessions about all manner of things, where, again, since you were invited, you will be expected to contribute.

17.3 …AND BEYOND

Apart from making sure you complete all your tasks on time and to a high standard, the first few months you should be a total sponge. Absorb everything you can, and not just about the industry and your particular skills, but, just as important, your employer.

It will be different working there than what you expected, no matter how much research you did before applying. Even if you worked there as an intern, being a full-time employee will be different.

You need to understand the structure of the company, the internal politics, the business decision-making process, and the reasons why the production process is the way it is. This goes beyond just learning about the corporate culture we spoke of earlier.

Knowing more about all these things will help make your life at the company easier in two key areas: making progress toward promotion and keeping yourself happy and motivated.

If you want to progress and be assigned to better, more important, more challenging, or more interesting tasks, then knowing who makes the decision about who works on what project (and what influences those decisions) is important. Knowing this will better enable you to show that you are the right person for that role or task.

Now, we are not saying to continually suck up to everyone, although in some companies that may be part of the office politics. We *are* saying: show a keen interest in and understanding of the background processes. This is in addition to showing you can carry out your assigned tasks.

Understanding how decisions are made concerning who gets to work on what projects also goes a long way toward avoiding frustration and disappointment. Knowing that not getting to do what you want when you would expect to has nothing to do with your lack of skill. It's not about you. The simple fact is that most companies never give out those roles to people until they have been there for at least a year. This is a good thing to know. Being happy, contented, productive, and motivated—especially when working on the menial tasks—is viewed as a great asset in many companies, one that is much more likely to get you that promotion and interesting work than complaining and whining all the time.

No, we are also not suggesting that you just hunker down and hope something better comes along. You need to show that you are interested and want to take on more, and seeing the bigger company picture really helps. Remember, those "menial" tasks are just as important as the glamour and glitz, and the game could not have been made unless those things had gotten done.

BE THE SHINY COG

A few years ago I (Adrian) attended a GDC meeting and heard a talk by a newbie in the industry. Wish I could remember his name, but I just can't. But he gave a very good talk about problems faced by newbies in the game industry, and one of the things that really stuck in my mind was his idea of being the shiny cog.

Production often involves being a cog in a big machine. One way to tackle the mundane and potentially soul-destroying boredom of your job is to make sure that, if you are going to be a cog along with a lot of other cogs, then be the shiny cog. The one who excels at being a small cog will get noticed by the bigger cogs and move on to greater things.

This really is good advice because it is all too easy, especially when you are just starting out, to get discouraged by the fact you are not doing the cool, interesting work you always envisioned doing. You then start to consider looking elsewhere way too soon. Persevere, and it will come.

Show that you have the character to own any job and make it great, and it will probably come more quickly.

FOR WANT OF A NAIL...

If you do not think menial tasks are important, then think of the old poem about a war that was lost because no one checked on the nails in the shoes of the messenger's horse:

For want of a nail the shoe was lost.
For want of the shoe the horse was lost.
For want of the horse the message was lost.
For want of the message the battle was lost.
For want of the battle the war was lost.
All for the want of a nail.

CHAPTER 18

A Day in the Life

UNLIKE MANY OTHER INDUSTRIES, there is no real standard workday in the game industry. This applies not just to the hours worked but also to the tasks you might be asked to perform. You are engaged in a creative endeavor, not working on an assembly line, and this is one of the biggest attractions about working this way.

Working in the game industry provides a variety of different experiences on a daily basis. There is no doubt that a lot of the time the work is exciting and challenging, with each day offering up new things to tackle and learn. On the other hand, there are also long periods where you will be doing the same thing or working on the same part of the game for what seems like forever. Recall what we said in the last chapter: those menial jobs are critically important, too, and somebody has to do them. The same thing happens when making a movie or staging a rock concert: quite a lot of the work is unglamorous, but has to be done. Ask any roadie or stagehand.

So if there is no standard day, how can we write a chapter about it? Well, just because there is no standard day does not mean there are no recurring patterns to discover.

18.1 THE PHASE OF THE PROJECT

What fills your day will almost certainly be driven by the phase of the project you are working in.

At the start of a project ("preproduction") there is a lot of documentation work, planning, iterating, and conceptualizing. This is possibly the most exciting part of the project because everything seems fresh, and all things are possible, yes, even if you are working on the sixteenth sequel of the game. Quite a lot of the raw creativity that will ultimately shape the finished game gets done here.

Once this phase is over, your work will shift to a more regular pattern of the "production" phase. It is during this stage that the game industry most resembles other production industries. There is a list of tasks you need to complete by a deadline, and you come in and grind away at them. While the details of the tasks will vary from week to week or even day to day, there will be an element of "samey" to it.

If you are an artist, for example, you will be creating art. Depending on the size and setup of the company and the project itself, you may at one point be working on character art or maybe heads-up display (HUD) art, for example. If you are more specialized, you will be tied to doing just one thing, for example, animation rigging. Regardless of your degree of specialization, your workday will be routine: arrive in the morning, work, go to lunch, more work in the afternoon, go home. Unless you are unlucky enough to be in a company that crunches from day one, then, apart from those busy times surrounding milestones, you will be relatively relaxed and comfortable. You'll know what to expect from one day to the next.

The closer you get to beta, the more stressed things will become. Your working day will probably lengthen and could now include weekends.

A lot of how this plays out critically depends on how well the project's producer has been filling the producer role (Chapter 7). As we say, the producer's job is to make sure all the work gets done when it is supposed to get done. Producers are the one who are really good at using Excel or Microsoft Project and will no doubt have created a pile of Excel files (plus, maybe, reports from some other project management software) to monitor the health of the project.

The producer's job is unglamorous and, in many cases, pretty thankless as well. When things are going smoothly, there is no drama, there are no explosions of temper and frustration, and the producer is, in effect, invisible. It's only when things go "off the rails" that you will need to deal with the producer.

18.2 THE BURN-DOWN CHART

One thing the producer maintains and updates daily is that "project plan" or "game plan" we saw earlier. From that, one useful chart the producer often generates—and keeps posted where everyone can see it—is the burn-down chart. This is a giant graph that plots the percentage of work completed on the vertical axis against time on the horizontal axis. There is a nice downward-sloping diagonal line showing 100% of the work to be done at time = 0, and 0% of the work that remains to be done by the delivery date.

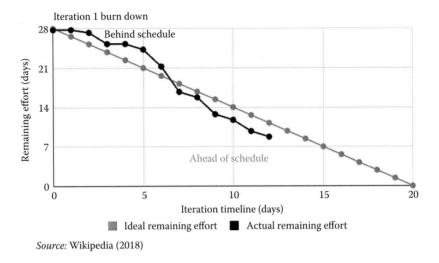

Iteration 1 burn down

Source: Wikipedia (2018)

Then there is that other line, the one showing actual progress. You hope—and do everything in your power as far as your own work is concerned—to see that line lying *below* the diagonal. When the line creeps up above the diagonal, trouble is brewing, and good producers will do everything in their power to (a) fix the problem right away and (b) prevent it from happening in the first place.

This is the reason for those daily scrum meetings. They are there to keep the project on track. A project that runs on schedule is a lovely thing. You don't get too stressed out or, worse, burned out, and the need for a lot of crunch time becomes much less urgent. There is yet another old saying in this business: Q: How does a project get to be a year late? A: One day at a time.

That old fable you heard as a kid about the tortoise beating the hare happens to be true. Every day, by everyone steadily hammering away at the project, the project gets done. If you prefer a different fable, recall the best way to eat an elephant: one bite at a time.

Great producers are worth their weight in gold.

18.3 SHIFTING RESPONSIBILITIES

Once past beta, your day will change depending on your responsibilities. You may be switched to a new project or you may be left on for the polishing stage. It is hard to say whether it is better to shift to a new project and get a fresh jolt of excitement or to stay on the same project and enjoy the satisfaction of seeing something through completion. A lot will depend on your personality and how well the project went.

Another factor is your seniority and how well you've demonstrated good design instincts. As your career advances, you are more likely to get placed on preproduction teams for new projects and, unless you are the lead or on the critical path, be switched off the project before it is actually finished. In the early days of your career, you are more likely to come on after preproduction and get switched off toward the end. Unless there are multiple projects already running or about to start up when you get asked which one you'd like to work on next, you are generally just told which project it will be and when you will start.

One reason we keep saying that you had better love games if you want to work in the game industry is that, while playing games is fun, or at least it should be, working on games can sometimes be extremely boring, especially toward the end of a project. The polishing stage as the projects nears completion will definitely test your resolve. You have been working on the game for months, and the initial excitement has worn off and been replaced by a desire just to get the darned thing over with and move on to something else. But before that can happen, numerous tiny, nagging details need to be dealt with, or a particularly tricky bug has

> "A video game is a piece of art. Art is a labor of love. Make games because you love them."
>
> SPYROS GIANNOPOULOS
> *Software Engineer &*
> *Game Industry Veteran*

to be squished, to bring the game to completion to the high standards you and your team entered the project with in the first place.

18.4 A DAY IN THE LIFE

So, there is no standard "day in the life" in the game industry. There are, in fact, multiple standard days, ranging from the truly awesome to the just plain horrible, and they are all dished up to you over time. If you have the personality to accept that, then you will probably survive. If, however, you want a workday where you know what you will be doing day after day, when you will be doing it, and when it will be finished, then choose a different career path while you still can.

CHAPTER 19

Teamwork, Part Two

WHILE IT IS NOT impossible to make a game entirely by oneself, especially with the advent of the latest engines and downloadable art, SFX, and music, this is far from the norm. The norm is to work as part of a team.

The size and makeup of the team varies from company to company and from project to project. In fact, unless the company you work for only makes one product at a time, "your team" can have different members as the project goes through its production cycle.

19.1 THE LIFE AND TIMES OF A TEAM

Typically, teams start small at the beginning, grow through the production phase, and then shrink again as production draws to a close. So unless you are the producer or lead designer (see roles below), it is quite possible you will not be on a project for its entirety but will join sometime after it starts and then leave sometime before it's over.

That said, there are some fairly standard formats for team makeups, so let us start there. We've already gone through some of this, but now we will expand on that previous discussion.

As we've seen, a standard team has people from four main disciplines, plus some additional people who may or may not be allocated exclusively to your particular project or who may only be part of the team for part of the project.

We saw that the four main disciplines are engineering, art, design, and production.

In additional, there can also be sound designers and sound effects creators, musicians and composers, tools programmers, and voice actors.

Not only that, the team you are on is itself part of an even larger team, even if that larger team is not within the office you work in or even within the company you work for.

Those other team members include clients and people in marketing, sales, and legal departments.

For a game to successfully reach the public, all of these diverse disciplines need to do their part. To be really successful, each part also has to understand and cooperate with the others.

Understanding the role each plays makes this a little easier, while understanding the hierarchy makes it a little less aggravating.

19.2 PRODUCTION HIERARCHY

At the top of the tree are the clients: they are the ones who are putting up the money and taking the risk, so at the end of the day, what they say goes.

Note that the term "client" includes cases where the publishing company owns the studio that is going to make the game. In this instance, the management of the publishing company is the client.

If the product is a licensed brand, then the owners of the license for the product are at least on a par with, and even sometimes above, the client.

In a close second comes legal. After all, you do not want to make a great game only to be sued over its content or over copyright infringement and lose everything.

Marketing and sales are next. It is no good having a great game if the public never hears about it and never discovers that the product is for sale.

WHAT'S WITH THE HUGE MARKETING BUDGETS?

It is interesting to note that marketing budgets are often double the production budget, especially for AAA titles.

This makes a lot of people—especially creative people—uncomfortable. Why, they ask, does marketing take such a big piece of the budgetary pie? Wouldn't the money be better spent on making sure the creative people have everything they need for a great game?

Well, no one is asking you to make a lousy game, and no one sets out to do that. There is a thing called Denki's First Law. It goes like this: *"Great games don't sell; well marketed games sell; and great games that are well marketed sell lots."*

ANDERSON 2016

Next, of course, are the company owners and managers.

Finally, we get down to the game production team itself. Yep, in terms of the hierarchy, you are right at the bottom.

19.3 TEAM HIERARCHY

On a day-to-day basis, the producer usually has the final say on key decisions because that person is responsible for making sure the product comes in on time, within budget, and of high quality. The producer works with the development team, but also works very closely with the other four production teams (clients, management, legal, and marketing). This is often an area in which intense discussions occur between the producer and the other production roles. The producer is the "front-facing" person on the team, the person that everyone not on the team comes into contact with.

Of the three major fields on the development team, design usually trumps engineering and art, except on specific technological issues. In some studios, this is not always the case. As we saw earlier, some studios might be said to be art-centric, story-centric, or maybe engineering-centric, reflecting what the founders of the studio feel most passionately about.

OK, so much for the hierarchy. What about the roles of each team member? We covered much of that in Chapter 7.

General Roles: On all but the smallest teams (six people or fewer) there will be at least two people in each of the three main disciplines, plus the producer.

On small teams people simply take on multiple roles.

Engineer: This role is responsible for creating the code that makes the game run. Depending on the size of the team, this could encompass all the game systems, sound, VO, music, AI, and shaders. In other words, everything you don't see but without which the game does not run! As the team size grows, some of these are split off and undertaken by dedicated or even specialized programmers.

Artist: This person is responsible for all the art in the game and possibly initial concepts as well. This covers the design of HUD objects and layouts, fonts and color palettes, character art, object art, backgrounds, level art, animating anything that moves…in other words, everything you see on screen. As the team size grows, these are also split off into specialty areas, for example, animation, rigging, textures, UI layout, concept art, backgrounds, and levels.

Designer: This person is responsible for maintaining the vision of the game, writing the narratives, laying out the levels, placing objects, tweaking the in-game stats, balancing the game, play testing, observing other play testers, and QA. If it is a licensed product, then the designer also ensures that the design adheres to the strict requirements of the license. The designer is also responsible for writing and updating the all-important Game Design Document. In small companies the designer is also often responsible for finding and implementing sound effects and music, in other words everything you hear over speakers. In short, the designer is ultimately involved in every aspect of the playability and fun of the game, as experienced from the player's perspective.

Sound Engineer: The person in this role is responsible for creating and recording, and possibly implementing, everything you hear in the game apart from music. Depending on the size of the company, this person may be a contractor and not even based in the production studio. Nonetheless, she is an integral part of the team. Can you really imagine a game without any sound?

Musician (or composer): The musician is responsible for creating and recording, and possibly implementing, the music within the game, although this is more commonly one of the engineers or the designer. Like sound engineers, the musician may be a solo contractor, but good music, especially as it changes to enhance atmosphere, makes the musician a team player, too.

Producer: The producer is responsible for the team's overall productivity. Most people who become producers usually move into that role after a few years in one of the other disciplines (engineering, art, design).

In smaller companies, producers (sometimes called *production coordinators*) may also have responsibility for doing actual production work. In larger studios, with larger teams, the producer's day is entirely filled with running the show, and he won't get to do as much coding or art or design as he once did. This alone sometimes puts people off the idea of becoming a producer; they miss the hands-on experiences.

The producer is also responsible for reporting up to the managers within his company or directly to the client on the progress being made. This includes the unpleasant task of making superiors aware of problems encountered and the solutions being explored. The producer acts as a buffer between the client and managers and the production team.

Producers report downward the need to make requested changes so that the team can start working on them. Part of this entails collaborating with the leads to determine how the changes can be accommodated within the schedule and budget.

Lead Roles: One person in each field may be designated the lead for that discipline, and that person is responsible for liaising with the other leads and the producer. This is to make sure that things are produced in the correct sequence and that no one is waiting around unable to work because they needed something from someone else. This is called a *dependency* in project management speak.

Leads are also responsible for mentoring others in their field, helping them when they get stuck, and suggesting better and faster ways to do things. Leads are responsible for working with the producer to come up with a feasible work schedule. As the team expands in size, there can be multiple leads within a discipline; for example, roles like lead artist, lead animator, lead designer, and lead level designer begin to appear. Really large teams, of the AAA title variety, may have even more levels of hierarchy than these such as senior lead *whatever*.

CHAPTER 20

Crunch Time

ANYONE WHO HAS WORKED in the game industry is aware of "crunch time," or simply "crunch."

People thinking of making the game industry their career should also be aware of crunch time, its implications, and how they will be affected by it.

So what exactly is crunch time?

20.1 THE IRON TRIANGLE

A simple way to view a complex economic situation is the iron triangle, also known as the production triangle.

The iron triangle

It takes the three main elements of production (scope, time, cost) and places them as the sides of a triangle. The sides and angles of the triangle are adjustable but are integrally linked to each other, so that if you lengthen one side, the other two sides must adjust in order to maintain the original external dimensions of the triangle, OR the triangle itself must get bigger or smaller.

So if you increase the length of the scope side—say by adding an extra level to the game—but you do not want to change the length of the time side, you *must increase the length of the cost side; otherwise, the triangle cannot remain intact.* The project will now cost more to compensate for the extra scope, but it will still be finished by the original time.

A slightly more involved version of the triangle places quality inside the triangle, so again as you increase or decrease the lengths of any of the sides, the area (quality) is also impacted.

A ruder way to say this is: fast, good, cheap. Pick two.

20.2 THE DYNAMICS OF CRUNCH

First, a little financial and economic background.

Almost every company in the industry bases the normal working week for pay calculations, and for profit and loss calculations, on a standard forty-hour week. Employee contracts are often worded along the lines of:

> *"Employees are expected to work an average 40 to 50 hours per week, but at times they may be required to work additional hours in order to bring a product to completion."*

The majority of employees, although not all, are classed as "salaried exempt." This means they do not work a fixed number of hours per week. They get paid the same whether they work 30 hours or 60 hours. Salaries are usually higher than a comparable hourly position, so this is generally considered perfectly reasonable and tends to even out over time. Salaried employees normally have a lot more flexibility in choosing their workday times as well. Some people like coming in early and leaving early, other people like coming in later and leaving later, and as long as the work gets done, that's fine.

There is one wrinkle to this: Many studios require a common block of time in the center of the day where everyone is expected to be there. For example, if your studio uses the Scrum methodology, then everyone on the team must be on hand for the daily scrum meeting.

Technically, while salaried employees are eligible for overtime, it is rarely paid. Instead, there are other compensations via bonuses, perks, time off in lieu of ("comp time"), and other considerations. Because of past labor abuses at some game studios, this has become a legal gray area, so we note that the relevant laws could change, at both the state and federal levels.

So how does this lead to *crunch*?

> An interesting thing is that people who work in the game industry tend to love their jobs so much that they often work longer hours anyway. As a producer and manager, Adrian was often in the unusual (some managers in other industries would probably say enviable) position of telling people to stop working and go home.

> In the case of making games that are slated to be released with a new hardware product or at the same time as a new movie, deadlines are even more critical. Sales can drop by 50% or more if you miss the deadline by even two weeks.

We noted that not only pay but also profit and loss (P&L) are calculated based on an assumption of forty-hour work weeks. Remember that the game industry is deadline and milestone driven. Missing deadlines can ruin P&L forecasts and shrink margins (or even make the studio unprofitable). Missing milestones can result in nonpayment or, at best, delays of payment of associated money from publishers and licensors. So there is a lot of incentive to meet both the agreed-upon deadlines and milestones.

The game industry is always cutting edge. Most studios try to achieve more on their latest game than their previous game achieved or to force the hardware to do more than it was designed for, just to gain an edge over the competition. It is not always easy to accurately predict how long a certain task will take. Even industry veterans can seriously underestimate how long some of this cutting-edge stuff will take, so the project starts to fall behind schedule.

The biggest reason for crunch is that a deadline is in danger of being missed. Perhaps initial estimates as to how long something would take were too optimistic and way off the mark, but that is not the only reason.

Expectations on quality and content within a game are often set at the maximum attainable level, sometimes even above what is reasonable. This may be where an independent company promises more, or in less time, just to outbid an opponent for a contract with a publisher. It also happens within owned studios where marketing or licensing requirements must be met. As we saw, any shortfall in matching an expectations set can result in loss of payment or, even worse, cancellation of the contract entirely.

Another reason for crunch is that expectations of quality or content are in danger of being missed, but there are still more reasons.

Sometimes pressures from outside force crunch time, for example:

- Another company is found to be releasing a competitive product before you are scheduled to release yours, so management wants to move up your release date.

- For reasons of its own, the film company decides to release the film that your game is based on earlier than originally planned, so you need to move up your release date to match.

- The publisher runs into financial problems because another product of theirs failed to make the expected sales, so they need an earlier release—from you—to compensate.

- Your company has the opportunity to work on another project, but its start date overlaps with the end date of the project you are already working on.

Finally, there can be a darker reason for crunch that you, dear reader, should be aware of so that you do not fall into the crunch time trap. To maximize profit, some companies deliberately schedule crunch time as a normal part of the production cycle, although, in our opinion, we don't see this as a true crunch. At best, it is poor management, and at worst, exploitation. To the greatest extent possible, you want to be aware of this before you start working for one of these less savory companies that deliberately abuse crunch time.

Note, this is *not* to be confused with crunch time as a recognized form of crisis management. Understanding that crunch is an inevitable feature of game production for all the reasons outlined earlier, some producers simply schedule one week of crunch for every five or so weeks of production in an effort to spread the workload and reduce the chances of needing a truly serious crunch at the end.

The last reason for crunch we will talk about here, although there are yet more, is that you screwed up. You completely underestimated a task and now need to work longer to get it done on time. You misunderstood what was needed and did the task incorrectly and have to redo it. Though again, maybe this is not really a true *crunch*; it is just you gaining experience. ☺

20.3 WHEN CRUNCH KICKS IN

Whatever the reason, the time comes during the course of a project—and trust us it will—when senior producers and managers start asking the question: *Is it crunch time?*

If the answer is YES, then they *ask* the staff to start working longer hours or to come in on weekends or holidays.

Depending on the company, *ask* may actually mean *require*.

The severity of the crunch obviously depends on the problem that caused the crunch in the first place. It may be as small as having to work twelve-hour days for two weeks or coming in every Saturday for a month. On the other hand, it could have a major impact on your life and that of your family. Seven-day weeks combined with twelve-hour days for a month or more put pressure on even the most stable families and relationships. So does having to sleep under your desk.

"We had been working 14 hour days 7 days a week for a month. The company did its best, free meals, etc. but I could tell it was getting to me. Trouble was I did not want to let my team down so I kept going, bolstered by the promise that we were only a few weeks from final master. We shipped—I left the company and the industry. I knew if I was placed in that position again I would do it again and, much as I love games and making games, I couldn't take that tiredness and wakefulness and pressure again."

ANONYMOUS BY REQUEST
Ex-Game Programmer

It is during crunch time that your passion for video games will be tested.

A lengthy crunch is obviously bad. Lengthy crunches can lead to burnout. For the most part, companies do not want to burn out their staff, so they try to ease the pressures as best they can. This comes in many forms, but some of the most common are free food, free laundry, free massages, or promises of free movie or theme park tickets when everything returns to normal. It can include things like supplying daycare for families and even supplying precooked dinners for the family when the game maker has to stay late. Then there are blowing-off-steam sessions, either organized or spontaneous, for example, a major Nerf™ gunfight throughout the office, mass snowballing or sledding, team yoga, and whatever else seems to work.

20.4 CRUNCH AND QUALITY OF LIFE

The good news is that the game industry has been burned enough in the past by highly visible crunch time scandals that many of today's studios have come up with more reasonable policies. This has come to be known as the "quality of life" issue. The International Game Developers Association (IGDA) has been leading the way on many of these reforms. Search the association's website (www.igda.org) using the term "quality of life" to locate dozens of reports and articles about this vital issue.

Another bit of good news is that the game industry now no longer hemorrhages experienced game design talent. During the worst of the crunch time years, the average career span of a typical game developer was only about five years. Developers would simply rage quit and take jobs in saner, if more boring, industries. Today, though, the average career span is over ten years and rising. This means that the industry gets to keep its best and brightest longer, and everyone's games are the better for it.

At the end of the day, though, if you work in the game industry long enough, you will undoubtedly come across crunch in some form or another, so just be ready. And, maybe more importantly, make sure your partner and family are ready for it as well.

But always remember:

"Making video games can be a challenging experience. Never forget to also have fun."

SPYROS GIANNOPOULOS
Vampire Hunter & Game Industry Veteran

CHAPTER 21

The Postmortem

T<small>HE PRODUCTION OF THE</small> so-called postmortem has become something of a sacred ritual at many studios, and there is a good reason for that: postmortems work.

21.1 WHAT IS A POSTMORTEM?

The postmortem takes place only after a project has shipped and is basically finished. There is still more work to do: dealing with last-minute issues, the emergency crash bug (very unwelcome), and the all-important task of backing up and archiving everything that was used to make the game (this is called the "closing kit").

The postmortem is the time when the team gets together to review how the project went. It is an essential part of the production process and, when done well, acts to improve the production process for all the games that the studio will make in the future. When done badly it can lead to recriminations and, at worst, team or company breakups.

So how do you achieve the former while avoiding the latter? *Professionalism is key.*

We have talked quite a lot already about the need to be able to accept criticism, and the postmortem is a place when this is especially necessary. No project, team, or individual will get everything right, and the fact that you, and your team, are being criticized should not be taken as a personal affront. It should be seen as an opportunity to improve. The tone of the postmortem (depending on how the project went) can be uncommonly blunt, but just remember, *it isn't personal!* A good postmortem says blunt things about the work, not about the people who did the work.

Another key element to a successful postmortem is the creation and nurturing of a company culture where postmortems are considered the norm and where everyone can have their input without fear of retaliation.

Of course, that is easier said than done, and many companies and teams fail at this. Among the more enlightened teams and studios, however, the postmortem really is the sacred ritual we talked about at the start, one that not only helps things work better next time but also provides, to use that cliché word *closure*, at the conclusion of a project—especially at the conclusion of a tough or dysfunctional project.

A successful postmortem must include the calling out of things that went wrong so they can be rectified, but it must not become a blame session. In essence, the postmortem revolves around answering—in detail—four key questions:

1. What went right?

2. What went wrong?

3. What are the main lessons we learned?

4. What can we do better next time?

21.2 RUNNING A POSTMORTEM

The best way to conduct a good postmortem is to have an "adjudicator" (basically a referee) who was not part of the team. The adjudicator starts by soliciting feedback from the team members in advance of the postmortem meeting. Ideally, this is done in such a way as to assure anonymity for the team members, for example by using survey software like SurveyMonkey.® Team members must be given assurances that their honest comments won't come back to bite them, and those assurances *must* be honored by management.

Having collected all this initial feedback, the adjudicator then collates it all together into something coherent and then organizes a meeting to discuss it. The adjudicator presents the feedback to the team, after which the discussion is off and running. (And there *will* be lots of discussion!)

The adjudicator tries to get everyone present involved in these discussions (even the shy ones), not only because the more people involved, the more solutions are generated, but also so people do not feel as if they are wasting their time. Any negative feedback will start more discussion on how each of the problems can be avoided or at least mitigated.

Once the discussion settles down, the adjudicator tries to obtain agreement from the team members about the most important problems encountered by the team during the project.

Finally, the adjudicator tries to build consensus toward answering the four questions. This really only works if all team members feel they had a fair chance to contribute their input.

From an organizational perspective, it is generally best to start with the negatives and end with the positives so that at the conclusion of the meeting people are thinking about how well they did rather than how badly they did. This also helps reduce recriminations and hard feelings.

Another way to collect feedback is the use of preset questions and online collection of data, again using something like SurveyMonkey, but this time asking for more details. For example, among a list of "what went right" items, team members might be asked to "rank order" them from most to least important.

While these can help people who are shy about giving negative feedback, the phrasing of the questions needs to be done carefully to avoid built-in bias. For example, "Name five things that went wrong" will produce different answers from "Name five things that could have gone better."

The timing of the postmortem meeting is important. Ideally the meeting should take place within a couple of weeks after the project is officially "completed," so things are fresh in people's minds. If it is known that this is not possible, then at the very least the feedback should be collected soon after so that important items are not forgotten.

In reality, the ideal is not what usually happens, and frequently the postmortem gets delayed or put off as staff are shifting to other projects or taking well-deserved time off. You may even not have been on the project to the end, so it is useful, if not essential, that you personally make your own notes as soon as you move off the project. That way, you won't have to struggle to remember things when the postmortem actually comes around.

On long projects team members should be encouraged to keep notes of things that they think are going well or badly so they can be added to the postmortem. Some team members may already be in the habit of maintaining journals or diaries about their day-to-day work on the project. These are valuable sources of information long after the details of the events that led to problems are forgotten.

But most people are generally poor at doing this on their own, so they will probably need to be reminded of it during the course of the project.

A less used way around this, although perfectly viable, is to have postmortems during production. These cover what has happened so far and highlight areas that need to be worked on going forward to keep production on schedule and reduce slippage. These are sometimes called critical stage analyses (CSAs). These are more appropriate for projects having very long timeframes and should be scheduled in so as not to put too much of a dent in production time.

While an important part of a postmortem is highlighting areas that went well and that should be repeated or not changed, it should not be forgotten that the main reason for the postmortem is to improve the production process itself. It is therefore essential that the postmortem include a discussion of possible solutions to any identified issues and agreement or consensus that changes will be made.

This might be a good time, for example, to bring up the matter of getting better tools in place. Maybe tedious, error-prone, manual processes can be automated or streamlined. Maybe the artists need better ways of managing or performing "batch" operations on large sets of art asset files. Maybe feedback from QA isn't getting to the right people fast enough. The postmortem is an excellent time to address those serious shortcomings in the pipeline and workflow processes that lead to error after error. See if these problems can't start getting fixed now, before the next project is under way.

This latter point is another area where many teams and companies fail. Having identified the problems and arrived at a set of possible solutions, management then does little or nothing to implement them or merely pays lip service to them. If this happens consistently, then people come to view the postmortem as a waste of time and won't participate fully. Worse, an opportunity to improve the production process is lost. In many ways, if management has no intention of making—or is unable to make—needed changes, then they are better off not bothering with a postmortem to avoid disillusionment within the team.

LEARN BY DOING

By the way, you can read a number of actual postmortems written by major design teams by simply Googling the term "game postmortem." You can find several delivered as actual talks at GDC in the GDC Vault, some of which don't require a subscription. An immense repository of postmortems (and plenty of other great articles) can be found in the pages of the defunct magazine *Game Developer*, which ceased operations in 2013. All back issues are available for free at www.gdcvault.com/gdmag/. Another source of postmortems, this time from a variety of high-tech companies, can be found at github.com/danluu/postmortems.

Since postmortems are so valuable, and since paying attention to their findings is so important to the industry, some studios choose to make their postmortems available for anyone to read. Try reading a couple, especially if you've never done one before. You'll learn a lot about the internal workings of real-world development teams.

CHAPTER 22

Your First Promotion

Y OUR FIRST PROMOTION MARKS an obvious personal step in your progress within the game industry.

You have been recognized by your peers and your bosses as having gained enough experience and to have shown enough skill that you can be trusted to work with less supervision, on more complex tasks, and possibly also to teach or oversee others.

We say possibly because "promotion" means different things to different companies and individuals. It is attained in different ways and can come with a whole range of different responsibilities and rewards.

22.1 WHAT IS A PROMOTION?

Perhaps we should start by clarifying what is *not* a promotion.

Monetary gain, while obviously nice, and often associated with promotion, is not by itself really a promotion. After all, you may have worked hard for a year at one company and were rewarded with additional compensation. Monetary gain, especially in large companies, may even be a standard factor, something that every employee receives after a certain amount of time has passed.

Similarly, growing respect for your opinions and your work among your peers and employers, again while nice, is not really a mark of promotion. In fact, if you are not gaining this respect, then you are doing something wrong.

So what does promotion really mean to you?

When can you say that you have been promoted?

To the authors at least, the main thing that defines a promotion is a change in your responsibilities or role. Also, while often it does include a change in compensation, this it is not always true, and not receiving more money does not mean that you have not been promoted.

There are also different types of promotion to consider.

"Upward" promotion, within a company, is the kind of promotion nearly everyone automatically thinks of. An obvious upward promotion would be to become a "lead" in your discipline, whatever that is.

"Sideways" (also called "lateral") promotion, while less obvious than upward, is an equally valid form of promotion. An example of a sideways promotion would be if you switched roles, for example, from a character artist to a concept artist, or from a designer to a producer.

Finally, there is promotion *within* the industry. An industry promotion is where you remain at the same level as you are now, or maybe even move down a grade, but you quit your present job to go work for a more respected or more highly regarded company, for example, switching from a company producing budget games to one that produces AAA titles.

Since there is a lot of job hopping (whether intended or thrust upon you) in this industry, a clever and ambitious individual might see strategic job hopping as a way to rise quickly within the industry. But be careful: This sort of job hopping is not looked upon favorably by prospective employers and is often treated as a red flag to possible personality issues. They like to see loyalty to a company.

Of course, some might not see this last one as a promotion, particularly if they went from being a big fish in a small pond to a small fish in a big pond. It is more a matter of personal perspective and what you ultimately want out of life.

Which leads nicely to the next section.

22.2 HOW TO EARN A PROMOTION

The first decision to make is yours. Do you even want to get promoted?

While this may seem like a no-brainer, especially if you have just entered the industry, promotion is not necessarily for everyone. Your view on promotion will also change during the course of your career.

When you are a new entrant in the industry, your first promotion will be, or should be, tucked in the back of your mind as a goal, right behind proving that you can do the job you were hired for. For example, a new software engineer would certainly want to get promoted from junior engineer to senior engineer, a process that might take three to five years.

However, the longer you are in the industry, and the more you learn about the different roles and responsibilities that promotions bring, there may well come a time when you decide that where you are, right now, and what you are doing, right now, are exactly what you want, and you do not want to change that.

For example, what we can say about practically all the terrific programmers we've ever known is that they *love* to code. An engineer might get promoted to lead engineer, for example, even before getting promoted to senior engineer.

When an engineer gets promoted to lead engineer, suddenly she finds she is either doing less coding or working longer hours—because there is less time available to do it. The lead engineer is necessarily concerned with other matters, and it will be the people who report to him or her who get to do all that cool coding stuff. To an engineer, this does not sound like much fun, even if the pay is usually higher. This becomes more and more the case with increasing team size. A lead engineer with only two engineers reporting to her will still likely get to do some programming, while a lead engineer with twenty reports will have her day filled with just wrangling all the complexity of what those twenty engineers are up to.

So yes, the first question is to yourself. Do you want that promotion? Then, assuming you actually want to be promoted, how do you achieve that?

You start by making it clear to the people that make these decisions that you are interested in getting promoted.

This may seem really obvious, but many people miss out on promotion simply because "the boss" is not aware they are looking for it. This is particularly true of sideways promotions.

Note here that "the boss" is not necessarily the CEO or the head of the studio. "The boss" is whoever it is that has the major say in deciding promotions, and "the boss" may be more than one person.

The next steps are going to depend a lot on the company structure and the promotion you are going after.

Promotions within a company may be handled very rigidly, with a formal application process and formal interviews, exactly as if you were applying for a new job. Which of course you are in a sense, because promotion involves a change of responsibility or role.

On the other hand, promotions can be handled in a more relaxed manner. Your boss walks up to you at the coffee machine one day and says, "Hey, I'm going to make you lead on the next project." Congratulations! It looks like you're getting a promotion.

Once you understand the way your company, or the company you want to move to, goes about handling the promotion process, it becomes easier to pursue one.

Rigid system: In some ways, rigid promotional systems are easier to handle because everything is laid out and you can make plans around that. On the other hand, that can also mean there are no shortcuts on the path to promotion.

In a rigid system, the key thing is to make sure you have all the right qualifications. This could include length of service; there is no point in applying for a lead role if you have only been in the industry two months and the company expects a two-year track record before they will consider a promotion.

Once you're "ripe," start keeping an eye on the company bulletin boards to see if a suitable vacancy is coming, and then apply for the position following the system's requirements.

Relaxed system: In a relaxed system, a key element is to talk to people in the company, especially those who are already doing the role you are after. Learn from them what it is that "the boss" looks for. This confers at least two benefits: (1) they can act as mentors to guide you about the steps you need to take and (2) you may be able to gain allies who can support your efforts later on.

A note about mentoring: Cultivating helpful mentors along your career path is a good idea. A mentor is someone who sees potential in you and is willing to help you in your career advancement. Sometimes the mentor is a master at the skill sets you hope to acquire; other times a mentor can be someone who can advise you about other aspects concerning work or even life.

When you seek out mentors, be aware that they are doing you a big favor by agreeing to take you on. Be respectful of their time, and listen—and act on—what they say.

If the company structure allows it, talk to "the boss" personally to find out what he looks for. Ask him what you may need to do to earn a promotion. Acquire those skills if you do not have them.

Whatever the system in place is, even when you have all the skills and the experience needed, there is still no guarantee of promotion.

Do not get disillusioned, and certainly do not become bitter or angry. Stay professional.

Getting a promotion, just like getting your first job, can still be a matter of being in the right place at the right time and of who your competition is.

Handling *not* getting a promotion in a mature manner says a lot about your character, and "the boss" may notice this and be impressed, certainly more so than if you go off on a wild rant about the unfairness of it all.

You can always try again in six months or a year.

CHAPTER 23

The Pink Slip

23.1 THRIVING ON CHAOS

It cannot be said often enough that the game industry is volatile and full of change. This can be rewarding and challenging, and it is what many in the industry really like about it. You are always trying new things, trying to do something bigger and better than before and pushing limits.

However, there is a downside. Failure to keep up with trends, failure to be as competitive and efficient as other companies, failure to meet deadlines and expectations almost inevitably lead to the failure of the company or the team itself.

If this happens, then you, as an employee, are usually among the last to know. You have your head down and are working hard on your project. Then, out of the blue, a company meeting is called, the axe falls, and you are suddenly out of a job.

This often means you are handed a package containing paperwork outlining any compensation you may be getting, and then you are asked to leave the building...right now. You can usually retrieve your personal effects that you may need right then, coat, lunch box, and so forth, but you are often escorted to and from your desk to make sure you don't attempt anything shady. You will then likely be asked to arrange to come back at a specific time to collect everything else.

Tales of walking into the office, thinking everything is great, and being handed a box to put your stuff in, before turning around and leaving, clutching your possessions and dismissal papers, are not uncommon. Being escorted to your desk and back to make sure you do not sabotage work or take company property is also common.

TALES OF WOE

Here are two true tales of woe from Adrian; only the names have been changed to protect the innocent.

Tale #1: I had been in the office for several hours as I always got in early when I started to notice that the usual crowd were not all there. Then a manager came in with a box and said, "Put your stuff in there and we will escort you from the building, you have been let go."

Tale #2: I arrived in the office and everyone looked sad. When I asked what happened, they said they had been told yesterday that the entire company was closing down. This was a blow to me as I had been out of the office the previous day. I had been in my new apartment as my furniture was being delivered by the moving firm—I had just moved across the country to start the new job.

Yes, it can be that brutal and that fast.

Sometimes it is not that brutal. For example, you are called in for an "all hands" meeting where you and your colleagues are told that you will all be let go at the end of the project in four weeks' time. At least you have a cushion of time to get ready for the inevitable. That month will go by all too quickly.

Either way, the net result is the same: your happy, comfortable life just came crashing down.

23.2 WHEN THE AXE FALLS

It could be a downsizing, where just a team or several individuals are let go, or it could be a complete studio shutdown where everyone goes. Neither makes you feel any better or keeps you from wondering if there was anything you could have done to prevent it.

Sometimes there are warning signs: sales for the most recently shipped game fell short of expectations; no new projects are appearing on the slate; people who left the company are not being replaced.

However, businesses do not like to advertise their potential failure, as it can make it harder to acquire the new clients and new investors they need to stave off the company's collapse. This is even more so for publicly owned companies, where any concern among shareholders could lead to a damaging sell-off of the company's stock.

So apart from keeping an eye out for potential problems with the well-being of the company, you could jump to another job before the crash happens. Just hope you have not jumped out of the frying pan into the fire as your new employer collapses.

What can you do to mitigate the disaster?

First, be prepared for it to happen. So now, even if it comes as a surprise, it does not come as a disastrous shock.

KEEP YOUR RÉSUMÉ FRESH

Keep your résumé up to date at all times. This is easier said than done as it is natural to get lazy about it, but it is much easier to do it every three or four months than suddenly find yourself having to remember what you did for the last three years. We've been guilty of this many times ourselves, although we have gotten better at it over the years. Trust us on this!

Keep in touch with all your friends in the industry wherever they end up; networking is very often the key to finding another position.

And there is always the Internet.

Second, apart from letting your network know that you are available, do nothing about applying for a new job for at least a week. This may sound crazy, but it is good advice. It was the same advice that was given to me (Adrian) once when I was let go. It was subsequently the same advice I gave to everyone I had to let go when I was a manager.

Why?

In the shock of unemployment, it is easy to panic and rush into grabbing anything that comes along. However, you need to be as careful about choosing your next employer as you were about choosing the one you're leaving. You should take the time to analyze what it is you want to do, where you want to do it, and what companies you would like to work for. Your choices should have improved over your first experience of trying to get a job because you now have additional experience.

Or maybe that experience has led you to think that you want to try something a bit different this time, maybe assistant producer instead of designer. You may even come to the conclusion that the game industry itself is not for you after all, or you have had your fill of it, and you want to change careers. It is essential in any of these cases that you spend some quiet time thinking about your future.*

Third, if you have a partner, hopefully you shared with that person the possibility that your job was not a permanent fixture; otherwise you may have issues beyond just being out of a job. Assuming your partner is supportive in your hour of need, this is a great time to

---

* If you were not careful about the last company you went to work for, perhaps read Chapters 12 and 15 for some advice so that you can pick a better one next time.

discuss all your employment options with him or her. This might include the need to move to another city, or to another state, or maybe even to another country! Your partner may have some opinion about this. ☺

If you think this is a bleak picture of employment in the game industry, it is supposed to be.

While it is certainly true that many people stay for years at the same company, it is equally true that a large number of people do not. From personal experience of both having to let people go and of having been let go, hoping for the best and preparing for the worst is definitely the way to go.

Finally, if you find yourself unemployed, you need to consider that it could take a while to find another job. While you search, be prepared to take on part-time, freelance, or temporary work, even outside the industry, because, unless you are independently wealthy, or your partner is, you still need to pay the rent and bills.

23.3 DEALING WITH UNEMPLOYMENT

Unless you are very lucky or extremely talented, sooner or later you will need to deal with being unemployed, even if it is only after you first leave college.

Here are some tips on making unemployment easier to cope with.

- It is *always* worst the first time.

- You will feel a sense of betrayal, rejection, and personal failure, but, unless you have truly screwed up, then it is probably not your fault. Just bite the bullet and accept it.

- Don't panic! Stop, think, plan.

- Don't let debt build up. If it becomes necessary, talk to the bank, the credit card companies, your landlord, and other creditors about short-term solutions.

WHY ME?

One of the most often asked questions when you tell someone she's out of work is

Why me?

Interestingly, it is also the most frequently question you ask yourself when *you* have been let go.

The Disheartening Truth

Unless the entire company or department closed down, when there was probably little you could have done about it, the disheartening answer is often that you were let go simply because they preferred to keep someone else instead.

Of course, you will never be told that. You will also not be told that many companies prerank their employees on a cut-back list so if the order comes down to reduce staff, they don't have to think about it; they simply count off the numbers needed from the list.

A Heartening Thought

The heartening thought is that the reason they preferred to keep someone else may have nothing to do with your abilities, although obviously it could.

It may have more to do with what projects are coming down the pipeline and what skills they will need for those. Possibly someone else happens to have more of those skills or experience than you do. That isn't your fault, as you can't be skilled and experienced at everything. You just happened to run into a bad mismatch.

It may be that they have been given a salary cap to meet and you were getting paid more than they could afford, even if they wanted to keep you.

It could even be a change in company direction from one type of genre to another or one platform to another, and they need different talents and skills.

Don't Agonize Too Long

Regardless of the WHY, one absolute truth is that agonizing about *why it was you* will not help you in any way to move forward.

Just try to get over the hand wringing and the blaming and the recrimination within a few days, as soon as you can, and move on to looking for the next job.

23.4 FINDING A JOB IS ITSELF A FULL-TIME JOB

Have a routine for searching job vacancies and stick to it. It is very easy to drift into lethargy. Put off the temptations to play your favorite MMORPG all day every day and playing through that stack of unplayed games you have lying around until *after* you have done your job searches and networking.

REACH OUT AND TOUCH SOMEONE

Our connected world has made it easier than ever to reach out and find employment opportunities. Here are just a few things you might investigate:

- Your personal network of friends and acquaintances
- The "trade" websites like Gamasutra.com and GamesIndustry.biz
- Online job-search websites like Monster.com, Glassdoor.com, and Indeed.com, and the many others besides these
- The social media you use, such as Facebook and, especially, LinkedIn.com
- Trade conferences like the Game Developer Conference (GDC) and many others like E3, PAX, ComicCon, and BlizCom
- Your local IGDA chapter meetings, if you have one, if only for the networking

Generally speaking, the conference route is the costliest way to go, and there may not be one when you need it, but the networking opportunities are unparalleled.

Expect to be unemployed for at least a few weeks. Even if you apply straightaway, it takes time for companies to go over your application and make a decision.

Try not to get disheartened if the first few jobs you apply for do not work out. Just keep searching and applying.

Depending on your previous situation, you might be able to collect unemployment for some fixed period of time. If so, great; this will make staying on top of your living expenses easier. But impose some fiscal discipline on yourself: cut expenses and frivolities to the bone while you weather the storm. This may mean no more lattés for a while.

Finally, if you are unemployed for an extended period of time and find that you really can't pay the bills, talk to the people you owe and try to arrange a temporary deal rather than letting it all slide. Maintaining your credit rating is important, too.

CHAPTER 24

Going Off the Rails

W<small>E TOUCHED ON GOING</small> off the rails a bit in Chapter 6. There, our concern was primarily with things that we've often seen go wrong in student teams. The biggest problems we observed there were lack of clarity, overscoping, project hogs, and procrastination. In this chapter, we talk more about the ways a project at an actual game studio, involving budgets and careers, might go off the rails and what can be done about it.

Certainly, some of the problems that often plague student teams might still be problems on a team of professionals, but by now we ought to expect that they have much less impact.

For example, by now most professionals have been burned often enough by overscoping that they routinely fear the creep. Some professionals who were project hogs early in their careers have gotten over it, whether through too many bouts of sheer overwork or by coming to the realization that this is no way to behave on a team. Procrastination, for most professionals anyway, is something they've worked through by developing whatever tricks and stratagems work for them to get them moving.

But lack of clarity is one thing we can say more about here, plus a couple of others that are much more likely to be problems in a commercial setting than on a student team.

24.1 DIAGNOSING THE PROBLEMS

When a project goes seriously off the rails, desperate measures are called for. But *ready… fire…aim* is no way to go about fixing a problem. This is why management charges the development team with preparing risk assessments and containment plans early on. Management needs to accurately diagnose the true causes of problems. Here are some more of them, besides the somewhat less likely problems with overscoping, the project hog, and procrastination noted earlier.

24.1.1 Lack of Clarity…Again

As the project wears on, perhaps your sense that there is something going awry is getting stronger and stronger. You feel increasingly that you're not really sure what you are supposed to be working on from one day to the next. Or you're working on one thing, and then suddenly the producer switches you over to something unrelated, and this is happening way too often.

This all might be due to a critical lack of clarity that was allowed to slip through from all the way back during the preproduction phase. Do you recall our example of a badly written GDD for the game of checkers? Or how a designer asked for a horse and got a camel and unicorn instead? Being even a little ambiguous in a design spec can lead to problems.

What can you do if you find yourself in this situation? Well, if things were allowed to fester to where they get to this point, the damage has already been done. More senior people will need to intervene and come up with a crisis resolution plan that lets the team salvage as much of the already finished work as possible while making sure the rest of the development stays much more focused, taking steps that are beyond the scope of this book. But, regrettably, the game may never reach the excellence of the original vision.

24.1.2 Hidden Agendas

Hidden agendas are another dark-side problem you may run into. Sometimes there will be someone on your team who has something else in mind besides the health and welfare of the team and the game the team is working on.

Hidden agendas can be anything: trying to get someone else on the team in trouble or fired, trying to make sure the game fails, getting ready to bail out of the project and go work somewhere else, or anything else a devious mind can devise. The problem is especially serious if the person with the hidden agenda is the game's producer or, worse, someone in management the producer reports to.

24.1.3 Micromanagement

A micromanager is not the kind of boss you want to have. A micromanager is someone who is constantly looking over your shoulder (even if only metaphorically), constantly monitoring your work, and constantly making helpful "suggestions."

There is not a lot you can do about this except to suffer through it. If the situation becomes intolerable, you may need to have another one of those uncomfortable, delicate meetings with your boss, wherein you try to come up with a new arrangement. But we caution you that this is unlikely to be successful and may be a great way to lose your job. Most managers hate to acknowledge that their management style sucks.

Just bear with it and make it a point never to work with that person ever again if you can help it.

There are several ways micromanagers can cause a project to derail: (1) they become a bottleneck to productivity because everything needs to go through them for approval; (2) they tend to make more damaging errors because they are so buried in work; (3) they can seriously demotivate a team, resulting in lower productivity.

24.1.4 Serving Two Masters

The Bible warns about this; no man can serve two masters, and this is sound advice. If you find yourself on a project where you have to report to two different people, you may find yourself with torn loyalties as you strive to keep both of them happy. It's worse when they are pulling you in different directions.

This is well understood in management circles—or should be—so most places have a clear "organizational chart" that shows who reports to whom. It is hierarchical, and there shouldn't be any places on the chart where one person reports to more than one boss.

Note that this isn't quite the same situation as a game developer who is finishing up one game while ramping up to work on a new game. Here, the two domains are separate and the developer is unlikely to be put in this sort of situation, except for the personal battle of how to divide up the hours in the workday.

But a project that has crossed lines of communication like the one just described is setting itself up for problems. Sooner or later, the conflicts inherent with a team member trying to satisfy two bosses will erupt and expose the fracture lines in the team.

24.1.5 Unexpected External Forces

Related to the serving-two-masters problem is another insidious problem that producers in particular need to be aware of. We mentioned earlier that the producer is the "front-facing" person on the team, the person who handles all outside communications and passes them along, as necessary, to and from the team.

A problem arises when some outside party establishes a line of communication with someone on the team that bypasses the producer. The producer is not "in the loop." This may be perfectly innocent or may have started with the best of intensions, for example, if an artist is communicating with someone in Marketing, which prompts the artist to veer away from the vision for the project by including or changing elements the marketer wants to see. If these communications do not also pass through the producer, so that they can be properly discussed as a formal request from Marketing, a lot of completed work may have to be scrapped or altered, negatively affecting the schedule.

It is hard to blame the artist here since he or she is simply trying to be helpful and is also in a junior position relative to the person from Marketing. Again, this sort of problem can unfold despite the parties having innocent intentions.

24.1.6 Unwelcome External Forces

One easy way to derail a project is simply for upper management or the client to order severe, abrupt, and unexpected changes to the schedule or budget, including such things as a budget cut, sudden layoffs of team members, or significantly moving up the scheduled release date.

Related to this would be the sudden loss of a key team member as a result of death or disability or from that member suddenly jumping ship or leaving the studio over "creative differences." These sorts of things can have a profoundly demoralizing effect on any team.

24.2 GETTING BACK ON THE RAILS

The key here is, of course, obvious, and that is for the producer and the management layer above the producer to always be acutely aware of the state of the project. Like a cancer, the earlier a problem can be detected, the earlier corrective measures can be put in place. Of course, some situations will be entirely unanticipated.

A project that is beginning to go off the rails usually reveals telltale signs of it early on. This is one reason burn-down charts are so handy. It is also why producers who can bring stability back to a project while remaining cool under fire are so valuable.

Even that may not be enough to put things right, but that issue is way beyond the scope of this book (and we don't want to overscope).

CHAPTER 25

A Continuing History of Change

25.1 EXPECT CHANGE... FOREVER

This chapter is about where we've come from and are going to in the world of PCs and game consoles and how that impacts work in the industry. If this piques your interest, then everything you could possibly want to know about the history of computers, or video games, or the Internet can be found all over the Internet itself.

The main takeaway here is to emphasize just how dramatic and rapid these developments have been and how there is no sign that this is going to stop anytime soon. So here we go.

25.2 THE EARLIEST PERSONAL COMPUTERS

The world of PCs really got under way in the mid-1970s with the introduction of the Apple II in 1977. But before the Apple II there were interesting hobbyist systems like the Altair, the North Star, and the Sphere.

These were all made possible by the introduction of the microprocessor chip, led primarily by two companies: Intel (the 8080, and all the Intel chips since then) and Motorola (the 6502, the 6800, and the 68000). There were a handful of other companies in the mix, but these were the main two. Intel will forever be associated with the IBM style of PCs running Microsoft's operating systems. Motorola was the predominant maker of chips for the Apple machines, and Apple went over to Intel only in 2006, with a stop along the way with their so-called custom PowerPC chip.

Today, it's all Intel or its archrival clone maker, AMD, for the PC. In the mobile space, Intel's other archrival, ARM, has been eating their lunch. The situation is less clear-cut for consoles: The Xbox One remains with Intel, the PlayStation 4 uses a custom CPU/GPU chip developed jointly by AMD and Sony, the Wii-U uses the "Espresso" chip developed by IBM and AMD, and the Nintendo Switch uses a chip called the Tegra 210, which itself is made up of ARM cores.

25.3 STORAGE DEVICES

In the earliest days of the PC revolution, a standard delivery system for games was ordinary audio cassette tapes. The cassette reader wasn't even part of the PC. You loaded the game by playing the cassette on an ordinary portable cassette player, feeding the audio output signal into a jack on the back of your computer. Depending on the size of the game, this could easily take ten or twenty minutes to load. Worse, if the load failed for any reason (and it often did), you had to try again. And if you managed to stretch the tape or warp the cassette shell, it was *game over, man*.

Things got better after 1977 when the 5.25″ floppy disk was introduced. The Apple II had it, but other cheaper machines like the Commodore Vic-20 still relied on cassette tapes.

You could get a drive for these floppies for your Apple II, and Commodore's next computer, the Commodore 64, could use 5.25″ floppies as well. The IBM PC, also introduced in 1981, had one or two floppy drives built in.

Floppies were better in every way: they were faster, somewhat more durable, and they could hold more data, about 100 kilobytes (Kb) (depending on a thing called "sectoring"). That's kilo, with a K, a mere thousand bytes (well, 1024 bytes if you want to get technical about it). This was a golden age for small, independent game publishers. You could literally run your studio from your kitchen table. In fact, many of the great game studios of that era, like Sierra and Broderbund, got started in exactly that way.

So all you needed to ship a game back then was one or a few floppies, pretty labels to put on them, some photocopied rules held together with a staple, and a zipper-locked bag to put them in. Then you punched a hole at the top so it could be hung by a peg. Little neighborhood computer stores were springing up all over the country, and they displayed their software offerings by hanging them on pegs.

Those days are long gone.

The 3.5″ floppy came along in 1982, and it was also a game changer. With a rigid casing and sliding protective metal cover, it was smaller and more reliable—and could store a lot more—than the 5.25″ floppy. The original Apple Macintosh, released in 1984, used this format. The 3.5″ floppy could store 720 Kb at first, later doubling to 1.44 Mb. One of us still has his original distribution of DOOM on three 3.5″ floppies. Yes, the original DOOM, one of the most important video games ever, fit in under 5 Mb of storage. (The recently reissued version of DOOM is much larger.)

Meanwhile, the first hard drive for the PC arrived in 1980. It could store 5 Mb (that's an M, a million bytes). It cost a mere $1500 in 1980's money. It was also rather fragile. But it arrived just in time for the mighty IBM PC the following year. Back then, hard drives were a luxury item for the poor computer hobbyist.

Prices have been quickly dropping ever since, and today we can buy a couple of terabytes (that's a T, a trillion bytes), all for less than $100. Today's drives are also far faster and more reliable. And while solid-state drives (SSDs) are a lot more expensive, they are even more reliable (no moving parts) and blindingly fast (again, no moving parts).

So why do we need so much storage? Images, movies, music, and, of course, games. People have also been known to store their work on them as well.

Game consoles developed more slowly, adding hard drives relatively late. For reasons of cost and mass-marketing considerations, these drives were at the low end of the storage capacity available to PC users. Not so long ago, the original Microsoft Xbox came with only a 40- or 80-gigabyte (Gb) drive, your choice, as compared to 250- or even 500-Gb drives available then for PCs.

Console manufacturers were slow to incorporate hard drives for several reasons, cost and reliability being two of them, but the main reason was to slow down piracy. Another way to slow down piracy were cartridges, a popular alternative, especially for Nintendo. Back then it was common for an entire game to have to fit into just 8 Kb of cartridge space, although later cartridges could hold more.

(The earliest home consoles, the Magnavox™ Odyssey® and the Atari™ Tele-Games®, didn't even have cartridges; the game logic was actually wired into the hardware. The microprocessor hadn't hit the market yet!)

The game cartridge was a plastic shell surrounding a little printed circuit board, with a ribbon of connector strips along one edge and a read-only memory (ROM) chip. Cartridges were relatively cheap to make but difficult to pirate. Nintendo, which has always run a tight ship, was the last console manufacturer to give this up.

The CD-ROM, another game changer, made its appearance in 1982. Originally used as a way to release record albums, its use as a storage medium for computers quickly followed.

All of a sudden, storage capacity went from a measly 1.44 Mb on a floppy to about 700 Mb on a CD. There was so much storage available that game developers could offer far more content than could fit in the machine's RAM, and so they devised ways of dynamically loading in levels on demand, allowing for far larger games.

The CD-ROM was later followed by the DVD (storing 4.7 Gb or more, released in 1995) and Blu-ray (storing 25 Gb, released in 2006). Computers and consoles started to include CD-ROM drives, and, despite the increase in the size of the games, they loaded faster and more reliably.

Today you can download games wirelessly from the cloud and play games on your mobile device—which has way more computing power than those early game machines. In fact, a relatively unimpressive mobile device has more processing power than the ancient room-sized mainframe computers.*

25.4 THE SOFTWARE

The massive increases in storage size were quickly gobbled up by game publishers, who could now pack hundreds of hours of game play onto a single disk. By 2009, slightly over twenty years after the Apple II, just a single texture, a face or a leather jacket, on a character model could take 256 Kb. RAM was now bigger than the entire hard drive of the earlier machines, and game sizes were measured in megabytes or gigabytes, not kilobytes.

And just eight years after that, in 2017, we think of system memory in terms of gigabytes and hard drive memory in terms of terabytes. We've come a long way; in fact, boosting memory capacities on the order of a million-fold. We can't think of any other product category (certainly not cars or agriculture or financial advising) that can make that claim.

It's also worth mentioning that game publishers, responding to the demands of the very demanding gamer audience, have always been quick to seize upon every new technological advance. In a very real way, one of the premier drivers of this technological explosion can be credited to (or blamed on) the insatiable demands of the video gaming audience.

These examples of the dizzying pace of advances in computer hardware are the kinds of things that the hard-working people in the game industry have had to adapt to. While it is true that the rate at which hardware speeds have been increasing has itself been slowing in recent years, it shows no signs of abating.

25.5 THE CHANGING MARKET

The market for video games has certainly changed. So have the people who play them.

In 1989, while there were exceptions, the audience was almost exclusively males between 15 and 25.

By 2009, the age range had broadened to 8 to 80, and while a majority, especially of hardcore gamers, were still male, about 40% of people playing games were female.

By 2017 it is now nearly 50/50 and, according to some reports, there are more female players than male.

The way people play games has changed, too.

In the early days of home computers, games were single player, or occasionally two players taking turns via "hot seat" mechanics. Some of the early game-specific consoles did allow for multiplayer controls using split screens or were turn-based action games like tennis.

Players therefore tended to play on their own, and social interaction was limited. This led to the popular stereotype of the antisocial gamer, playing in his (because players were usually male) parents' basement.

---

* Or if you want to get really scary, today's average small car has more computing power than the entire Apollo lunar lander and orbiter.

Nowadays, thanks to the Internet and Wi-Fi, a large majority of console and PC games support simultaneous actions from multiple players. Nowadays, whether it is cooperative or competitive, social interaction is a major component of game play. This should not be surprising; we've been playing board games and sports that way for thousands of years.

While they tend to follow a more regular pattern of improved development and release to market, game-specific consoles have also followed a path similar to that of computers. One thing the console manufacturers figured out very early on (beginning with the very first console, the Magnavox Odyssey) was that people did want to play with others and so provided for two-player, and later four-player, controls.

All of the changes we have been discussing have affected the way games are made, the content they include, and, perhaps most important of all, the expectations of the players themselves.

Gone are the days when the top-selling games could drive trends in what games were really about and the audience would lap it up. Players today have many more options to choose from. Companies and their employees, especially designers, marketing, and sales, must keep abreast of the latest trends or their games will not sell well.

Gone are the days of trying to save that elusive byte, at least for PCs. Programmers have to constantly learn new coding methods, adapt to ever-changing hardware and software environments, find more efficient ways to include better art, better sound, better AI. It is still important even now to worry about every byte and every CPU clock cycle, but these concerns have receded relative to having great game play, great graphics, and great characters and story.

Gone are the days when there were only four colors on screen. Artists have to produce photorealistic graphics, movie-quality cut scenes, and animations.

Gone also are the days when the only sounds you could get were "beep" or "ding." Sound engineers and musicians now produce complete ambient worlds of sound with accompanying orchestra-sized scores.

All this has firmly and forever established the video game as an entertainment medium par excellence. The video game industry now outperforms the U.S. domestic box office for movies and has become an international success, rivaling film and television everywhere on Earth.

25.6 KEEP YOUR SKILLS SHARP

With a constantly changing work environment and market, the most important thing for you is to keep your skills sharp. This is especially true if you are an engineer. Your skills can go from sharp to dull in a matter of months.

What to do? You already know the answer. Read the trade magazines and websites. Try to get to the GDC every once in a while. Visit the massive library of videos available on the GDC Vault. Make sure you learn as much as possible about the tools you use daily.

This is scarcely less important for artists, designers, writers, and the sound and music folk, although it doesn't get quite as insane as it does for programmers. The tools you use are constantly improving, and new features and capabilities are always appearing.

And for artists, mastering Maya is no longer enough; there is a constant parade of new software tools for artists and designers that raises the bar for what is possible.

CHAPTER 26

Going It Alone

Tʜɪs ᴄʜᴀᴘᴛᴇʀ ɪs ᴀʟʟ about leaving the safety and comfort of a steady (?) job and going it alone. Let us state right up front that this path is not for everyone.

26.1 ARE YOU AN ENTREPRENEUR? DO YOU WANT TO BE?

You may already know this about yourself, that you're a born entrepreneur. Perhaps you had a lemonade stand, made money trading *Magic: The Gathering* cards during recess, or did deals at the skate park. Perhaps you made money the more modern way, with a successful YouTube channel or by generating Bitcoins.

To be sure there are "born" entrepreneurs, but most people who go into business for themselves are "made" entrepreneurs.

Was it your intention all along to start your own studio? There have been wildly successful game studios started by people who just graduated college, and nothing says you can't do that, too. Be aware, however, this is super tough and you need exceptional skills, stamina, perseverance, and luck to make it happen. You could even start a studio outside of high school, and that has happened, too. Do a search for "Richard Garriott," who, along with this brother, started Origin™, the makers of the classic *Ultima*® series.

Earlier we advocated taking a job in the industry and "learning on someone else's dime." We still think this is sound advice—for most people. But if you have the burning passion to go your own way much earlier than that, don't let us rain on your parade.

However, and whenever it happens, at some time or other in your career, you are almost bound to wonder if you can "go it alone."

It may be right at the start of your career when, full of enthusiasm, full of bright new ideas that will wow the game industry, you know the only way to go is to set out on your own.

It may be later when, having gotten a feel for the industry, having gotten some published games under your belt, feeling that, with the benefit of experience, you can now do things better or in a different way from the industry around you.

It may be forced on you when the company you work for goes down, and you find yourself without a job, but, owing to family or other personal reasons, you do not want to move to a new location.

Whatever the reason for going it alone, you will face a swath of hurdles: personal, industry-specific, and maybe the hardest to overcome, financial.

Before looking at these in more detail, now is probably a good time to say that there are two ways to go it alone:

- Solo freelancing

- Startup company

Each faces similar and slightly different problems, I (Adrian) have done both; and they are BOTH HARD!

26.2 SOLO FREELANCING

Note we are not talking about getting a short-term contract working within a company for the length of a project here; we're talking about actually working from home or from your own office or studio.

This is where you are literally going it alone. There is only you!

The most important thing you MUST have if going this route is self-discipline.

Even more important than finances? Yes, although they come in a very close second.

If you are not able to get up in the morning and start work and, more importantly, stay working for the entire day, you will fail. Meeting deadlines and turning out quality work is just as vital, maybe more vital, when you are the boss of yourself as when there is someone looking over your shoulder.

As we said earlier, this route is most definitely not for everyone, but if you have the character for it and can make it work, there are advantages to being your own boss, with no one else to tell you how and when to do things.

The main thing to master is time management.

As long as you meet your deadlines, you can work what hours you want and what days you want. You do not need to worry about taking time off from work to meet contractors or the cable guy. Taking the kids to school or worrying about "snow days" are not issues.

For me personally one of the great bonuses is having a commute that is not affected by weather or traffic conditions, that costs nothing in gas or wear and tear on the car, and that takes only two minutes.

I (Adrian) walk downstairs, sit at my desk, and I am at work. When I walk upstairs, I am home.

SEPARATING HOME AND WORK

This is also a good illustration of how to maintain self-discipline and manage one's time. At the desk I (Adrian) am working, away from the desk I am not working.

Drawing a sharp line of demarcation between "home" and "work," and not allowing yourself to violate it, is key.

The main disadvantage is not having a team around you that you can bounce ideas off and socialize with.

This is potentially huge, and you may need to put in place other ways to satisfy these social needs.

A lack of criticism affects your judgment about what is a good or bad idea.

A lack of general chatter affects your overall personal psyche.

Of course, just because you are your own boss does not mean you are not answerable to someone. You will have a client, and, unless you are a millionaire and this is just a hobby for you, they will hold the purse strings, so you better listen to what they want.

This is true even if you intend to publish your work yourself. In this case, your client is your target audience, so you better deliver what they want; otherwise your game will not sell enough to make enough profit to live on.

Which brings us to the next most important element of freelancing: How are you going to pay your rent, utility bills, and food bills while you're working on your blockbuster?

This will partly depend on your own financial situation. If you are straight out of college and have college loans, for example, then you are probably not going to be able to finance yourself. You are going to have to convince someone to pay you.

If you have been working for a while, you might have built up enough savings to keep you going for a few months, maybe even a year. In that case, your initial financial problems are not so pressing, but you better make sure that your business plan and delivery dates do not extend beyond your savings, otherwise it will all come crashing down when the money runs out. This is about as common a cause of small business failure as anything.

So let us assume that you are not self-sufficient financially and actually need some income to survive from day to day.

Here are several routes you can try:

- Contract work

- Advance on royalties

- Loan

- Crowd funding

26.2.1 Contract Work

This is the most straightforward and common way for freelancers to make a living.

You reach an agreement with a third party to complete a specific project, by a specific date, and, assuming you complete this task, they pay you an agreed amount of money. If it is a long project, there may be interim deadlines at which you receive partial payments, assuming you stay on schedule along the way.

Alright, so at the start of this section we said this was not about getting a short-term contract and working in the client's office. But sometimes, just so you can keep paying your bills, you may have to sacrifice some of your principles on this point.

While video conferencing makes it much easier to work outside of an office, the contract may specifically require you to work at the client's office a few days a week, or at least be in the office at certain times. It will almost certainly include the requirement to be in fairly constant contact.

Getting a contract in the first place will depend on a number of factors:

1. Your experience and reputation

2. Your Area of Specialization

3. Your ability to sell yourself

4. The size of the project

5. How much you are going to charge

6. Current demand for your particular skills

1. Experience and Reputation

There is just no way around this.

The more experienced you are, the greater your reputation is, the easier it is to land contracts.

The longer you have worked in the industry, the more contacts you will have, and the more likely you are to hear about opportunities. This is where networking really counts.

2. Your Area of Specialization

Programmers are always in short supply, so in general it is easier for them to pick up contracts.

Sound and music is very often contracted out, so you may have an advantage in that it is considered the norm to operate like this. But you will probably need to have amassed a solid track record of successful projects, and people need to know that your unique talents are on the market. This will require a fair amount of hustling. Making it in the music business, if anything, may be even harder than making it in the game industry. At least the game industry has a constant need for new soundtracks and new SFX.

Artists, this is tricky, because it depends on the type of work you are prepared to do. There are usually opportunities for artists, but not necessarily in the game field. This is where you may need to be practical and gain experience and a reputation outside games while still looking for that opportunity within games.

Designers, it is tough, especially if you are just starting out. Most design work is done in-house, and there are few outsourced opportunities.

The main exception is narrative design, where you may be able to land a contract to write a script or a background story. Writers, like sound and music people, are often contracted out, especially by smaller companies who cannot maintain a permanent in-house writer.

3. Selling Yourself

It does not matter how experienced or brilliant you are, a big part of success in gaining contract work is getting out there, finding it, then convincing someone that you are the right person. This may also include convincing someone that a contractor makes sense rather than a full-time hire.

4. Project Size

This is an odd one. On the surface, opportunities for short-term contracts may appear easier to obtain on small projects. The client does not want to commit to hiring a full-time employee for something that will only last a few months. However, the client might simply look at rescheduling within their current workforce to cover it. Large projects, on the other hand, need more staff, and there just may not be enough qualified people around, so the client is forced to look for contractors. Bottom line, it is going to depend on what clients are looking for.

5. Your Fees

As we say in other parts of this book, making games is a business, and businesses must make a profit, or they go out of business.

This applies both to your prospective client, who will have done a detailed P&L and decided on their budget, and to yourself. The client will generally not pay you more than they have planned on; you must not charge less than you can live on.

Do your own P&L <u>for each contract</u> you pursue. It is really important to do this on a contract-by-contract basis. Travel, software, hardware, and peripheral equipment you need to buy or rent in order to fulfill a particular contract will be different from one project to the next.

The temptation, especially when you are starting out, is to grab a contract for whatever you can get. After all, some income is better than none right? Not necessarily!

You have no idea whether a better contract is just around the corner.

You have no idea how desperate the client is. They may say no initially but come back later with a different offer.

You have no idea about the budgets of your competitors, who may be able to undercut you because their money outflow is less, and they can still make a profit at a price you can't.

There is also the question of reputation. If you sell yourself short, it will be harder, if not impossible, to come back for a follow-on project and ask for a significantly larger amount of money.

All that said, if the wolf is really at your door and you desperately need money, going low may be a temporary solution. Emphasis on "temporary." At this juncture, you should really start looking at whether freelancing is for you, or even if the game industry is for you.

You cannot sell yourself short forever.

6. Current Demand

Demand is going to vary both with your location and with the time of year.

If you are living/working in a gaming hub, where several game companies are doing business, then your opportunities will generally be greater because there is more work.

On the other hand, there will also be more competition for those jobs.

If you don't live in a gaming hub, all is not lost. Gaming hubs tend to be in major cities where living expenses are higher. If you are working from home or a small office in a less urban location, then your expenses, apart from travel, will be less and you can charge less, making you more attractive.

While games are not as tied to Christmas releases as they used to be, it is still true that the vast majority of games have ship date deadlines that come in the fall. December to February are quiet months when it comes to new projects. Having the discipline to put aside some of the money you make to cover the lean periods is simple common sense.

During these months, your bills will remain about the same, so you may want to consider looking outside the industry for short-term work just to bring in some income.

Or maybe you managed to do your P&L well and you earned enough throughout the year to take a well-deserved vacation. Of course, being a solo freelancer means any vacation you take comes directly from your profits, but trust us, freelancers need vacations too.

26.2.2 Advance on Royalties

This is a sweet spot if you can get it. If gaining a contract is tough, gaining an advance on royalties is even tougher.

It has all of the problems associated with gaining contract work, and your reputation or contacts are often key. You have to convince a publisher that your game fits into their publishing schedule and is going to be good enough to ensure they will recoup what they are going to advance you. In addition, you expect to continue receiving money if the game sells well.

The big win is that you are being paid up front for <u>your own work</u> that is not completed yet.

We say "not completed" because you must have done some of the work already; otherwise you would have nothing to use to convince the publishers to give you the advance. You may want to build a marketing-oriented prototype or a "vertical slice" to secure the deal.

An advance on royalties is almost exclusively going to be where you provide the entire game, the entire design for a game, or the entire script or story for a game.

Yep, for once designers get a break here because they can sell a package that is complete within one discipline.

Providing an entire game when there is only one of you, even with all the available tools and middleware now available, is a real challenge because very few individuals are a great programmer, a great artist, and a great designer all wrapped up into one.

There is also the issue of delivery times. If you are doing all the work, it is just going to take three times longer to do than if there were three of you (programmer, artist, designer).

If you get a large enough advance, or you have some free cash of your own, you could consider hiring a contractor to cover the bits you can't do yourself, but remember that what you pay them comes out of your money. Also, you will be responsible for ensuring their work is on time and to the standards your publisher wants. This doesn't go quite as far as forming a company but blurs the edges a bit about whether this is solo freelancing.

26.2.3 Loan

We are not talking about borrowing money from friends and relatives or living off your parents. We mean borrowing enough money to live on for at least six months, plus any expenses you incur during production.

If you have just finished college, then this is going to be the toughest route. You probably already have debt in the form of college loans and maybe credit cards as well. You really should consider whether the risk of long-term damage to your creditworthiness is worth taking.

Banks and similar financial institutions are not known for their generosity when it comes to giving out money without good collateral. The people who make that decision are also not likely to be interested in your game.

You are going to need an excellent business plan, showing exactly how you intend to pay them back. Actually, scratch that. What you want to do, if you want to take entrepreneurship seriously, is adopt more modern ways of going about it. The business plan, long the traditional way of setting up an operation, has given way to a better system, the Business Model Canvas. We include two significant books about entrepreneurship in the appendix.

Even with all that, however, the bank may be just antiquated enough to want a business plan, and you will have no choice but to burn hours to put one together.

You may stand a better chance with capital investors, but again you will need that excellent business plan or Business Model Canvas to convince them. The good news is that some investors are interested in the game industry, so you may find a friendlier ear. The bad news is they also know what they are talking about and so will want to see something from your game as well as the business side of the business. Also good news is that many of these people are a lot savvier about the real nature of startup ventures.

If you can, seek out business gatherings in your area and start networking. Also, if you can get into a "business accelerator" program, where you get a crash course in starting a startup, these are well worth your time if you are a relative noob to business.

26.2.4 Crowd Funding

Crowd funding is a fairly recent phenomenon, and the growth of social media has not only allowed it to happen but has also facilitated the self-advertisement of its successes.

It's simple, right: you build part of a game, call it a beta, and post teasers and small playable demos on all the social media sites. You ask people to pay you to finish the game in exchange for some type of reward like input into the game, free copies, free T-shirts, and so forth.

Then sit back and wait for the money to roll in.

The truth, though, is of course not as simple or as rosy. Yes, there have been hundreds of success stories, but there have also been thousands of failures. There is an art to doing a crowd-funding campaign successfully.

Along with the growth of crowd funding, there has been growth in legal checks and balances to prevent fraud. If you use any of the well-known companies, you will have to meet their criteria before you gain access to their support.

You cannot just put up a single post and expect results.

The work involved in successfully running a crowd-funding scheme and managing social media sites adds many hours to your weekly schedule. While essential to keeping your clients (the people who are funding you) happy, it is not game production work. That work still needs to get done.

Meanwhile, although technically not crowd funding, we do want to mention here an alternative offered by several companies. These are companies who will publish your game online for free in exchange for advertising revenue.

This is actually a good way to get your game in front of a very large and avid gamer base, who will also act as reasonable critics and offer advice on improvements. They will also act as a major playtesting or QA group. All things a solo operator needs.

If you are new to the industry, it also gives you experience facing the competition and meeting deadlines and customer expectations. These experiences will prove invaluable.

The down side—and yes, there is always a downside—is that the competition is huge.

Hundreds, even thousands, of games are put on these sites every month. Your game needs to receive a significantly large number of hits (thousands) on a regular basis for you to receive a percentage of the advertising revenue. I (Adrian) have done this, and my return was negligible, certainly not enough to live on. Of course, maybe my game just sucked. ☺

26.3 STARTUP COMPANY

The first thing to remember is that getting together with a group of friends to make a game and putting it out there is <u>not</u> the same as forming a company.

First, you should all have written contracts and written job descriptions and expectations. We cannot recommend this enough. Whether the company is a great success or a terrible flop, having these items written down will save a lot of arguments and might preserve friendships.

Next, your company should have goals and ideals beyond "let's make a game and publish it." These goals and ideals should be agreed upon by the principals of the company and again written down. They should also go on your website. This may seem lofty if there are just three of you, but, like written contracts, having goals keeps things focused in times of crisis and also shows potential publishers, banks, crowd funders, and others that you are a serious company. Lastly, if the company really takes off, you are not left struggling for what to do next. Your goals will guide you.

Name your company and create a logo and corporate image, to the best of your ability, making sure that no one else is already using them, of course. Make sure all the principals in the company like these identifiers.

Don't give your company a stupid name because you think it is funny or satirical. Not everyone will agree with you, and they will not treat you seriously. Sound like you mean business.

Similarly, don't pick a name or logo that could be offensive to someone, and remember that what is offensive can vary from country to country. When you go international, which you do as soon as you put yourself on your website, that matters.

Don't pick a "temporary" name or one you don't like. When you become a huge success, changing the name of your company will be awkward at best and may even cost you money.

We highly recommend reading any of the many really useful books or online articles on starting a company that this book does not have the space to cover.

We also recommend you contact the local Chamber of Commerce and your local business community for advice, some of which may be free. You will probably find, to your delight, that most business people are not the money-grubbing ogres depicted in the movies but genuinely want the local community (and you) to prosper.

OK, so you have a group of business associates (not friends), you have contracts lined up, you have set up your website, have plans, goals, a design, and maybe a demo.

Now what?

EVERYTHING we said about solo freelancing applies to startup companies—and then some.

Your income must now cover not just your expenses but also that of however many people are in the company. On top of this, there are day-to-day expenses of running a company that you did not have when you were running solo.

As a company, you have to meet more legal requirements. These will vary from state to state, so research what you have to do.

Unless you are all working in your parents' basement, you will need an office or studio big enough for everyone in the company, and you will need to pay the rent and utilities on it, often up front.

Depending on the size of your company and who you hire, you may need to provide health insurance and minimum wages, and a whole lot more.

26.4 ARE YOU PREPARED?

Going off on your own and being absolutely responsible for what happens to you is one of the most exhilarating experiences you can have. Exhilarating and frightening. If you know in your heart that you must do this, get ready to make the jump and then jump.

Remember that whether you are soloing or starting up a small studio, apart from the expertise needed to actually make a game, you also need to know about the business side of business.

Fortunately, there are vast resources for this and you don't necessarily have to earn an MBA to be successful. We've included some resources to get you started in the appendix. Meanwhile, we cover more of what you will need to know in the next chapter, "The Exploding Gig Economy."

Beyond these recommendations, we cannot advise further. All we can say is that if you go your own way like this, you are in for the ride of your life.

Make sure you turn your brain into a sponge. There is going be a lot to learn.

And who knows, you could end up as the next EA or Activision. But…probably not. There we go again, raining on your parade.

Bottom Line:

However you do it, going solo ain't easy! But if it's successful, the rewards are great.

CHAPTER 27

The Exploding Gig Economy

THIS CHAPTER IS A continuation of Chapter 26, but it also looks at going it alone with an eye on the Internet and social media and the huge impacts they are having—and will no doubt continue to have—on the work environment.

While nobody was looking, a new way of working has come into being. Well, not quite; freelancing or "contract work" has been percolating along for quite a few years now, but the exploding gig economy has grown large enough for the mainstream media and mainstream economists to notice.

What is the exploding gig economy? Simply put, it is working without an employer, that is, working freelance or as a "contract worker." This is by no means a new idea. What is new is how the Internet and social media have transformed this way of working into a large, and increasingly important, way in which people find work and get paid for it. Uber is one go-to example of this phenomenon.

The term "gig economy" has been applied to the situation that many millennials find themselves in, especially since the Great Recession of 2008. Regular forty-hour-a-week jobs for new college hires were scarce, and many young people just out of college (and usually carrying a lot of student debt) were often forced to take jobs well below what their freshly minted degrees would suggest they were worth. "Should I leave room for cream at the top?" was uttered by many a college grad.

Enter the gig economy.

27.1 ARE YOU READY FOR IT?

As we said in the previous chapter, freelancing isn't for everyone, but the exploding gig economy has forced people to revise long-standing work traditions. We've heard that some people are even predicting the death of the forty-hour work week and, with it, the traditional employer–employee relationship. We think the rumors of this death have been greatly exaggerated.

For many industries, freelancing simply won't work except in certain limited situations. A restaurant cannot continually scout out freelancers for the position of head chef. Too much depends on the restaurant maintaining the quality of its food, and that critically depends on the personality, style, and talent of the head chef. In fact, for many successful restaurants the head chef and the owner are the same.

Yet the other restaurant staff changes constantly. Waiters, bartenders, and line chefs (the ones who actually crank out all the dishes) come and go. It's the nature of the restaurant business that many of its employees are highly mobile and transient. But not the head guy. If a restaurant loses its star chef, its days may well be numbered.

Most other businesses require stability and continuity to function properly. Think of banks, hotels, doctors' offices, construction companies, mail delivery, and so much else. No, the traditional employer–employee relationship isn't going anywhere soon.

But for other companies in other industries, freelancing makes a lot of sense. These notably include businesses that make up the entertainment industry, of which video game development is an increasingly important part.

To make a movie, for example, dozens, hundreds, or even thousands of people are assembled together—for a limited time—to perform all the tasks that go into making a movie. The period of time actually on the set shooting the movie (called "principal photography") will definitely need the actors, stagehands, production people, and others on hand while all this is going on, but before that (preproduction) and after (postproduction), they are not needed. No production company can afford to keep these expensive artists and craftsmen hanging around doing nothing. If the studio is large and well managed, they could be kept on full-time, rotating from project to project. But this is out of the question for a small studio or an independent production company with only one current film project.

So many people who do this for a living do so on a freelance basis. A freelancer with the right skills and talent is brought in for a fixed period of time, under contract, and that person works on the project (oftentimes exclusively) during that time.

27.2 FREELANCING AND THE GAME INDUSTRY

Freelancing is also quite common in the various tech industries, and that includes video game development. Some occupations in the game industry are nearly always performed by freelancers. These especially include game writing, sound design, and music composition. People in these jobs are usually needed only for short periods of intensive work, and only the largest studios can maintain them on their payroll full-time.

If you are a game writer, sound designer, or music composer, you probably already have found this out. But what about engineers, artists, and animators? There is freelance work for them as well. The main difference here is that engineers, artists, and animators generally find it easier to get steady employment than those other people.

27.3 IS FREELANCING RIGHT FOR YOU?

Writers and sound/music people don't have much choice; freelancing is thrust upon them. This has been historically true and is not new just because the game industry got rolling. We could even say that this kind of itinerant, freeform lifestyle is part of the attraction of working this way.

This is probably mostly true for artists and animators, but less so for engineers. A lot depends on your personality. Do you like the thrill of not knowing where the money for the next rent or mortgage payment is going to come from? Do you enjoy knowing that there won't be a steady stream of payroll checks or unemployment checks? Do you know when your next meal will be?

We're just trying to scare you a little here. Things aren't actually going to be that bad unless you start slacking off or the economy hits the wall. In the next section we talk about all the things that come under the heading of "taking care of business" when you freelance.

27.4 THINGS TO CONSIDER

When you land your first gig and see the size of your paycheck, you'll enjoy that wonderful sense of "Wow, that's a lot of money for doing _____." Enjoy it while you can, because that's the gross payment amount. From that you'll need to subtract money for all sorts of things, beginning, unfortunately, with taxes. But before we get into that, let's look at a few other important matters.

27.5 WORK FOR HIRE

When you are getting paid under contract to perform work for a client, you are technically "working for hire." That is, your relationship to your client is legally referred to as "work for hire." This has a number of important implications you need to be aware of if you go down the freelancing road.

First, since you are getting paid, the client—not you—owns the work you produce. Entirely. In exchange for getting the money, you agree to surrender all intellectual rights to your creations. If you are a programmer, the client owns the source code, not just the resulting executable. If you are an artist or animator, the client owns the art you create, and this means not just the art itself but the "concept" behind it.

An example will make that clear. Say you are asked to draw an anime character from a set of guidelines supplied by the client. What you come up with is amazing. It's also not yours, and this means additionally that you cannot draw that same character again for any other purpose later on. Small tweaks won't work either. Disney would still sue you if you came up with a character that "sorta" looks like Mickey Mouse but isn't.

You want to be very clear in your own mind about this. If you have your own intellectual property that is yours and you treasure it and you want to do something with it in the future, don't turn that work over in exchange for a check. Don't turn in something close, either, for the same reason you can't draw "sorta Mickey Mouse." Instead, crank out what the client wants, turn it over, get paid, and move on.

This doesn't mean you turn in substandard work. Do the best work you can; just don't fall in love with it.

Keep in mind also that your work must be *your work*. You simply cannot use other copyrighted materials in the creation of whatever it was you are hired to do. This gets complicated fast, involving such things as stock photo and footage libraries, sound loop and sample audio libraries, "royalty-free" music compositions, various forms of software libraries and APIs licensed in various ways, and so forth. Any of these will require that you make sure you're in the clear, and you might need the help of an attorney who specializes in intellectual property law to make sure.

27.6 TAX MATTERS

When you freelance, you are not working for an ordinary paycheck where taxes are taken out. When you are an employee, you get a Form W-2 at the end of the year, showing your gross pay, taxes and other deductions, and net pay, the amount you actually get to put in the bank.

Not so when you are freelancing. There, you get the entire amount you contracted for, with no taxes or any other deductions taken out. You are now responsible for paying those taxes, and you had better remember to do so.

At the end of the year, you get a different piece of paper, Form 1099, which shows the amount the client paid you that year. Anyone hiring someone else is legally required to keep track of the money paid out and report it at the end of the year on Form 1099. You get a copy and the IRS gets a copy. If you don't pay the taxes you owe, you will eventually get found out. If you go without paying your taxes for a few years, then when the IRS does catch up to you, you will owe so much additional in the form of penalties and interest that you will wish you had done this correctly from the beginning.

When you set out on the freelance route, be sure to talk to an accountant, especially one who works with people in your situation. In fact, it's a good idea to form a long-term relationship with a good accountant. For one thing, you are now "self-employed," and many of the costs you incur just doing your job are tax-deductible, and only an accountant can set things up so you can deduct the maximum amount without running afoul of the law. For example, if you have a home office and do all your work out of it, you can probably deduct a fraction of all your apartment or house expenses because of it. But this deduction is often abused, and the IRS regards such deductions as "red flag" items that can trigger getting audited. There are strict rules for determining how and when such deductions are legit, and you will want the help of an accountant to make sure.

27.7 HEALTHCARE

Another bit of bad news. When you are on your own, you are on your own for providing healthcare, insuring yourself against various forms of loss, and putting aside money for retirement.

At the time of this writing (speaking here of the U.S.), healthcare is quite an unsettled issue, and there is no way of knowing what the healthcare terrain will look like in the future. But we think we can safely say that you're going to want it and it is going to be expensive.

For a lot of young people health insurance doesn't seem to make economic sense: You're young and in good health, so why does it cost so much? You already know the answer. You are paying for the health care of people much older and sicker than you are. That's what insurance is all about. When you get old, you are going to want the system to take care of you.

If you are married, you may be able to get coverage if your spouse is covered. The costs for healthcare are still borne by the marriage or relationship, but they won't have to be borne by your freelancing revenue. (You should be fair about this with regard to your spouse or partner, however.) If you have children, then healthcare is not an option; you're definitely going to need it.

The good news is that, with the gig economy exploding as it is, expect to see more and more ways to obtain insurance through freelancer associations. The IGDA, for example, offers a limited form of health insurance for its members. What you would be doing here is buying "group insurance" from an association of freelancers who all face the same situation you do. This is a dynamically shifting scene, and for professional freelancers, it pays to keep an eye on emerging trends. We expect new associations to form as gig work becomes more common. You may need to shop around.

27.8 OTHER INSURANCE

Health insurance is just one kind of insurance you might need. Here we talk about a few others.

Disability Insurance. This is insurance designed to carry you through while you are disabled and unable to work. The idea here is that, should you be injured in a car accident or suffer some other disaster, you can receive a fixed amount of money for some period of time as you get rehabilitated and make your way back into the workforce. This sort of insurance may also be offered through freelancer associations in the same manner as health insurance.

Should you get disability insurance? It does cost a fair amount of money, month after month, year after year, and as long as you don't need it, it will feel like a colossal waste. Until you do need it. Young people, as we old folks have observed, like to think they are invulnerable.

If you are married, and especially if you have children, the answer is easy: YES, you should have it because you have a responsibility to your family.

Catastrophic Health Insurance. Related to disability insurance is catastrophic health insurance, but it is not quite the same. Disability insurance allows you to cover your every-day expenses like rent, utilities, and food. Catastrophic health insurance pays for expensive hospital stays, doctor bills, physical therapy, and so forth for truly major health issue like cancer, heart disease, or anything that is life-threatening and that definitely takes you out of the workforce.

Again, the question is whether you should get it. First off, this sort of insurance has changed since passage of the Affordable Care Act (ACA) (also known as Obamacare). It used to be more common prior to Obamacare, but now the assumption is that coverage under the ACA includes coverage for catastrophic illnesses as well. But again, as of this writing, we have no idea how the political terrain will shape up, and you will need to do your homework. We suggest you start by asking parents and relatives what sorts of things have worked for them, then get on the Internet and do some solid probing. There are plenty of scams and plain old bad advice out there, so be careful.

Liability Insurance. This insurance is for something entirely different. It's to cover you against lawsuits for things like copyright infringement and nonperformance of what you promised on a contract you signed. If you are working on small projects where your pay is in the three to four digits, this is probably not going to be a problem; the amount at stake won't be enough to trigger an actual lawsuit.

But here be dragons. The contract you sign when you are hired for a project will likely contain the phrase "indemnify and hold harmless." What this means (keeping in mind that we are not lawyers and we are not rendering legal advice) is that if your client gets sued for copyright infringement or nonperformance because of your work, you agree to let them pass the blame down to you, meaning you, not they, are on the hook for a large damages settlement. This is what liability insurance is for. Note that if you were genuinely "negligent" (to use the legal term), even this insurance may not cover you for the entire amount. Don't be negligent; it's that simple.

Of course, if you are actually in harm's way here, your pay ought to be in line with the higher risk. If you do enough freelancing and are working on large high-risk projects, you may want to consider doing your work under a corporate structure, perhaps a Limited Liability Corporation, or LLC. This should give you a hint as to why you might want one. Even then, if you are grotesquely negligent, good attorneys can "puncture" this protection. You also have to run such a corporation "at arm's length," for example, by maintaining careful records and a separate checking account for the business.

If things get to this point, you're definitely going to want to seek the advice of the right kind of attorney. In fact, forming a productive long-term relationship with the right attorney can greatly help you prosper in the long term. Yes, sometimes even the lawyers are good guys.

Life Insurance. This one is easy. If you are young and single, you don't need life insurance. If you are married, especially if you have children, you do. Life insurance is for your survivors, not for you. You might want to consider a tiny policy to cover your funeral expenses. It's so much fun thinking about insurance, isn't it?

27.9 PENSION PLANS

Another item that needs your attention is putting away money for the future. When you were an employee, you probably set up a 401(k) pension plan and put money into it every pay period. Your employer might also have matched your contribution to some extent, making it even more valuable. Generally, you should always max out your pension contributions when you work for someone else, especially if they match funds.

If you leave the company, the 401(k) leaves with you, and you can "roll it over" into a new one at your new employer. There are strict laws governing this: you can't actually make use of the money (except in very limited circumstances), only transfer it "at arm's length" from one 401(k) plan to another.

For freelancers and the self-employed there is a different mechanism called the IRA, or Individual Retirement Account, specifically the SEP-IRA, where "SEP" stands for "Self-Employed Pension."

Fortunately, it's never been easier to set up this sort of pension plan. This is a way to set up an investment account with a firm like Fidelity or Ameriprise for the purpose of making regular contributions into and, hopefully, letting the money grow. You can even roll over your 401(k) into the new plan. You will probably need the help of your accountant to make sure this gets done correctly.

You should try to contribute the largest allowable amount to your retirement account. What is less easy is staying disciplined about making those regular payments. You may find you need to employ some tricks to ensure that happens. One such trick is to have some amount of money automatically withdrawn monthly and put into your retirement account. That way, you don't even see the money and you won't be able to spend it on something frivolous. It doesn't take long to get used to this arrangement. If you can consistently spend less than you make (and who can't do that with a little effort?), you can make this work.

Beyond this, all we can do is point you in the direction of a good financial advisor so you can set up a plan that works for you. You might start by asking family members and maybe your accountant.

27.10 SAFETY NETS

Another good idea when freelancing is to put aside money to begin building a cushion for lean times. And there will be lean times, when the economy is in a slump and no one seems to be hiring anyone for freelance work.

The idea here is to put aside three to six months of money to cover your ordinary living expenses. It doesn't necessarily have to be six months, but this seems to be a good rule of thumb if you can manage it. Even longer is better, if you can swing it.

Ideally, you put this money into a bank account separate from your checking account, lest it become too tempting to dip into. As with your retirement account, you can set this up to work automatically. With online banking as easy as it is today, this takes almost no effort to set up.

We've noticed a nice psychological benefit that happens when you have a safety net like this in place. The very knowledge that you have this cushion available means you have more latitude to decide how often and under what circumstances you are going to freelance, and on what terms.

27.11 PROTECTING YOUR REPUTATION

As we've said, when you are employed in the traditional way, you don't want to become known as a complainer or difficult person. It's the same thing, if not more so, when freelancing. Your ability to get more work in the future greatly depends on how you get to be known for the work you do in the present.

Most importantly, a satisfied customer is more likely to give you repeat business. After all, if you've consistently turned in quality work at a fair price, you become a known quantity, and nearly everyone who shops for professional services is going to want to go with a known quantity. Think of your own purchasing behavior. Don't you tend to go to the same restaurants and hair stylists if you like their work?

This is more important than you think. It will take you far more effort to land a new client than to keep an existing client. Of course, not every client can promise you more work in the future, but you certainly don't want to spoil your chances by poor performance in the present.

It is also costly for clients to make the switch as well, not only in terms of money but in anxiety. So one success factor is your ability to relieve clients' anxieties by reassuring them that their projects are in good hands.

More often than not, a client will stay with a freelancer who produces excellent work but will be willing to pay the price to switch to someone new if the quality of the work starts to fall short. The process is not entirely fair, though. Clients may very well switch to someone new if they want to take their business in a new direction or they simply want a new look. *Them's the breaks*, as they used to say. As with so many other things in life, having a thick skin helps get you through a lot.

27.12 POLITICAL IMPLICATIONS

In city after city, Uber has been challenging the dominance of traditional taxi services, and the taxi industry is not taking this lying down. Same for AirBnB in relation to the hotel industry.

These traditional industries are old enough and wealthy enough to hire lobbyists to put as many obstacles in the challengers' way as they can legally get away with. Sometimes they aren't even entirely legal and get thrown out after a successful court challenge.

The gig economy similarly challenges the traditional employer–employee relationship. A lot of laws govern this relationship, some designed to protect the employer, others to protect the employee. Many of these laws are complicated and all too easy to violate. It is for this reason that once companies reach a certain size, they hire out their human resource (HR) activities to a professional HR firm. Beyond an even larger size, they create their own HR departments. These people are the ones responsible for staying legal.

But what about the poor freelancer? It is certainly true that in the client–freelancer relationship, much like the employer–employee relationship, the person cutting the checks has the upper hand. It's the Golden Rule in action: he who has the gold makes the rules.

This is where the law comes in. Much federal labor legislation has been put in place to curb the worst employer abuses. While many of these protections have been weakened in recent decades, many laws remain on the books governing overtime pay, exposure to toxic substances in the workplace, and much more. Even these are not always properly enforced.

Historically, trade unions arose to curb the worst employer abuses as well, although they have not been exempt from their own forms of abuse and corruption.

Today, however, except in the "public sector" (government jobs), trade union membership is at its lowest level in decades, after having been in steep decline since the 1960s.

But the game industry today is virtually entirely nonunionized. The same cannot be said of the movie industry, where practically everyone works for one trade union (often called a "guild") or another. For example, there is the Screen Actors Guild, the Writers Guild of America, the Directors Guild of America, the Producers Guild of America, not to mention the American Society of Cinematographers, the International Alliance of Theatrical Stage Employees (the "stagehands" union), and the Teamsters. Even casting directors and makeup artists have guilds.

Working for the film industry is quite a bit different from working in the game industry, even though both are "show biz."

The IRS also may weigh in on the whole 1099 economy. There are so many opportunities for tax evasion shenanigans that just working this way opens you up to a higher likelihood of getting audited. One reason we highly recommend a good accountant is that they put their livelihood on the line on your behalf and the fact that they submit your taxes as being genuine, while not removing any chance of an audit, does make it less likely.

A lot of people in the political sphere may want to weigh in by imposing restrictions on this sort of employment. We've already seen this at the local and state level with the attempts to restrict Uber, Lyft, and AirBnB.

As for us, we like videogames and we like technology, so our view is that if the Internet and cell phones can make lining up a room or a ride easier and cheaper, we're all for it. If you have the right personality and attitude to flourish in the world of freelancing, we're all for that, too. We agree that freelancers may need some legal protection from time to time, but let's be sure that they are true protections and not schemes by special interests to limit the bright future of the exploding gig economy.

CHAPTER 28

There Is More to Life Than Games

Y ES, THERE REALLY IS one. ☺

28.1 PERSONAL GROWTH

Life is more than just creating and playing video games, no matter how passionate you are about them. If you're young when you read this, you may not think so, but there will come a day when you crave something else, something more. If you are old, like us, when you read this you will just nod your head in a sagely fashion.

One of these will be a relationship, one you will have to carefully nurture and maintain. Too many marriages and relationships have been wrecked by ignoring this. All we can say is, try to be mature about this and be mindful of the warning signs of a relationship about to go off the rails. Since we're not psychologists or counselors, we recommend you seek the counsel of professionals.

But that isn't all. You have intellectual needs, aesthetic needs, spiritual needs. Again, we can't say much here except to encourage you to keep an open mind. Read a lot. Get out more. Try new things. Listen to experimental music. Go to art galleries.

When the time comes, you'll know what to do. As the old saying goes, when the student is ready, the teacher appears.

28.2 LIFE OUTSIDE OF WORK

One of the perennial problems faced by the game industry is the exodus of skilled and talented people from its ranks. As we saw earlier, though, the situation is better now ever since several major labor abuse scandals erupted within the game industry in the mid-2000s. People working in this industry should have the expectation of being able to live ordinary lives, raise a family, take vacations, and so forth, and not have to sleep on a cot under their desks during crunch time.

Again, if you're very young, you may think that this doesn't apply to you, but sooner or later it will.

28.3 FAMILY VERSUS GAME INDUSTRY

As we hinted at earlier, family life and personal relationships can be put at risk by excessive devotion to your game industry job, whether that was your choice or not.

One life decision you'll want to make, fully understanding that things will change anyway if you meet the right person, is just what sort of life and work balance you want. For some people, the ones who are madly driven in one area, it may well be the case that starting a family simply won't be on their radar. Or, if they do, they may be opening themselves up to a world of hurt for themselves and those around them, unless they are able to refocus at least some of their attention away from their madly driven area toward their family.

This is something only you can figure out for yourself. We're just pointing it out to you here so you can be thinking about it. Maybe you set yourself timelines, for example, I am going to be single and dedicated to my job and career until age XX, or until I am a senior engineer, or until I am earning enough money to buy a house. Then I am going to settle down.

In theory, this is a great plan, but like so many great plans, it rarely quite works out as planned. What if you meet Mr(s). Right five years before your timeline, what if you can't quite get that promotion, or where you live the house prices are just way out of your reach?

Well, then do the sensible thing and revise the plan, be flexible and adaptable, and be willing to learn new things. Actually, exactly the steps you take to succeed in your job work just as well in your personal life. Funny That.

28.4 TAKING RESPONSIBILITY FOR YOURSELF

In the end, how your life ends up is largely up to you, but ducking responsibility for your life's decision—a far-too-common occurrence—is no way to live, and you may as well own up to it now.

This is how you gain respect among your peers. You're a gamer, right? Deep down you know that respect has to be earned; it isn't just granted automatically.

This is also how you can become a leader, if you so desire. People will only follow people they respect, and they can't respect anyone who is too cowardly to take responsibility for the work they do and the decisions they make.

28.5 KNOW YOURSELF

All this can be pretty overwhelming. One way to help yourself through life is to "know thyself." Let's give credit to those ancients who had a lot of this figured out. Even if it does not let you change yourself, simply knowing yourself and why you do the things you do might just help you overcome some hurdles.

Well, how do you do that? Here are a few tools we've encountered along the way. Keep in mind that, in the grand scheme of things, this is a pretty paltry offering, but consider it a start.

28.5.1 The MBTI

MBTI stands for the Myers-Briggs Type Inventory. This is a psychological test based on the theories of the famous early psychologist Carl Jung. We discussed this briefly earlier in this book.

By answering a set of about 150 questions, you get placed in one of sixteen possible "types," a combination of four pairs of letters, each representing two extremes along four axes.

- Introvert/Extrovert (**I** or **E**) is one you probably already know about.

- Sensing/Intuitive (**S** or **N**). Are you the kind of person who is "in the moment" (**S**) or are you more reflective, seeing the less obvious bigger picture (**N**)?

- Thinking/Feeling (**T** or **F**) is also pretty obvious.

- Perceptual/Judgmental (**P** or **J**). Do you experience things as they are (for good or ill) with or without passing judgment?

Even though there are sixteen types in this system, don't make the mistake of thinking that there are only sixteen kinds of people! First of all, each of these four axes is a continuous scale, and for any one of them you could be at one extreme but are more likely to be somewhere in the middle.

Also, the MBTI only captures a little bit of who you are as a person. The publishers of the MBTI will be the first to tell you that.

It's entirely possible you've already taken this test, possibly in school or on a job. Use it as a way of learning something about yourself.

It is a commercially published test, and only people certified in the method are supposed to administer it, so you can't just "take it." You can, however, find tests similar to the MBTI out there, for example the Kiersey Temperament Sorter (http://www.keirsey.com/).

28.5.2 The Gallup StrengthsFinder

This is another commercially published test that serves an entirely different purpose. As the name suggests, it helps you find out your strengths, that is, what you're good at. You can find it at https://www.gallupstrengthscenter.com/.

The premise of the StrengthsFinder test is that while, yes, it is possible to devote hours and years at improving the things you are weak in, you'll advance much faster if you concentrate on mastering the things you are strong in. This isn't to say that you shouldn't try to fix those things you are weak in if they cry out for attention. Just spend most of your self-improvement time on your strengths. Makes sense, doesn't it?

Two versions of the test are available: the $15 version that identifies your top five strengths and the $89 version that evaluates you along all thirty-four of the fundamental strengths in the theory (also includes the e-book that explains the theory in complete detail).

This test can be quite the eye-opener. One of us who took the $15 version wasn't too surprised by three of the identified top strengths but was quite surprised by the other two. (We're not going to say what those were, though.)

If you buy into the idea that greater success and happiness in life is more likely ʰ
you do the things you are best at, this test can be of considerable help, especially when o
discover a strength you didn't know you had.

28.5.3 The Big Five (OCEAN) Personality Test

The Big Five Theory of Personality distills about a century's worth of psychological reseaʳ
on personality into a clean set of five axes that are the major determiners of personaliᵗ
These are not the only ones, but nowadays many psychologists would agree that they aᵣ
the most important.

One version of the Five Factor theory expresses the five using the acronym OCEAN, which
stands for **O**penness to new experience, **C**onscientiousness, **E**xtraversion, **A**greeableness,
and **N**euroticism. Actually, in the full form of the theory there are six subfactors for each
of the major ones, for a total of thirty.

As with the MBTI, taking the Big Five test may help you understand yourself a little
better.

The full form of this test is quite lengthy and usually administered by a psychologist. The
magazine *Psychology Today* offers a short form of this test, which you can take for free at
http://psychologytoday.tests.psychtests.com/take_test.php?idRegTest=1297.

28.5.4 Other Tests

There are myriad psychological tests out there with words like "profile," "assessment,"
"inventory," or "measure" in their names. They vary greatly in quality, from low-end "tests"
like "Are you good in bed?" that you might see in a cheesy popular magazine to properly val-
idated psychological instruments developed and refined by psychologists over many years.

The Gallup organization, the publishers of the StrengthsFinder test, for example, also
publishes the Entrepreneurial Profile. Find out if you have what it takes to go into business
for yourself.

This always fascinating website also offers a variety of tests, measuring all sort of things,
at http://psychcentral.com/quizzes/.

28.6 ONLINE COURSES

Living in the modern age is great. One thing we can all do nowadays is keep our skills
sharp and our brains operating at 100% by taking online courses.

There are courses for everything, not only those you need to maintain your professional
skills. Check out Udacity, Coursera, and the increasing number of college courses offered
by the likes of MIT and Stanford.

And let's not forget the thousands of hours of useful tutorials offered by software publishers and third parties on YouTube.

You have no excuse for not making use of these. What's keeping you?

28.7 MINDFULNESS

We'll close this chapter by commenting on something that sounds more like "woo-woo"
than practical advice.

Woo-woo (or just "woo") is a pejorative term properly applied to worthless activities like astrology or gazing at crystals.

We're speaking again here of the practice of meditation, specifically "mindfulness" meditation. We bring this up not because it's BS, but because it is not. We are learning from more and more scientific research that mindfulness meditation confers a variety of benefits and, moreover, actually works.

It's not easy to do it or do it well, and in fact it can take years to really get the hang of it and derive all its benefits. But what it can do for you, if you give it an honest chance, is help you maintain your poise (and sanity) when things get tough, to help you make better and more thoughtful decisions, and to improve the quality of your life in subtle and far-reaching ways.

You are, after all, about to enter a crazy, dynamic, high-pressure industry, and you can use all the help you can get. We listed a couple of resources in the appendix.

28.8 LIVING LEAN AND MEAN

Coming straight out of college to a new job in a new environment is tough.

If you just moved from a small town to start working for a major studio in a major city, you've already experienced the shock of high rents. You're probably spending most of your paycheck on rent, and you are probably splitting the rent with roommates as well.

The problem with paying rent is that it's pure waste as far as your bottom line is concerned. This is a number you want to keep as low as possible. We're not suggesting you live in the worst parts of town, but you probably don't need to spend extra for luxury living. Part of being able to do this is to live lean and mean, that is, not accumulating a lot of needless stuff.

Clearly, we don't mean your game collection or your game consoles. But it is so easy when you are starting to see regular paychecks to blow a lot of money on stuff you don't need.

Now, we're old. We have families, and houses crammed with stuff, stuff that took decades to accumulate. We're at the point where we are trying to get rid of stuff, not accumulate more.

But as you set out, you might want to consider starting off with the kind of lifestyle where all your stuff can fit into a few boxes and you can stuff those boxes into a car or SUV. If you can, you become incredibly mobile. If you lose your job in Los Angeles to take a job in Boston, you can cross the country in a few days, and you'll be all set. And a cross-country drive can be a blast if you have the extra few days to stretch it into an adventure.

After you settle down, buy a house, maybe start a family, this becomes much harder to do quickly and comfortably.

Henry David Thoreau once advised us to "Simplify, Simplify." Nearly two centuries later, it's still good advice. There is an emerging national trend toward tiny houses, sustainable farming and living, and "minimalism," trying to live in a more economical and human-scale way.

WAY AHEAD OF HIS TIME

We once knew of a guy who lived in an RV parked right in the parking lot of the high-tech company he worked for (he had permission). His cost of living was laughably low.

About a year after he started doing this, he got a visit from some company accountants. They were puzzled. The books for the payroll didn't balance. Turns out, he had a drawer full of uncashed checks. He'd cash one only once in a while when he needed money for groceries.

This was about three decades ago, but this guy is an inspiration to the Live Lean, Live Mean lifestyle.

28.9 CLOSING THOUGHTS

We have covered a diverse range of subjects concerning games, game production, and what it takes to survive what can be a harsh and brutal environment. While the aim of this book is certainly to remove some of the glossy veneer that surrounds video games, this was only to enable you to make informed and objective decisions rather than blindly going, "Wow, what could be better than working on games?"

We really hope that some of the homely truths and hard-won experience we have shared do not put you off entirely from considering a lifelong career in game development.

Adrian was once asked by an eighth grader what he would like to do if he didn't make games. His honest answer: "I cannot think of anything else I would rather do."

Despite its many ups and downs, even after twenty-five years, yeah, Adrian still thinks, "Wow, what could be better than working on games?"

Appendix 1: Resources for Game Development

Nowadays, there are plenty of tools, game engines, art assets, royalty-free music, and much else available to the aspiring game maker. Many are free, or reasonably priced, and it is possible to get going on a game of your own with no money out of pocket.

You will, of course, need a reasonably modern PC, generally running Windows 10. While there are also game development resources for Mac and Linux, there simply aren't as many, but Mac and Linux users are by no means shut out of the game. Nonetheless, this listing will center around conventional PCs, but keep in mind that many of these are also available for those other operating systems. We will note these as necessary.

Let's begin with Python.

PYTHON

Python has become widely popular, with a huge and generally helpful base of users who will often happily answer your questions. (But keep in mind what we said about making the effort to find answers on your own before bothering the gurus.)

Why Python? Python has been said to "fit the brain." What this means is that, if you are trying to learn programming for the first time, Python is a great choice for your first language. As you start to learn the essentials, Python will feel quite natural, and you can begin to build your procedural literacy in a mostly effortless way. Don't try this with C++, which is at the other end of the complexity spectrum. The grocery store examples we gave in the text were basically little Python programs.

Python is renowned for the many "libraries" it supports. There are libraries (which you can think of as collections of useful functions and data structures) for practically anything you can throw a computer at: math, statistics, robotics, artificial intelligence, machine learning, astronomy, meteorology, chemistry, graphics, engineering, network communications, scientific research, and many more. And, of course, making games. In fact, it is hard to think of a domain that computers can be turned loose on that doesn't have a Python library or two written for it.

While Python is a great learning language, it isn't quite the language for making games unless you are willing to work at a relatively low level. By this we mean that you, as the game developer, will necessarily work with lots of code doing very elementary things, and this can be time consuming. By contrast, a complete game development environment, like

Unity or Unreal Engine 4, lets you work more with visual dragging-and-dropping, setting values for various things in a user interface, and actually trying out your game while in the middle of developing it. Working at a low level isn't quite that easy or convenient.

You can get Python here (by the way, Python runs on everything):

http://www.python.org

This is an immense site, fully documenting the language and providing links to all those libraries, among other things.

What game development libraries are available for Python? Many have come and gone, but many older ones are still in use. Some of the best are these:

Pyglet	http://www.pyglet.org
Pygame	http://www.pygame.org
Cocos2s	http://www.cocos2d.org/

These hardly exhaust the category. For a more complete list, this page on the Python site gives several dozen:

https://wiki.python.org/moin/PythonGameLibraries

Remember that with any of these you are working at a low level and responsible for a lot of the fine details of the programming to get the effects you want. Expect a steep learning curve no matter how you go about it. If you want to work at a more convenient high level (and many do, even professionals), you will want a complete game engine and development environment.

There are two ways you can go: with a system more targeted at beginners, like GameMaker and RPGMaker, and more full-strength solutions, like Unity and Unreal Engine 4.

GAMEMAKER AND RPGMAKER

Both of these applications have been around for a while and continue to get more and more powerful. Although both have "Maker" in their names, they are two different product lines offered by two unrelated companies.

GameMaker, full name GameMaker Studio 2 (https://www.yoyogames.com/), can be thought of as a game development environment with training wheels. Its drag-and-drop way of working and intuitive scripting make it an excellent platform for beginners to learn game development.

GameMaker is also popular among professional developers, who often use GameMaker to quickly build prototypes for things like proving that an untried new game mechanic works and is fun. The actual game, however, gets made using a more powerful game engine.

But GameMaker is capable of far more than that. In its early days, it was ideal for making 2D platformer and side-scroller games, and it still is. Indie developers have made great games using its powerful feature set. We can see that in the recent games *Undertale* and *Hyperlight Drifter*. GameMaker is available for all three operating systems and at several price points.

If your tastes run more to role-playing games, then consider RPG Maker (http://www.rpgmakerweb.com/). The newest version is called RPG Maker MV, and still available are the older RPG Maker VX and RPG Maker VX Ace versions. RPG Maker MV is available for all three operating systems. The makers of RPG also offer a large number of art assets and music for purchase as well.

Any version of RPG Maker lets you design 2D RPGs with its capable map editor, character stats system, inventory management (e.g., for items, weapons and armor), and a versatile event-driven programming model. RPG Maker is a surprisingly capable development environment for old-school 2D RPGs, and you can go very far with it.

GAME ENGINES

For larger-scale projects, there are many game engines to choose from. Some have been around for a while; others are relatively new and kept current. For our purposes, to make use of a powerful development environment without paying any money, two stand out: Unity and Unreal Engine 4.

This is not to say that they are entirely "free." If you want to make a commercial game and the game makes money, you will need to pay the companies an appropriate licensing fee, which is perfectly fair and reasonable. We won't get into what that involves here; see their websites for details.

Unity

Unity (https://unity3d.com/), formerly known as Unity3D, is a game engine and development environment that lets you do much of your development without ever leaving the confines of Unity itself. You can develop a piece of your game and test it (run it) right then and there. You can be remarkably productive with it. Unity is available for PC, Mac, and Linux.

It too has a steep learning curve, mainly because it does so much for you, and learning most or all of it takes time. For example, you can handle physics and collisions with it, do some AI, build the HUD and UI, and everything else that is going to need attention.

Programming in Unity is done with your choice of two languages: JavaScript or C#. C# definitely has the edge here, and we recommend making that your first choice. If you are making games on a PC, you will most likely "compile" the code using Microsoft Visual Studio (also free, and something you install alongside Unity and works alongside Unity). For the other operating systems, you use the open-source C# alternative called Mono.

Unity currently dominates the indie development scene and is also widely used in college programs for game development. If you get into game school, you will definitely run into it. Don't let the steep learning curve throw you; it's rather fun to go exploring all the cool features this game engine has. You may even run into a feature that inspires you to rethink how you are going to build your game, just because it reveals a capability you didn't know you had available.

Unity also has the Asset Store, a place where you can buy (at reasonable prices or free) all sorts of things you may find will simplify your life, including art assets and useful code modules. Need a "hex grid" setup for an old-school war game? They have it. Do you want to implement a "behavior tree" for some sophisticated NPCs? They have it. You won't need to reinvent the wheel.

Unreal Engine 4

If you think Unity is powerful, just wait until you try out UE4 (https://www.unrealengine.com/). This is a full-strength, AAA-title-grade development environment, loaded with advanced features and a truly fearsome learning curve. It is coming up strong against the leader, Unity.

A key reason for wanting to get good at UE4 is that this is the engine of choice for many major titles, and people who know how to program for UE4 are in rather more demand than Unity programmers. This is, perhaps, in part due to the fact that programming in UE4 is done in UE4's native language, C++. Don't say we didn't warn you.

GAME STORYTELLING

If your tastes run more toward building story-based games, there are several excellent development environments available.

Most everything we discuss here is centered around the notion of the "branching narrative." That is, some bit of story is displayed, the player makes a decision or engages in dialogue, more story is displayed based on that decision, and on and on. Stories built this way can be remarkably subtle; your imagination is the only limiting factor.

Twine (http://twinery.org) is one system for building such stories that uses a visual layout approach where blocks on the screen (called *passages*) display text and provide one or more links to other passages, thereby creating the branching structure of your story. You can have variables, random number generation, and other forms of control to achieve whatever level of complexity you desire. You use it by downloading and installing the app to your machine, and all three operating systems are supported. You can also use it online with a browser.

Inklewriter is similar, except that you use it entirely within a browser. There is no download; everything is served from the company website. As with Twine, inklewriter uses a visual block metaphor where each block represents a piece of story you want to display and the ways it connects to other blocks.

Both Twine and inklewriter do their display magic using regular HTML and CSS style sheets; thus, you are not limited to merely displaying plain text.

Still another system is **Choose Your Story** (http://chooseyourstory.com/).

A couple of older environments deserve a brief mention: **Inform** (http://inform7.com/) and **TADS** (http://www.tads.org/). Neither is in active development. These are more script-like; there are no visual tools (or not much of one) to help you create your story. They make up for it by offering rather more powerful programming structures, if you want to take the time to explore.

Finally, there is **Ren'Py**, which, as the name suggests, has something to do with Python. Ren'Py is a system for building so-called visual novels, where static images (displayed in several "planes" from back to front) are moved around to create a kind of simple cartoon. The story is advanced by having the player make decisions at key points you specify. If you want to get more hardcore with Ren'Py, you can combine it with PyGame (described earlier) by adding PyGame and another library, a sort of "glue" library called RenPyGame, which lets them both be put to use in a single game. This would let you build a point-and-click visual novel, add particle and animation effects, and mini games within the story.

A commercial alternative to Ren'Py is TyranoBuilder, available from Steam for USD$14.99.

Before we leave this part of the appendix, we will mention two other development environments for you to explore: Haxe (http://haxe.org/) and Construct 2 (https://www.scirra .com/).

TOOLS FOR ARTISTS

If you are set up with Adobe Photoshop, and maybe Adobe Illustrator, you are pretty much set as far as creating decent 2D artwork is concerned. The free alternative to these tools is GIMP (https://www.gimp.org/downloads/), which has been around for quite a while. It isn't as full-featured as the Adobe products, but until you get more advanced, you may find it has everything you need.

For 3D, the commercial solution is Autodesk's Maya, with 3D Studio running second. These are definitely expensive products, although students can get access to them while in college at deep discounts.

If you prefer not to go down that route, then Blender (https://www.blender.org/download/) is your most likely alternative. Blender certainly cannot compete with Maya in terms of features, but you'll be surprised at how much it can do, given that it's free.

There are plenty of other, more specialized tools for artists, like Mudbox and Houdini. These don't really have decent open source alternatives. Like the Maya and Adobe products, you can probably use them on your school's computers or get them at deep student discounts.

There are also tools for working with "sprites" and "tiles," which come up a lot in 2D games. Pyxel Edit (http://www.pyxeledit.com/get.php) is one such tool, in both free and paid versions (USD$9.00), and you can find others at the Humble Bundle Store (https:// www.humblebundle.com/store).

For art itself, just use your favorite search engines to find art. By now there are probably literally millions of art objects, sprites, tiles, textures, 3D models, and so forth that you can access. Keep in mind, though, that there is a bit of a stigma attached to using the same models a lot of other people are using; it seems lazy and uncreative. There are plenty more resources for art assets that you pay for. Generally, they are better in quality than free materials, because you do get what you pay for.

SOUND AND MUSIC

Just as with art assets, there is a vast assortment of sound effects libraries, sample libraries, and royalty-free musical pieces, all only a search away. Similarly, those same resources are available at a price (sometimes a high price).

If you want to make your own music, FL Studio and Abelton Live are popular tools, each with a very different way of handling "workflow." FL Studio is essentially a multitrack recording environment with built-in synthesizers and effects. Abelton Live uses a sample loop metaphor to construct music from loops, samples, and built-in synthesizers. It can also be used as a more conventional multitrack recording system.

Some very sophisticated music can be made with these if you have the talent and patience to master them.

FL Studio (http://www.image-line.com/flstudio/) offers a free version with some features disabled and paid versions starting at USD$99 all the way to $899. You can get perfectly good results with the USD$99 version, or maybe the USD$199 version, the next one up. A very nice thing about FL Studio is that once you pay for it, you get updates forever after.

Abelton Live (https://www.ableton.com/), as noted, is quite a bit different and lets you approach music construction in an entirely different way. We don't have space here to get into how it works, but there are plenty of demo and tutorial videos on YouTube and other places.

An affordable alternative multitrack recording environment, yet with a decent feature set, is Reaper (https://www.reaper.fm/index.php), available for both Windows and Mac.

If you want to edit actual wave files for sound effects or other purposes, the barebones solution is Audacity (http://www.audacityteam.org/), available for all three operating systems. The commercial equivalents are SoundForge (http://www.magix.com/us/sound-forge/), available in USD$60 and USD$300 versions, and Adobe Audition, part of Adobe's Creative Suite.

Note that all these products can use—and share—standard "plug-ins," small software objects that can perform all the tricks a recording engineer might want: delay, reverb, compression, equalization, distortion, time-stretching, and much more.

Appendix 2: Top Schools for Game Development and Game Design

DISCLAIMER

This list is simply a guideline to over eighty universities and colleges that offer or have at some time offered relevant courses in game development or game design. Note that the authors are *not* making recommendations here. Inclusion in or exclusion from this list does not imply any sort of judgment on the authors' part.

This list does not attempt to be comprehensive, and the information it contains should only be considered correct at the time the authors compiled the list. Courses and offerings by universities and colleges change every year, with new programs coming online and others closing down all the time. You will need to do your own research to determine which courses and which programs are right for you.

The list is presented alphabetically. To see how they actually rank, check out the latest *Princeton Review*. Please note that, since we are listing over eighty institutions, and the *Princeton Review* lists only the top 50, not all institutions here will make it onto that list!

https://www.princetonreview.com/college-rankings?rankings=top-50-game-design-ugrad

If you are an administrator or faculty member of an institution that you think deserves to be included on this list, please contact the authors via the publishers for inclusion in subsequent editions.

Abertay University
Address:
   Bell Street
   Dundee, Scotland, DD1 1HG

Character: small, dynamic urban environment
Program Names:
   B.Sc. (Hons) Computer Game Applications Development
   B.Sc. (Hons) Computer Games Technology
   Sound and Music for Games

Main Website: http://www.abertay.ac.uk
Main Phone: 44 (0)1382 308000

Abilene Christian University
Address:
    1600 Campus Court
    Abilene, TX 79699

Program Names:
    Digital Entertainment Technology, Game Development Track

Main Website: http://www.acu.edu/
Main Phone: 325-674-2000, 800-460-6228 (admissions)

Academy of Art University
Address:
    79 New Montgomery St.
    San Francisco, CA 94105

Character: An art school in a dynamic urban environment
Program Names:
    Game Development (B.F.A.)
    Animation & Visual Effects
    Motion Pictures & Television

Main Website: http://info.academyart.edu/?pmcode=PMDIR
Main Phone: 888-366-6016, 844-437-3108
Program Phone: 800-544-2787, 415-274-2222

Adelphi University
Address:
    1 South Ave.
    Garden City, NY 11530

Program Names:
    Computer and Management Information Systems: Game Development Concentration, B.S.
    Computer Science: Game Development Concentration, B.S.

Main Website: http://home.adelphi.edu/
Main Phone: 800-233-5744
Program Website: http://catalog.adelphi.edu/preview_program.php?catoid=4&poid=1469

American University
Address:
    4400 Massachusetts Ave NW
    Washington, DC 20016

Program Names:
   Game Lab
   Also relevant:
   Business and Entertainment
   Computer Science
   Film and Media Arts

Main Website: http://www.american.edu/
Main Phone: 202-885-2940
Program Website: http://www.american.edu/gamelab/
Program Phone: 202-885-2040

Amherst (Mass.) College
Address:
   Amherst College
   P.O. Box 5000
   Amherst, MA 01002-5000

Main Website: https://www.amherst.edu/
Main Phone: 413-542-2000

Angelo State University
Address:
   2601 W Ave. N.
   San Angelo, TX 76904

Main Website: http://angelo.edu/dept/
Main Phone: 800-946-8627
Program Website: http://angelo.edu/dept/computer_science/

Arizona State University
Address:
   Various locations
   Tempe, AZ 85281

Program Names:
   Computing and Mathematics

Main Website:
Main Phone: 480-965-2100
Program Website: http://engineering.asu.edu/cidse/

Art Institute of Vancouver

Game Art & Design/Visual & Games Programming

Address:

2665 Renfrew

Vancouver, British Columbia V5M 0A7

Canada

Character: art school, top urban environment

Program Names:

Animation

Audio Production

Digital Film

Game Design

Game Programming

Main Website: www.artinstitutes.edu

Main Phone: 888-411-7731, 604-683-9200

Program Website: https://www.artinstitutes.edu/vancouver/Programs/Game-Art-and-Des ign/136

Becker College

Address:

61 Sever St.

Worcester, MA 01609

Character: Small liberal arts college, with computer science, urban environment

Program Names:

Game Design and Game Programming (which of these is correct?)

Game Design

Game Development and Programming

Main Website: http://www.becker.edu/

Phone: 508-791-9241, 508-373-9727

Program Website: www.becker.edu/gamedev

Bradley University

Address:

1501 W Bradley Ave.

Peoria, IL 61625

Program Names:

Game Design (in Department of Interactive Media)

Main Website: http://www.bradley.edu/

Main Phone: 309-676-7611

Carnegie Mellon University

Address:
5000 Forbes Ave.
Pittsburgh, PA 15213

Main Website: http://www.cmu.edu/index.html
Main Phone: 412-268-2000
Program Phone: 412-268-2000

Case Western Reserve University

Address:
10900 Euclid Ave.
Cleveland, OH 44106

Character: Urban, on 155 acres
Program Names:
Computer Science (B.S. and B.A.)

Main Website: http://www.case.edu
Program Website: http://bulletin.case.edu/schoolofengineering/

Champlain College

Address:
163 S Willard St.
Burlington, VT 05402

Character: Small private, co-educational undergraduate college with a small-town vibe
Program Names:
Game Art & Animation
Game Design
Game Programming

Main Website: http://www.champlain.edu/
Main Phone: 802-860-2700
Program Website: http://www.champlain.edu/academics/undergraduate-academics/majors-and-specializations/

Clarkson University

Address:
8 Clarkson Ave.
Potsdam, NY 13699

Program Names:
    Computer Engineering
    Computer Science
    Computing Programs

Main Website: http://www.clarkson.edu/
Main Phone: 315-268-6400
Program Website: http://www.clarkson.edu/digitalarts

Cleveland Institute of Art
Address:
    11610 Euclid Ave.
    Cleveland, OH 44106

Program Names:
    Game Design

Main Website: http://www.cia.edu/
Main Phone: 800-223-4700, 216-421-7000

Cogswell Polytechnical College
Address:
    191 Baypointe Parkway
    San Jose, CA 95134

Character: This is a for-profit institution
Program Names:
    Game Design and Development
    Digital Art and Animation

Main Website: www.cogswell.edu
Main Phone: 800-264-7955

The College of New Jersey
Address:
    2000 Pennington Rd.
    Ewing Township, NJ 08628

Character: 289-acre suburban campus
Program Names:
    Interactive Media
    Computer Science

Main Website: http://www.tcnj.edu/
Phone: 609-771-2131
Program Website:
   http://www.tcnj.edu/~imm
   https://bulletin.tcnj.edu/files/2015/06/Computer_Science.pdf

Columbia College Chicago

Address:
   600 S Michigan Ave.
   Chicago, IL 60605

Program Names:
   Game Art, B.A.
   Game Design, B.A.
   Game Design, Game Development, B.A.
   Game Programming, B.A.
   Game Programming, B.S.

Main Website: http://www.colum.edu/
Main Phone: 312-369-1000

Cornell University

Address:
   Ithaca, NY 14850

Program Names:
   Computer Science
   Independent Major
   Information Science
   Information Science, Systems, and Technology
   Performing and Media Arts

Main Website: http://www.cornell.edu/

Dartmouth College

Address:
   Hanover, NH 03755

Program Names:
   Tiltfactor
   Computer Science
   4+1 MS in CS with Digital Arts
   Film and Media Studies hosts the game program

Program Website:
> http://www.tiltfactor.org
> http://researchguides.dartmouth.edu/gaming

DePaul University
Address:
> 2320 N Kenmore Ave.
> Chicago, IL 60614

Program Names:
> Computer Game Development

Program Phone: 312-362-8300

DigiPen Institute of Technology
Address:
> 9931 Willows Rd.
> Redmond, WA 98052

Program Names:
> B.S. in Computer Science in Real-Time Interactive Simulation
> B.S. in Computer Science and Game Design
> B.S. in Computer Science
> B.A. in Game Design
> (among others)

Main Website: https://www.digipen.edu/
Main Phone: 425-558-0299

Drexel University
Address:
> 3141 Chestnut St.
> Philadelphia, PA 19104

Character: Located in Philadelphia, very close to U. Penn
Program Names:
> Game Design and Production
> RePlay (Digital Media & Computer Science)

Main Website: http://www.drexel.edu/
Main Phone: 215-895-2000
Program Website: www.replay.drexel.edu

Eastern Kentucky University

Address:
521 Lancaster Ave.
Richmond, KY 40475

Program Names:
EKU Gaming Institute—On the Frontier of Play

Main Website: http://www.eku.edu/
Main Phone: 859-622-1000
Program Website: http://gaming.eku.edu/

Ferris State University

Address:
1201 S. State St.
Big Rapids, MI 49307

Program Names:
Bachelor of Applied Science—Digital Animation and Game Design

Main Website: http://www.ferris.edu/
Main Phone: 231-591-2000

Full Sail University

Address:
3300 University Boulevard
Winter Park, FL 32792

Program Names:
Game Art Bachelor's
Game Design Bachelor's
Game Development Bachelor's

Main Website: http://www.fullsail.edu/
Main Phone: 877-611-5420, 800-226-7625, 407-679-6333

Georgia Institute of Technology

Address:
North Ave.
Atlanta, GA 30332

Program Names:
Computer Science
Computational Media

Main Website: http://www.gatech.edu/
Main Phone: 404-894-2000

Hampshire College
Address:
   893 West St.
   Amherst, MA 01002

Program Names:
   Game Design and Development

Main Website: https://www.hampshire.edu/
Program Website: http://hampshire.edu/lspector

High Point University
Address:
   One University Parkway
   High Point, NC 27268

Program Names:
   Game and Interactive Media Design

Main Website: http://www.highpoint.edu/
Main Phone: 800-345-6993 or 336-841-9000
Program Website: http://www.highpoint.edu/communicationmajor/game-and-interactive
-media-design/

Indiana University
Address:
   107 S Indiana Ave.
   Bloomington, IN 47405

Character: Very large state university
Program Names:
   Game Design at the Media School

Main Website: http://www.iub.edu/
Main Phone: 812-855-4848

Kennesaw State University
Address:
   1000 Chastain Road
   Kennesaw, GA 30144

Program Names:
  B.S. in Computer Game Design and Development

Main Website: http://www.kennesaw.edu/
Main Phone: 470-578-6000
Program Website: http://ccse.kennesaw.edu/swegd/programs/bscgdd.php

Lawrence Technological University
Address:
  21000 W 10 Mile Rd.
  Southfield, MI 48075

Program Names:
  Computer Science
  B.F.A. in Game Art

Main Website: www.ltu.edu/
Main Phone: 1.800.CALL.LTU

Lycoming College
Address:
  700 College Pl.
  Williamsport, PA 17701

Character: Liberal-arts
Program Names:
  Computer Science

Main Website: www.lycoming.edu/

Lynchburg (Va.) College
Address:
  1501 Lakeside Dr.
  Lynchburg, VA 24501

Program Names:
  Computer Science

Main Website: http://www.lynchburg.edu/
Main Phone: 800-426-8101
Program Website: http://cs.lynchburg.edu/briggs
Program Phone: 434-544-8609

Marist College

Address:

3399 North Road
Poughkeepsie, NY 12601

Program Names:

Games and Emerging Media
Computer Science B.S. with a Concentration in Software Development

Main Website: http://www.marist.edu/
Main Phone: 845-575-3000
Program Websites:

http://www.marist.edu/compscimath/undergraduate/cs.html
http://www.marist.edu/commarts/film-television-games-media/gamesandemerging
media.html

Marshall University

Address:

1 John Marshall Dr.
Huntington, WV 25755

Program Names:

Computer and Information Technology
Game Development Minor

Main Website: http://www.marshall.edu/
Program Website: http://www.marshall.edu/isat/cit/

Massachusetts Institute of Technology

Singapore-MIT GAMBIT Game Lab

Address:

77 Massachusetts Ave.
Cambridge, MA 02139

Character: Urban Northeastern, near Harvard University and Boston, MA.
Program Names:

Electrical Engineering and Computer Science
Media Arts and Sciences (primarily graduate)

Main Website: http://web.mit.edu/
Main Phone: 617-253-1000

Miami University

Address:

501 E High St.
Oxford, OH 45056

Program Names:

Computer Science
Digital Game Studies (minor)

Main Website:

https://www.miamioh.edu/
http://aims.muohio.edu

Main Phone: 513-529-1809
Contact:

Armstrong Institute for Interactive Media Studies
2045 FSB
513-529-1637

Michigan State University

Address:

220 Trowbridge Rd.
East Lansing, MI 48824

Program Names:

Game Design & Development (minor)

Main Website: https://www.msu.edu/
Main Phone: 517-355-1855
Program Website: https://reg.msu.edu/academicprograms/ProgramDetail.asp?Program=6315

New England Institute of Technology

Address:

1 New England Tech Blvd.
East Greenwich, RI 02818

Program Names:

Game Development & Simulation Programming (associate's)
Game Development & Simulation Programming (B.A.)

Main Website: http://www.neit.edu/
Main Phone: 401-467-7744

New Jersey Institute of Technology

Address:
University Heights
Newark, NJ 07102

Program Names:
B.A. in Digital Design

Main Website: http://www.njit.edu/
Main Phone: 973-596-3000
Program Website: http://design.njit.edu/school-art-design/

New York University—Tisch School of the Arts

Address:
721 Broadway
New York, NY 10003

Program Name:
NYU Game Center (B.F.A.)

Main Website: http://tisch.nyu.edu/
Main Phone: 212-998-1900 (undergrad)

North Carolina State University

Address:
Raleigh, NC 27695

Program Names:
Computer Science
Bachelor of Art + Design: Animation + Interactive Media Concentration

Main Website: https://www.ncsu.edu/
Main Phone: 919-515-2011

Northeastern University

Address:
360 Huntington Ave.
Boston, MA 02115

Program Names:
B.F.A. in Games
Digital Arts and Game Design
B.S. in Computer Science and Game Design

Main Website: http://www.northeastern.edu/
Main Phone: 617-373-2000

Northern Michigan University
Address:
  1401 Presque Isle Ave.
  Marquette, MI 49855

Program Names:
  B.F.A. programs in Computer Art, Digital Cinema, Human Centered Design
  Computer Science (emphasis on network computing)

Main Website: http://www.nmu.edu/admissions
Main Phone: 906-227-1000

Oklahoma Christian University
Address:
  2501 E. Memorial Rd.
  Edmond, OK 73136

Program Names:
  Computer Science
  B.F.A. Gaming and Animation

Main Website: http://www.oc.edu/
Main Phone: 405-425-5000
Program Website: www.oc.edu/academics/arts_sciences/art_design/

Old Dominion University
Address:
  5115 Hampton Blvd.
  Norfolk, VA 23529

Program Names:
  Computer Science

Main Phone: 757-683-3000 (switchboard)
Program Website: http://www.ece.odu.edu/~yshen
Program Phone: 757-683-3114

Parsons School of Design: The New School
Address:
  66 5th Ave.
  New York, NY 10011

Program Names:
Design and Technology (B.F.A.)

Main Website: http://www.newschool.edu/parsons/
Main Phone: 800-292-3040, 212-229-8900

Pace University
Address:
1 Pace Plaza
New York, NY 10038

Character: Urban
Program Names:
Computer Science (B.A. and B.S.)

Main Website: http://www.pace.edu/
Main Phone: 914-773-3648
Program Website: http://vulcan.seidenberg.pace.edu/~skevoulis/

Polytechnic Institute of NYU, Brooklyn
Address:
6 MetroTech Center
Brooklyn, NY 11201

Character: Brooklyn!
Program Names:
Brooklyn Experimental Media Center
Computer Engineering, B.S.
Computer Science, B.S.
Integrated Digital Media, B.S.

Main Website: http://engineering.nyu.edu/
Main Phone: 646-997-3600
Program Website: http://bxmc.poly.edu/
Program Phone: 646-997-0720

Purdue University
Address:
610 Purdue Mall
West Lafayette, IN 47907

Program Names:
Game Development and Design

Main Website: http://www.purdue.edu/
Main Phone: 765-494-4600
Program Website: http://www.admissions.purdue.edu/majors/a-to-z/game-studies.php

Quinnipiac University

Address:
275 Mt Carmel Ave.
Hamden, CT 06518

Program Names:
Game Design and Development

Main Website: https://www.qu.edu/
Main Phone: 800-462-1944, 203-582-8200

Rensselaer Polytechnic Institute

Games and Simulation Arts and Sciences
Address:
110 8th St.
Troy, NY 12180

Program Names:
Computer Science
Games and Simulation Arts and Sciences (B.S.)

Main Website: http://www.rpi.edu/
Phone: 518-276-6000
Program Website: http://www.gsas.rpi.edu

Rice University

Address:
6100 Main St
Houston, TX 77005

Program Names:
Computer Science
Cognitive Science

Main Website: http://www.rice.edu/
Main Phone: 713-WELCOME (935-2663) (welcome center)
Program Website: http://www.cs.rice.edu/~jwarren

Ringling College of Art and Design

Address:

2700 N. Tamiami Trail

Sarasota, FL 34234

Program Names:

Computer Animation

Game Art (B.F.A.)

Main Website: http://www.ringling.edu/

Main Phone: 941-351-5100

Rochester Institute of Technology

Address:

One Lomb Memorial Drive

Rochester, NY 14623-5603

Program Names:

Computer Science

Game Design and Development B.S.

Main Website: http://www.rit.edu/

Main Phone: 585-475-2411

Sacred Heart University

Address:

5151 Park Ave.

Fairfield, CT 06825

Program Names:

Game Design & Development

Computer Science

Main Website: http://www.sacredheart.edu/

Main Phone: 203-371-7999

Program Website: http://www.sacredheart.edu/academics/collegeofartssciences/academic departments/computerscienceinformationtechnology/undergraduatedegreesandcertificates/ gamedesigndevelopmenttrack/

Savannah College of Art and Design

Address:

SCAD Admission Department

22 E. Lathrop Ave.

P.O. Box 2072
Savannah, GA
31402-2072 USA

Program Names:
    Animation
    Interactive Design and Game Development

Main Website: https://www.scad.edu/
Main Phone: 800-869-7223, 912-525-5225

Shawnee State University
Address:
    940 2nd St.
    Portsmouth, OH 45662

Program Names:
    Game and Simulation Development Arts

Main Website: http://www.shawnee.edu/
Main Phone: 740-354-3205
Program Website: http://www.shawnee.edu/academics/fdpa/majors/gaming.aspx

---

Southern Methodist University
Address:
    P.O. Box 750100
    Dallas, Texas 75275-0100

Program Names:
    Guildhall (This is a graduate program)

Main Website: http://www.smu.edu/
Main Phone: 214-768-2000
Program Website: https://www.smu.edu/Guildhall/Academics/Curriculum/GameDesign

---

Southern Illinois University Carbondale
Address:
    Carbondale, IL 62901

Program Names:
    Game Design and Development Minor

Main Website: http://siu.edu/
Main Phone: 618-453-2121

Program Website: http://isat.siu.edu/undergraduate-minor/game-design-and-development/

Stetson University
Address:
   421 N. Woodland Blvd.
   DeLand, FL 32723

Program Names:
   Computer Information Systems
   Computer Science

Main Website: www.stetson.edu
Main Phone: 386-822-7000 (DeLand campus)

Texas A&M University
Address:
   400 Bizzell St.
   College Station, TX 77840

Program Names:
   Department of Visualization
   B.S.-Viz, minor in art

Main Website: http://www.tamu.edu/

University of California, Riverside
Address:
   900 University Ave.
   Riverside, CA 92521

Program Names:
   Computer Engineering
   Computer Science

Main Website: http://www.ucr.edu/
Main Phone: 951-827-1012

University of California at Santa Cruz
Address:
   1156 High St.
   Santa Cruz, CA 95064

Program Names:
  Computational Media

Main Website: http://www.ucsc.edu/
Program Website: https://www.soe.ucsc.edu/departments/computational-media

---

University of Delaware
Address:
  Newark, DE 19716

Program Names:
  Computer & Information Sciences
  Both B.S. and B.A.

Main Website: http://www.udel.edu/
Main Phone: 302-831-2792
Program Website: http://www.cis.udel.edu

University of Denver
Address:
  2199 S. University Blvd.
  Denver, CO 80208

Program Names:
  B.S. and B.A. in Game Development
  Daniel Felix Ritchie School of Engineering & Computer Science

Main Website: http://www.du.edu/
Main Phone: 303-871-2000

University of Illinois at Chicago
Address:
  1200 W Harrison St.
  Chicago, IL 60607

Program Names:
  Computer Science

Main Website: http://www.uic.edu/index.html/
Main Phone: 312-996-7000

University of Maryland, Baltimore County
Address:
  1000 Hilltop Circle
  Baltimore, MD 21250

Program Names:
  Animation & Interactive Media
  B.S.CS with the Game Development Track

Main Website: http://www.umbc.edu/
Main Phone: 410-455-1000
Program Website: http://art.umbc.edu/varts/faculty/mcdonald.php

---

University of Michigan—Dearborn
Address:
  4901 Evergreen Road
  Dearborn, MI 48128, US

Program Names:
  B.S. in Computer and Information Science

Main Website: https://umdearborn.edu/
Main Phone: 313-593-5000
Program Website: https://umdearborn.edu/cecs/departments/computer-and-information-science/undergraduate-programs/bs-computer-and-information-science

---

University of North Texas
Address:
  1155 Union Circle
  Denton, TX 76203

Character: Denton is a college town
Program Names:
  Computer Science

Main Website: https://www.unt.edu/
Main Phone: 940-565-2000, 800-868-8211 (admissions)
Program Website:
  http://www.eng.unt.edu/ian
  redirected to: http://engineering.unt.edu/

University of Pennsylvania
Address:
  Philadelphia, PA

Program Names:
  Master of Science in Engineering in Computer Graphics and Game Technology

Main Website: http://www.upenn.edu/
Main Phone: 215-898-5000

University of San Francisco
Address:
  2130 Fulton St.
  San Francisco, CA 94117

Program Names:
  Computer Science

Main Website: https://www.usfca.edu/
Main Phone: 415-422-5555
Program Website: https://www.usfca.edu/arts-sciences/undergraduate-programs/computer-science

---

University of Southern California
Interactive Media Division
Address:
  Los Angeles, Calif.

Program Names:
  USC Interactive Media & Games

Main Website: http://www.usc.edu/
Main Phone: 213-740-2311
Program Website: http://interactive.usc.edu

University of Texas at Dallas
Address:
  800 W Campbell Rd.
  Richardson, TX 75080

Program Names:
  Bachelor of Arts in Arts and Technology

Main Website: http://www.utdallas.edu/
Main Phone: 972-883-2111
Program Website: http://iiae.utdallas.edu
  redirects to http://www.utdallas.edu/atec/
  also: http://www.utdallas.edu/atec/artstechnology/gamelab/

University of Tulsa

Address:
   800 South Tucker Drive
   Tulsa, OK 74104

Program Names:
   Tandy School of Computer Science

Main Website: https://utulsa.edu/
Main Phone: 918-631-2000
Program Website: https://engineering.utulsa.edu/academics/computer-science/

University of Utah

Address:
   201 Presidents Circle
   Salt Lake City, UT 84112

Program Names:
   Game Arts Track
   Game Engineering Track
   Game Production Track

Main Website: http://www.utah.edu/
Main Phone: 801-581-7200
Program Website: http://www.eae.utah.edu

University of Wisconsin—Stevens Point

Address:
   2100 Main St.
   Stevens Point, WI 54481

Program Names:
   WDMD Major
   Computer Information Systems
   (Options: Application Development and Support, IT Infrastructure)
   WDMD Major

Main Website: http://www.uwsp.edu
Main Phone: 715-346-0123

University of Wisconsin—Stout

Address:
   712 Broadway St. South
   Menomonie, WI 54751

Program Names:
  B.F.A. in Game Design
  B.S. in Game Design and Development-Computer Science

Main Website: http://www.uwstout.edu/
Main Phone: 715-232-1122

Vancouver Film School
Address:
  198 W. Hastings St.
  Vancouver, BC V6B 1H2
  Canada

Main Website: https://vfs.edu/
Main Phone: 604-685-5808
Program Website: https://vfs.edu/programs/game-design

Western University (Canada)
Address:
  1151 Richmond St.
  London, Ontario, Canada, N6A 3K7

Program Names:
  Computer Science with minor in Game Development

Main Website: http://www.uwo.ca/
Main Phone: 519-661-2111
Program Website: http://welcome.uwo.ca/programs/programs_by_faculty/science.html

---

Worcester Polytechnic Institute
Address:
  100 Institute Rd.
  Worcester, MA 01609

Program Names:
  Interactive Media & Game Development

Main Website: http://www.wpi.edu/
Main Phone: 508-831-5000
Program Website: http://www.wpi.edu/academics/imgd

References

INTRODUCTION

Paul, R. 2016. "Pinball prohibition: The arcade game was illegal in New York for over 30 years." Retrieved from: https://www.6sqft.com/pinball-prohibition-the-arcade-game-was-illegal-in-new-york-for-over-30-years/

Princeton Review date unknown. "Top 50 Game Design: Ugrad." Retrieved from: https://www.princetonreview.com/college-rankings?rankings=top-50-game-design-ugrad

Totilo, S. 2016. "Antonin Scalia's landmark defense of violent video games." Retrieved from: http://kotaku.com/antonin-scalias-landmark-defense-of-violent-video-games-1758990360

June. L. 2013. "For amusement only: The life and death of the American arcade." Retrieved from: https://www.theverge.com/2013/1/16/3740422/the-life-and-death-of-the-american-arcade-for-amusement-only

Seneca, L. A. 1932. *On the Shortness of Life*, translated by J.W. Basore. Retrieved from: http://www.forumromanum.org/literature/seneca_younger/brev_e.html

CHAPTER 1

Sineta, M. 1987. *Do What You Love, The Money Will Follow*. New York: Paulist Press.

Videogames. 2014. "Videogames in the 21st century: The 2014 report." Retrieved from: http://www.theesa.com/wp-content/uploads/2014/11/VideoGames21stCentury_2014.pdf

CHAPTER 2

Danielle Douglas-Gabriel. 2016. "Feds found widespread fraud at Corinthian Colleges. Why are students still paying the price?" Retrieved from: https://www.washingtonpost.com/news/grade-point/wp/2016/09/29/feds-found-widespread-fraud-at-corinthian-colleges-why-are-students-still-paying-the-price/?utm_term=.05bae2c1b3fb

Danielle Douglas-Gabriel. 2016. "ITT Technical Institutes shut down after 50 years in operation." Retrieved from: https://www.washingtonpost.com/news/grade-point/wp/2016/09/06/itt-technical-institutes-shut-down-after-50-years-in-operations/?utm_term=.f1a814e26831

Association for Computer Machinery. 2013. Computer science curricula 2013: Curriculum guidelines for undergraduate degree programs in computer science. Retrieved from: http://www.acm.org/education/CS2013-final-report.pdf

CHAPTER 3

Heinlein, R. 1961. *Stranger in a Strange Land*. New York: Ace Books.

Peters, A. K. 2014. *The Art of Game Design: A Book of Lenses*. CRC Press; 2nd edition (November 8, 2014).

CHAPTER 4

Goleman, D. 2006. *Emotional Intelligence: 10th Anniversary Edition; Why It Can Matter More Than IQ*. New York: Bantam Books.

CHAPTER 5

Allen, D. 2002. *Getting Things Done*. London, England: Penguin Books Publishing.

Global Game Jam. 2017. "About Global Game Jam." Retrieved from: https://globalgame-jam.org/about

CHAPTER 6

Dwight, D. Eisenhower. date unknown. Retrieved from: https://www.brainyquote.com/quotes/authors/d/dwight_d_eisenhower.html

Fulghum, R. 1988. *All I Really Need to Know I Learned in Kindergarten*. New York: Villard Books Publishing.

Greenfield, R. 2014. "Brainstorming doesn't work; try this technique instead." Retrieved from: https://www.fastcompany.com/3033567/brainstorming-doesnt-work-try-this-technique-instead

Brinkman, R., Kirschner, R. 2003. *Dealing with difficult people: 24 lessons for bringing out the best in everyone*. New York: McGraw-Hill Education.

Kruger, J., Dunning, D. 1999. "Unskilled and unaware of it: How difficulties in recognizing one's own incompetence lead to inflated self-assessments." Journal of Personality and Social Psychology. American Psychological Association. 77 (6): 1121–1134.

Sedita, S. 2014. *The eight characters of comedy: Guide to sitcom acting and writing*, 2nd edition. Los Angeles: Atides Publishing.

Wikipedia, Waterfall model, https://en.wikipedia.org/wiki/Waterfall_model. (Last modified January 19, 2018).

CHAPTER 8

Alexander, C. 1964. *Notes on the synthesis of form*. Cambridge MA: Harvard University Press. Retrieved from: https://books.google.com/books?id=Kh3T3XFUfPQC&pg=PA60&lpg=PA60

Wikipedia, There are known knowns, https://en.wikipedia.org/wiki/There_are_known_knowns (Last modified January 3, 2018).

CHAPTER 9

Allen, Woody. date unknown. "Eighty percent of success is showing up" Retrieved from: https://www.brainyquote.com/quotes/quotes/w/woodyallen145883.html

American Psychological Association. 2006. "Multitasking: Switching costs." Retrieved from: http://www.apa.org/research/action/multitask.aspx

Keller, G. and Papasan, J. 2013. *The ONE Thing: The Surprisingly Simple Truth Behind Extraordinary Results.* Austin, Texas: Bard Press.

CHAPTER 11

Berger, W. 2010. *CAD monkeys, dinosaur babies, and T-shaped people: Inside the world of design thinking and how it can spark creativity and innovation.* New York: Penguin Books.

CHAPTER 12

Wikipedia, List of video game developers, https://en.wikipedia.org/wiki/List_of_video_game_developers. (Last modified January 18, 2018).

CHAPTER 15

Wikipedia, Gamification, https://en.wikipedia.org/wiki/Gamification. (Last modified December 16, 2017).

CHAPTER 16

QuickBase. 2014. "6 dimensions of organizational culture—which one is right for you?" Retrieved from: http://www.quickbase.com/blog/6-dimensions-of-organizational-culture-which-one-is-right-for-you

CHAPTER 18

Wikipedia, Burn down chart, https://en.wikipedia.org/wiki/Burn_down_chart. (Last modified January 17, 2018).

CHAPTER 19

Anderson, C. 2016. "What role does an office play in game development?" Retrieved from: http://www.gamasutra.com/blogs/ColinAnderson/20160615/275048/What_Role_Does_An_Office_Play_In_Game_Development.php

Suggestions for Further Reading

GENERAL GAME DESIGN

The Art of Game Design: A Book of Lenses, 2nd Edition, 2014
    by Jesse Schell
    Published by A K Peters/CRC Press
    ISBN-13: 978-1466598645
    ISBN-10: 1466598646

One of the best books about game design we've ever encountered is Jesse Schell's *The Art of Game Design: A Book of Lenses*. This is the sort of book that you keep around. You'll get a lot out of it on the first reading, but pick it up again a few years from now and you get a lot more that didn't quite register the first time.
    It became a classic the moment it was published.

Game Design Workshop: A Playcentric Approach to Creating Innovative Games, 3rd Edition, 2014
    by Tracy Fullerton
    Published by A K Peters/CRC Press
    ISBN-10: 1482217163
    ISBN-13: 978-1482217162

A terrific book for the classroom, Tracy Fullerton's book will supply the beginning to intermediate game designer with plenty of essential knowledge to get you started.

Chris Crawford on Game Design, 1st Edition, 2003
    by Chris Crawford
    Published by New Riders
    ISBN-10: 0131460994
    ISBN-13: 978-0131460997

Chris Crawford's game design book was one of the first books about designing video games in print. It has hardly aged, and the principles he discusses are timeless.
    Also recommended are game design books by Richard Rouse and Andrew Rollings & Ernest Adams, among others.

Donald Featherstone's War Games Battles and Manoeuvres with Model Soldiers: The Book That Launched Modern Wargaming, 2014
> by Donald Featherstone, edited by John Curry
> Published by History of Wargaming Project
> ISBN-13: 978-1291851427

Originally published as *War Games* in 1962, this 2014 revision of the book is the main go-to reference for builders of table top war games. It does not stop there, however. The basic design principles developed in this book have wide applicability to both board game and computer role-playing games and real-time or turn-based strategy games. This is only the first of a series created by Donald Featherstone, one of the grandfathers of war gaming of all sorts.

How to Lie with Statistics, 1993
> by Darrell Huff
> Published by W. W. Norton & Company
> ISBN-10: 0393310728
> ISBN-13: 978-0393310726

Why would we include a book with a title like this in a section about game design? The answer is that, once you are deep into developing, balancing, and tweaking the math that underlies your game mechanics, you will soon get swamped with mountains of survey results and log file data that have information you can use. But can you make sense of it, and how would you know if the data aren't leading you seriously astray? This little book can help.

A final note here: we've hardly scratched the surface for books about making board games and video games.

GAME STORYTELLING

Video Game Storytelling: What Every Developer Needs to Know about Narrative Techniques, 2014
> by Evan Skolnick
> Published by Watson-Guptill
> ISBN-10: 0385345828
> ISBN-13: 978-0385345828

This book will give you advice not only about the detailed goings-on when writers write stories for games and, necessarily, interact with the rest of the design team, but also solid advice about writing in general.

Video Game Writing: From Macro to Micro
> by Maurice Suckling
> Published by Mercury Learning & Information (January 24, 2012)
> ISBN-10: 1936420155
> ISBN-13: 978-1936420155

As with other books directed specifically at game writers, this book not only covers the fundamentals of the craft of storytelling but delves into the details of how to put the craft to work in the interactive settings of games.

Character Development and Storytelling for Games, 2013
    by Lee Sheldon
    Published by Course Technology
    ISBN-10: 1435461045
    ISBN-13: 978-1435461048

Here is another book about the art and craft of game storytelling with plenty of anecdotes and tales from the trenches. It's a book intended for classroom use, which is why many game storytelling classes make use of it.

GAME PRODUCTION

The Game Production Handbook, 3rd Edition, 2013
    by Heather Maxwell Chandler
    Published by Jones & Bartlett Learning
    ISBN-10: 1449688098
    ISBN-13: 978-1449688097

This is a book directed at industry practitioners, not a textbook. Even so, one of us (Mike) uses it as the text for his Intro to Game Production course. It gets into everything you need to know from the production side of things, at least as far as can be communicated in a reasonably sized book. Of course, actually engaging in the production of a game is another matter entirely.

DESIGN, THE D-WORD

These books are all about "design" in the grand sense of the term. While none of these books will magically turn you into a designer, they might illuminate a little of what goes on in the mind of the designer, and maybe some of that will rub off.

A More Beautiful Question: The Power of Inquiry to Spark Breakthrough Ideas, 2014
    by Warren Berger
    Published by Bloomsbury USA
    ISBN-10: 1632861054
    ISBN-13: 978-1632861054

This is a book about asking questions, the right sorts of questions. The book is a handy adjunct for brainstorming and other sorts of design activities and offers practical advice for getting to the heart of the (design) problem, whatever that happens to be.

CAD Monkeys, Dinosaur Babies, and T-Shaped People: Inside the World of Design Thinking and How It Can Spark Creativity and Innovation, 2010
    by Warren Berger
    Published by Penguin Books
    ISBN-10: 0143118021
    ISBN-13: 978-0143118022

This rollicking little book offers a nice window into the minds of designers and the work they do, plus it gives plenty of practical advice that you can use in your own work. Think of this book as food for the brain.

Notes on the Synthesis of Form, 1964
    by Christopher Alexander
    Published by Harvard University Press
    ISBN-10: 0674627512
    ISBN-13: 9780674627512

A foundational book about architectural design by one of its most noteworthy practitioners and theorists. Although it talks in terms of architecture, the design lessons apply to design work of any sort. Dating back to 1964, this book has become a classic and one any designer (or architect) can benefit from.

SCRUM AND AGILE METHODOLOGIES

There is a wealth of information about Agile development—and Scrum in particular—on the Internet, but if you want to tackle it all inside one place, here are a couple of titles to get you started.

Scrum: The Art of Doing Twice the Work in Half the Time, 2014
    by Jeff Sutherland and JJ Sutherland
    Published by Crown Business
    ISBN-10: 038534645X
    ISBN-13: 978-0385346450

This is it, the book that will take you through the Scrum methodology, the reasons why it is set up the way it is, and the reasons why it works. We discussed Scrum somewhat deeply in this book, but there is much more to Scrum than we could get into. That's why the book clocks in at 256 pages. Can you really do twice the amount of work in half the time? Put Scrum into practice and find out.

Scrum for Dummies, 2015
    by Mark C. Layton (Author)
    Publisher by For Dummies
    ISBN-10: 111890575X
    ISBN-13: 978-1118905753

Clocking in at an even longer 408 pages, this is another way to approach Scrum. We don't have both copies of the book in front of us for comparison, so we're guessing the print is larger and the info is presented in a less dense way. Either or both books will get you started.

MOTIVATION

Rather than try to come up with our own list, we're just going to send you to this excellent compilation, courtesy of Inc.com:

https://www.inc.com/geoffrey-james/top-10-motivational-books-of-all-time.html

For the most part, the books listed there are classic titles, many in print for decades, that have stood the test of time. Our list wouldn't have looked much different.

But their list leaves the #1 spot open for your own personal favorite, so here we go with ours:

Managing Oneself: The Key to Success, 2008
    by Peter F. Drucker
    Published by the Harvard Business Review Press
    ISBN-10: 163369304X
    ISBN-13: 978-1633693043

If you are in business for yourself, sooner or later you're going to have to read Peter Drucker. This short book gets to the heart of the matter, how best to run your own life as effectively as possible, thereby freeing up the necessary time and resources for success.

PROCRASTINATION AND TIME MANAGEMENT

Ultimately, fixing your personal hang-ups about time management and procrastination will simply lead to a better, more productive life, even if the recommendations seem painful to implement at first.

Getting Things Done: The Art of Stress-Free Productivity, 2002, 2015
    by David Allen
    Published by Penguin Books
    ISBN-10: 0143126563
    ISBN-13: 978-0143126560

This book goes well beyond the mere to-do list. It will revolutionize the way you work. Every college student…wait, everyone should read this book.

The ONE Thing: The Surprisingly Simple Truth Behind Extraordinary Results, 2013
    by Gary Keller and Jay Papasan
    Published by Bard Press
    ISBN-10: 1885167776
    ISBN-13: 978-1885167774

This quick read is another book that will revolutionize the way you work. It is also incredibly liberating. Once you start to live by its principles, you'll be amazed at how much of your day opens up to new possibilities. After you finish reading it, might we suggest passing it along to the other members of your team?

The Pomodoro Technique Illustrated: The Easy Way to Do More in Less Time, 2012
    by Staffan Noteberg
    Published by Pragmatic Bookshelf
    ISBN-10: 1934356506
    ISBN-13: 978-1934356500

We discussed this in the body of our book. This book isn't quite so much about time management as giving you a life hack to deal with procrastination. The technique is simplicity itself: you merely train yourself to work in finite blocks of time, marked off by a kitchen timer, agreeing to shut out all distractions during that time block. Simple, but easier said than done!

BOOKS ABOUT BUSINESS

The many motivational books we linked to earlier overlap to some extent, but here we concentrate more on the matter of running a business. We can hardly do this section justice, as the business literature is vast, with thousands of titles, some good, some not so good.

    Since we're speaking in particular about how to start a game studio, we're going to recommend just three books here. Keep in mind that in this short space we can hardly do justice to the whole body of possible books, online courses, and other materials that can help you succeed at business. We're just going to recommend three.

The Lean Startup: How Today's Entrepreneurs Use Continuous Innovation to Create Radically Successful Businesses, 2011
    by Eric Ries
    Published by Crown Business
    ISBN-10: 0307887898
    ISBN-13: 978-0307887894

This book changed the way startup companies get started. Most new businesses don't survive for even five years, and this book was among the first to try to fix that.

    Gone are the days of the tedious "business plan" and other failed techniques. The Lean Startup™ shows you a whole new way to proceed, one that promises (although it can't guarantee) a better chance of success. This book was such a game changer that The Lean Startup is a trademark of Eric Ries.

The Startup Owner's Manual: The Step-by-Step Guide for Building a Great Company, 2014
    by Steve Blank and Bob Dorf
    Published by K & S Ranch
    ISBN-10: 0984999302
    ISBN-13: 978-0984999309

The title gives it away. The authors instruct you to hang onto this book as you build your company until it is in tatters and falling apart. That's how often you're going to be going back to it.

Talking to Humans, 2014
    by Giff Constable, with Frank Rimalovski
    Published by Giff Constable
    ISBN-10: 099080092X
    ISBN-13: 978-0990800927

This short volume is a useful tool for helping you talk to people, to find out what they are thinking and what they want, especially if you are not particularly comfortable about the process. The book is primarily concerned with talking to customers, something every startup venture needs to do well. You can use the same principle to talk to gamers, to help you find out what they would love to see in the games your new studio is going to make.

LIFE HACKS AND LIFESTYLE

Just as we did for the motivation list, rather than try to come up with our own list, we're just going to send you to another solid compilation:
    www.lifehack.org/articles/communication/10-books-that-will-change-your-life.html
    It's interesting to note that these two lists have three titles in common.
    To the preceding list we would also add a few more titles. They aren't all similar to each other, which is part of the fun of reading them.

The 4-Hour Workweek, 2009
    by Timothy Ferriss
    Published by Harmony
    ISBN-10: 9780307465351
    ISBN-13: 978-0307465351

Don't take the title too seriously. Your workweek will no doubt be longer than that. What this book is, however, is a compilation of clever techniques you can use to streamline your life, automating the dull parts so you don't have to deal with them so much.

    This book could easily have been put under Motivation or Business, but the author's innovative ideas on how to live life in the modern age make it more of a Lifestyle entry. What Ferriss has to say applies especially well for people who want to live a mobile lifestyle, as we discussed in Chapter 26.

The Drunkard's Walk: How Randomness Rules Our Lives, 2008
 by Leonard Mlodinow
 Published by Vintage Books
 ISBN-10: 9780307275172
 ISBN-13: 978-0307275172

Think you are in charge of your life? Think again. While there is plenty that you can control, there is plenty more you cannot: a chance encounter with a stranger, an accident, a missed phone call, getting struck by a meteor.

This book explains to you just how much influence random chance has on our lives, providing a gentle introduction into how probability works. Worth reading if only for the perspective it gives.

All I Really Need to Know I Learned in Kindergarten: Uncommon Thoughts on Common Things, 1988
 by Robert Fulghum
 Published by Ballantine Books
 ISBN-10: 034546639X
 ISBN-13: 978-0345466396

Don't let the title throw you. This book is a collection of essays about human universals and advice for the right way to live. We pointed out in our book that this is a kind of life-hack book, and that's as reasonable a way to approach it as any. Now you won't have any need to climb a mountain in the Himalayas to find a spiritual teacher.

MINDFULNESS

Everyone's spiritual life is an intensely personal affair, and we are not going to claim there is only one way to lead what philosophers would call the "good life." What we offer here are a few noteworthy titles that we have found to be of value.

We already mentioned Seneca the Younger's *On the Shortness of Life.* We think the earlier in life you can read it, the more profound will be the effect. We're sorry we didn't read it decades ago.

Another ancient writer whose advice still applies over the centuries is Marcus Aurelius, author of *Meditations.* Marcus Aurelius was the emperor of Rome from 161 CE to 180 CE. The *Meditations* are actually his own personal journal, not intended for publication, but we're happy that word got out.

The *Meditations* were about life and conquest, leadership, and living well. We still read it almost 2,000 years later.

His *Meditations* have nothing to do, however, with the entirely unrelated practice called "mindfulness meditation." Mindfulness meditation has grown immensely popular in recent years, and one of us (Mike) advocates its practice.

Just don't expect immediate results, and try not to give up too soon. This is a practice that requires patience, both during the actual meditation sessions and also over the months and years it takes to experience its profound benefits.

You can find many practical clips on how to do this on YouTube. Since everyone is different and gets different results, you will likely need to shop around to find a particular technique that works for you.

One resource that Mike found useful is a course available through The Great Courses, a seller of CD and DVD educational programs. They frequently hold sales that make their products available at deep discounts.

Practicing Mindfulness: An Introduction to Meditation, 2011
   by Mark W. Muesse
   Published by The Great Courses
   ISBN: 159803792-7

The Great Courses company offers CD and DVD educational programs in hundreds of topics, each equivalent to at least several weeks of a full-length college course. This course gets into the theory into why it works and takes you through a number of practical approaches to doing meditation and making it a part of your life.

Emotional Intelligence: 10th Anniversary Edition; Why It Can Matter More Than IQ, 2006
   by Daniel Goleman
   Published by Bantam Books
   ISBN-10: 055338371X
   ISBN-13: 978-0553383713

There are verbal and mathematical intelligences, what IQ tests claim to measure. Daniel Goleman argues that there is also an emotional intelligence, a measure of how skillfully one can read the emotional states of others and how well one understands one's own emotional behaviors.

Index